More
Tricks & Tips
for the Amiga

Bleek
Maelger
Weltner

A Data Becker Book
Published by
Abacus

First Printing, March 1989
Printed in U.S.A.
Copyright © 1989

Copyright © 1989

Data Becker, GmbH
Merowingerstraße 30
4000 Düsseldorf, West Germany
Abacus
5370 52nd Street, SE
Grand Rapids, MI 49508

Every effort has been made to ensure complete and accurate information concerning the material presented in this book. However, Abacus Software can neither guarantee nor be held legally responsible for any mistakes in printing or faulty instructions contained in this book. The authors always appreciate receiving notice of any errors or misprints.

AmigaBASIC is a trademark or registered trademark of Microsoft Corporation. Amiga 500, Amiga 1000, Amiga 2000, Amiga and C64 are trademarks or registered trademarks of Commodore-Amiga, Inc. Lattice C and Lattice are trademarks or registered trademarks of Lattice Corporation. Aztec C and Aztec are trademarks or registered trademarks of Manx Software Systems. IBM is a trademark or registered trademark of International Business Machines, Inc. Atari ST is a trademark or registered trademark of Atari Corporation.

ISBN 1-55755-051-4

Table of Contents

Foreword   vii

1.   New Tricks and tips   3
1.1   Tips for the CLI   3
1.2   Tips for AmigaBASIC   8
1.3   Printer tips   11
1.4   Tips for working with the Amiga   13
1.5   Secrets and hidden messages   14

2.   AmigaBASIC tricks and tips   19
2.1   An Intuition window   19
2.1.1   Gadgets   23
2.1.2   Gadget borders and text   29
2.1.3   User-friendly gadgets   34
2.1.4   Filled gadgets   40
2.1.5   Scrolling tables   45
2.1.6   Proportional gadgets   52
2.2   A file monitor   58
2.2.1   Using the file monitor   72
2.2.2   Patching files with the monitor   74
2.2.3   Patching AmigaBASIC   74
2.3   Accessing AmigaDOS from AmigaBASIC   76
2.3.1   File access through AmigaDOS   77
2.3.2   File, directory and disk information   84
2.3.3   Direct file control   90
2.4   Libraries and applications   92
2.4.1   Directory manager   92
2.4.2   Program documentation   99

3.   Machine language   105
3.1   Division by zero handler   106
3.2   Attention: Virus alarm!   109
3.2.1   The ultimate virus killer   110
3.3   Machine language and BASIC   114
3.3.1   Assembler and C programs from BASIC   116
3.3.2   BASIC enhancement: ColorCycle   118
3.3.3   Putting the mouse to sleep   121

4.	Hardware hacking	125
4.1	Disabling memory expansion	127
4.1.1	The 2000A board	127
4.1.2	The Amiga 500: printed circuit board	128
4.2	Disk drive switching	130
4.3	Installing the MC 68010	131
4.4	The roar of the fans	134
4.5	New processor information	135
4.5.1	The 68010: high power, low price	135
4.5.2	The 68012: low cost, high memory	137
4.5.3	Monster processors: 68020, 68030, 6888x	137
5.	Workbench 1.3	141
5.1	Using Mount	141
5.1.1	Renaming commands	143
5.1.2	Less is more	144
5.2	Improvements to DOS 1.3	146
5.2.1	The PIPE device	146
5.2.2	The Speak command	147
5.2.3	The NewCon device	148
5.2.4	The FastFileSystem	148
5.2.5	FFS and hard disks	149
5.2.8	The new math libraries	150
6.	The printer device	157
6.1	Controlling printer parameters	157
6.2	Graphic dumps with the printer device	163
6.2.1	Hardcopy as an application	167
7.	Workbench and extras	171
7.1	Preferences	171
7.1.1	Reading and setting Preferences data	172
7.1.2	The new Preferences (Version 1.3)	176
7.1.3	The 1.3 Utilities drawer	180
7.1.3.1	Other Workbench 1.3 utilities	184
7.2	Tools on the Extras disk	185
8.	Personalizing the Workbench	191
8.1	Making preparations	192
8.2	Getting started with text editing	194
8.2.1	Starting messages and the AmigaDOS window	194
8.2.2	Changing the title bar and menus	196
8.2.3	New menu items and messages	197
8.3	A guide to Kickstart messages	200

Appendices
A.   Error messages   205
B.   CLI shortcuts   208
C.   Printer escape sequences   210
D.   Guru meditation codes   212

Index   215

Foreword

We were very happy when the new Kickstart and Workbench Versions 1.3 were released. Commodore added several new commands, better applications and many enhancements to the operating system. So we did some research to find out what was new, unfamiliar and worth knowing about Kickstart and Workbench 1.3. We looked for changes and improvements so we could describe them in detail, and compare them with the program data on Workbench 1.2.

More Amiga Tricks and Tips is the result of our research and experimenting. The concept of this book is similar to our previous book, *Amiga Tricks and Tips*. You'll find important information and many, many new programs which you can adapt to your own needs.

Here is a book that tells about both Workbench 1.2 and Workbench 1.3. From software to hardware, from the old operating system to the new operating system, you'll find plenty more Tricks & Tips that will help you get the most out of your Amiga.

Bleek, Maelger and Weltner
December 1988

1.
New tricks and tips

1.   New tricks and tips

This chapter contains many small hints and bits of information that could be thought of as "mini tricks and tips." These include information specific to both Workbench 1.2 and 1.3. These tricks and tips will hopefully make your sessions with your Amiga more productive and more enjoyable.

1.1   Tips for the CLI

#1:
Automatic
backups

Have you ever edited your startup sequence using ED, quit ED, and then realized that your Amiga won't boot without the line you just deleted from the startup sequence? Don't panic. ED always creates an automatic backup of the last file edited, and places this file in the t: (temporary) directory. The t: directory keeps temporary files available on disk, just in case you mess up the file you're currently editing.

To restore the old startup-sequence file, copy the file ed-backup located in the t: directory to the s: directory as the startup-sequence. The CLI command sequence is as follows:

```
copy t/ed-backup to s/startup-sequence
```

Note:

Do <u>not</u> copy the t: directory to the RAM disk. If you do, the t: directory will be deleted after a reset, and you'll be unable to access it after a crash.

#2:
Interrupting
CLI output

You can pause text scrolling in the CLI window (i.e., whenever you execute the list, dir or type commands, or any command which displays large amounts of data in one group) by pressing any character key. The CON handler stops the text display until you remove this character by pressing the <Backspace> key. Once you press <Backspace>, the output resumes. You can easily pause and restart a disk directory display by pressing <Space> and <Backspace>.

#3:
New CLI text
modes

You may have seen some disks which displayed text in different colors and type styles during booting. There's no magic here: You can change colors without any problem. Also, you can display text in italic, bold or underlined text. The normal Echo command permits these changes.

To use these text features, you need control characters to inform the computer that the next characters are escape sequences, and must be executed rather than printed. These command characters are enclosed in quotation marks, and always begin with the sequence "*e". The "*e" combination represents the <Esc> key and signifies an escape sequence. After this initialization, characters and numbers follow. Some of these characters are separated from one another by semicolons, and comprise the control sequence itself. For example, the number "4" enables underlining and the number "42" represents a black background color (see the values in the following tables for the styles available). The control sequence concludes with "m" and the text you want displayed.

Try the following: Create a file named UNDERLINE using ED or another editor. Enter the following in this file:

```
echo"*e[4mUNDERLINE on"
echo"*e[0mNormal"
```

Save the file and exit the editor. Now enter Execute Underline and press <Return> to see the results:

Underline
Normal

The following list documents control sequence values:

Typestyle	Number	Remarks
normal	0	
bold	1	
italic	3	
underline	4	
inverse	7	
Foreground color	Number	Remarks
normal	30	set using Preferences
white	31	
black	32	
orange	33	
Background color	Number	Remarks
normal	40	set using Preferences
white	41	
black	42	
orange	43	

**#4:
<Ctrl> key
combinations**

Key combinations can accomplish many things. Most of these key combinations are actuated in conjunction with the <Ctrl> key. When you press and hold the <Ctrl> key then press another key, the combination usually affects control of a screen or program. This combination usually bears the name *control key*.

The first four control keys allow you to stop the execution of many programs.

<Ctrl><C>   stops a CLI command
<Ctrl><D>   stops a running script file
<Ctrl><E>   executes a break of higher priority
<Ctrl><F>   executes a break of higher priority

Here are a few of the most used screen control combinations:

<Ctrl><G>   screen flash (without signal tone)
<Ctrl><H>   same as the <Delete> key
<Ctrl><J>   same as the <Tab> key
<Ctrl><K>   same as <Cursor up>
<Ctrl><L>   erases the window (same as <Esc><C>)
<Ctrl><M>   same as the <Return> key
<Ctrl><N>   activates a new (an alternative) character set
<Ctrl><O>   restores the original character set (same as <Return>)
<Ctrl><X>   deletes the contents of the current line

#5:
Copy more!

The Copy command copies files from within the CLI. There are many variants to this command that are poorly documented (if any documentation exists at all). One application of Copy allows you to copy several files that have nothing to do with one another. These files cannot be grouped together using the wildcard characters (* and ?).

The solution is very simple: You can copy files with the same names but different extensions using the bar character (|). The following example copies three files of the same name (test.c, test.h and test.o) to the RAM disk:

```
Copy :test.(C|H|O) to RAM:
```

We can use this in a different way by viewing the entire filename as an extension and creating a multiple copy from that. This avoids loading the Copy command for each copy. The following example copies the three CLI commands Dir, List and Rename from the c: directory of the current disk to the c: directory of the RAM disk:

```
Copy C:(DIR|LIST|RENAME) to RAM:C
```

#6:
CLI windows
and script
files

You can supply your own dimensions and title when opening a new CLI window. In addition, you can assign the new CLI task to execute a script file. That looks like this:

```
NewCLI Outputdevice: Script-file
```

In Version 1.2 the device for the Outputdevice argument should be CON: with its window size arguments. The script file executes after the NewCLI opens. You can execute a script file in parallel with another process in another window.

Workbench 1.3 owners should either use `NewCon:` as the `Outputdevice` argument (this keeps all the `Shell`'s editing features resident in the new window), or `NewShell` without an output device.

#7:
Disk icons

Workbench 1.3 has a slightly different look from the previous version. All old devices are represented by their old icons. The RAM disk and the new RAMB0 disk still use the old plain disk icon. The icon used by the Workbench disk can also be used by the RAM and RAMB0 disks by adding two small `Copy` commands in the startup sequence. The following lines perform this task:

```
Copy Disk.info to RAM:
Copy Disk.info to RAD:
```

Place copy commands before the `LoadWB` command and you will have a uniform icon design. This method can be applied to any other disk as well.

#8:
One window,
two CLIs

You cannot have two `CLI`s operating at once in two windows. However, it's possible to have two `CLI`s in one window. This is simply done with the following command sequence:

```
NewCLI *
```

This command redirects the `NewCLI` output to the present window, without opening a second window. You alternate between the first and second task. This saves you the somewhat complicated trouble of switching windows. If you do this, use `Run` to execute a program instead of `Execute` for a direct program call.

#9:
Borderless
CLI

There are programs that try to eliminate the border of the `CLI` window by using complicated methods. Many of the developers of these programs seem to have forgotten that the `CLI` is created using the Console device. The Console device contains commands which let you change the border's appearance using escape sequences. These sequences let you do just about everything with the size and appearance of the window:

Sequence	Explanation
<Esc> [n u	sets the window width at n characters
<Esc> [n x	sets the left border at n pixels
<Esc> [n y	sets the upper border at n pixels
<Esc> [n t	sets the number of lines at n
<Esc> c	sets everything back to normal

The `Echo` command is used to call each sequence. It is also possible to link multiple sequences using semicolons. The window must be resized after <Esc><c> to display the border. Here is an example:

```
;This sequence configures for border OFF
echo "*e[80u*e[0x*e[0y*e[31t"
;Press <Ctrl><L><Return> to actuate borderless window

;This sequence returns system to normal mode
echo "*ec"
```

#10:
Quick
messages

Usually the startup sequence displays messages about the Workbench version number and the current date. If you wish, you can add your own messages to this data.

The problem in doing so is that when the Echo command displays text, the command must be reloaded every time, which is quite time consuming. You can speed this up by writing the entire text to a file and using the Amiga's multitasking capability to display the new text on the screen during the startup sequence.

Enter the following line in your startup sequence file to call the text file that you want displayed:

```
Run Type Textfile
```

1.2   Tips for AmigaBASIC

#11:
Closing with
standard icons

AmigaBASIC uses one particular icon for all the programs created from AmigaBASIC, as well as files created from AmigaBASIC programs. There are two ways to change this:

The first deals with the BASIC program icon. You can edit this icon using the icon editor after you finish developing the program. Assign this new icon to the finished program and copy it into the correct directory. The trick is to set the delete flag in the info file so that the info file cannot be deleted. This ensures that the icon doesn't get overwritten the next time you save the program.

There is a simpler method when it comes to data files. These data files should have an icon relating to the program (e.g., text files written in Notepad have a note icon). First you draw the desired icon with the icon editor. This icon is stored in the same directory as the main program. Then you read the icon at the beginning using the function GetDiskObject. Every time you save a file this icon gets saved under the same name. The result: Your icon replaces the AmigaBASIC icon. Here is an example program that gives a BASIC program the Shell icon, you will have to change the drawer and disk names (T&T2:Chapter1) for your own setup:

Program start:

```
REM IconInstall in Chapter1 drawer on disk named T&T2
LIBRARY "T&T2:bmaps/icon.library" :REM use ConvertFD
DECLARE FUNCTION GetDiskObject& LIBRARY
DECLARE FUNCTION PutDiskObject& LIBRARY
FileName$ = "SYS:Shell"+CHR$(0)
DiskAdr& = GetDiskObject&(SADD(FileName$))
```

After closing
file:

```
File$ = "T&T2:Chapter1/IconInstall"
File$ = File$+CHR$(0)
status = PutDiskObject&(SADD(File$), DiskAdr&
```

#12:
Modular work

You should try to use modular program structure whenever possible. This makes the listing easier to follow and modify. Another advantage is that many of these modules can be merged into later programs that you write. This saves alot of work. You have two possibilities which you can apply to merge modules into other listings:

The first is to load the BASIC interpreter and copy the module from the source program into the clipboard. This clipboard can then be pasted into a second BASIC program. Load the second program and paste this stored section back into the listing using the Paste function.

The second method requires that you save the program block to a file. Be careful that you use ASCII format—you cannot use the other formats for this method. You can then merge the new block into a program with:

```
MERGE Filename
```

This saves a lot of work and allows you to build a library of independent function modules.

#13:
Changing
window and
screen names

In AmigaBASIC you can specify a window name when opening a new window, but you can't change the window name later on. The Intuition library offers a solution.

Open the library at the beginning of the program. This lets you specify both window and screen names by calling `SetWindowTitle()`. The following demonstration program renames your BASIC window to `test` and your Workbench screen to `Screen`. Please notice that the variables used to pass parameters to the `CALL` must be ended with null bytes, `(Chr$(0))`.

```
REM WindowTitle
LIBRARY "T&T2:bmaps/intuition.library":'set path name for
'wherever you have intuition library stored
CALL SetTitle("test","Screen")
END

SUB SetTitle(WinNam$, ScrNam$) STATIC
 WinNam$ = WinNam$ + CHR$(0)
 ScrNam$ = ScrNam$ + CHR$(0)
 CALL SetWindowTitles(WINDOW(7), SADD(WinNam$),
SADD(ScrNam$))
END SUB
```

#14:
More memory

Normally `Clear` allocates more memory in AmigaBASIC. But this command often doesn't work if it can't find the desired memory (a bug in AmigaBASIC). First it tries to provide new memory and then it tries to release old memory. When you want to change your memory only a little, you must have double the amount needed available, which is often not the case. There is only one method to achieve this goal— simply set the area to the smallest size, then enter the desired number:

```
CLEAR ,1024
CLEAR ,500000
```

We don't recommend this method when you're in program mode instead of direct mode. Use the following in program mode:

```
CLEAR ,25000-FRE(0) 'only the necessary program memory
CLEAR ,FRE(-1)-50000 'entire free memory - security
```

#15:
Editing
BASIC
programs

The BASIC editor is a nuisance sometimes. It scrolls horizontally with difficulty and scrolls up or down slowly. In addition, you cannot search for commands because no search function exists. AmigaBASIC offers some help. You can save programs as ASCII text with `Save "name",a` and then edit the program using a word processor such as TextPro or BeckerText from Abacus. The programs can also be transferred to other computers in this manner.

Word processors allow many more editing features than the Amiga-BASIC editor. Since the Amiga is multitasking, the word processor and BASIC can be running at the same time. This lets you quickly move the edited program to AmigaBASIC for easy testing.

#16:
Faster
AmigaBASIC

AmigaBASIC could be faster. Consider this; when you start Amiga-BASIC from the Workbench, the task priorities are not optimally set for AmigaBASIC operation.

Two functions in `Exec.library` offer a cure for this problem. `SetTaskPri()` allows you to view the priorities of your tasks and BASIC. You can choose a value from 1 to 127. The larger the number, the faster AmigaBASIC runs. That means that other programs (tasks) receive less processor time. This method works especially well for calculations that take a lot of time, and for graphic output.

First you access `Exec.library`. Then the task is found with `FindTask()` and changed with `SetTaskPri()`. When the BASIC program ends, it is important that the priority be reset so other programs can run. Here are the program segments:

Program start

```
LIBRARY "T&T2:bmaps/exec.library"
DECLARE FUNCTION FindTask& LIBRARY
BASICTask& = FindTask&()
CALL SetTaskPri(BASICTask&, 80)
```

Program end

```
CALL SetTaskPri(BASICTask&, 0)
```

#17:
No overflow
in line buffer

Do you recognize this? The AmigaBASIC editor occasionally won't let you go back over a line using <Backspace>. It responds with the error message "line buffer overflow". You can easily get around this. Select a space with the mouse and then cut it with <Amiga><X>. Now the editor will work correctly again.

#18:
Reset

When you would like your BASIC program to reset the Amiga, use the following code (with caution):

```
bye = 16515072
CALL bye
```

1.3   Printer tips

#19:
Changing
printers
without
Preferences

Very few people know that the printer driver is a standalone program and can be started by itself. It's not handled as a program in the usual sense, so you can't access it through the CLI. The Workbench knows where the driver must be placed in memory. Copy the necessary driver from the DEVS:Printers directory into the main directory of the Workbench disk. Then you need a Tool type icon like the clock or the CLI icon. Give the one of these icons the same names as the printer drivers. When you click on the icon from the Workbench the corresponding printer driver initializes. Here are the CLI commands for the Epson printer driver:

```
1> copy sys:devs/printers/epson sys:epson
1> copy CLI.info Epson.info
```

#20:
Indirect
printing pays
off

When you would like to use the functions of your printer in a BASIC program, most people access the printer directly by using the PAR: or SER: device. Normally, all printer output should occur over the printer device PRT:.

Commodore-Amiga implements generic sequences that control printer effects. The corresponding printer driver converts the sequences that are necessary for that particular printer. This ensures that the print routines for one printer can run on all others as well. The following table lists the command codes that can help you to achieve all different print styles. All sequences begin with <Esc>. It is best to define this with a string, as in the example below:

ESC$=CHR$(27)

The above CHR$(27) signifies the <Esc> key. This character string tells the printer to prepare for special codes to control the printer or other device.

The following is a table of type styles and escape sequences:

Typestyle	Sequence
Italic	on: ESC[3m off: ESC[23m
Bold	on: ESC[1m off: ESC[22m
Underlined	on: ESC[4m off: ESC[24m
Elite	on: ESC[2w off: ESC[1w
Compressed type	on: ESC[4w off: ESC[3w
Wide type	on: ESC[6w off: ESC[5w
NLQ	on: ESC[2"z off: ESC[1"z
Proportional type	on: ESC[2p off: ESC[1p
Superscript	on: ESC[2v off: ESC[1v
Subscript	on: ESC[4v off: ESC[3v

A command sequence can be sent together with the text to the printer with LPRINT:

```
LPRINT ESC$;"[4m";Text$;ESC$;"[24m"
```

1.4 Tips for working with the Amiga

#21:
Faster, faster,
faster

It helps speed up the Amiga during long computation times if you close all unnecessary screens. That way the graphic processor and the entire system runs faster.

#22:
Stop!

Pressing the left mouse button stops text output. When you release the mouse button, the text output can continue. This is especially useful when text is scrolling past rapidly in some CLI commands (e.g., the Dir, List and Type commands).

#23:
DiskDoctor
First aid

Have you ever deleted a file that you really didn't want deleted? If you act promptly, you can recover the file. The Amiga doesn't really delete files. It simply resets the directory entry and the disk's bitmap.

You don't need a disk monitor to rescue the file, just the DiskDoctor program. DiskDoctor replaces deleted files providing that you haven't written to the disk since you deleted the files.

#24:
One Guru less

When you start a program from the Workbench, it runs without hesitation. When you start it from the CLI, it takes five seconds longer to execute. Why? Many Amiga users have asked this question, so here's the answer: On a multitasking computer every program has its own stack where a return address is stored. When a program starts from the Workbench, this stack is created using the value in the Info file.

It's different in the CLI. Here the CLI's stack value comes into play instead of the stack value of the info file. This is usually rather small. Remember when you start a program from the CLI, it takes on the current CLI stack size. This may not be enough memory, and you may end up getting a Guru Meditation. If that's the case you should enlarge the stack before running the program. The stack size needed for a program can be seen by selecting Info in the Workbench menu.

#25:
More of the
same

The file System-Configuration can be found in the devs: directory of any given boot disk. This file contains all the parameters set by Preferences. Copy this file onto each boot disk you have. This gives you the same Preferences setting on all your boot disks. Here's a sample CLI command:

```
1> copy sys:devs/system-configuration df1:devs
```

1.5   Secrets and hidden messages

Many pieces of hardware and software contain extra messages conveying greetings to users, names of developers, political attitudes, love affairs, etc. These hidden texts go under a number of titles: "Easter eggs," "wasted memory", and others. Here are a collection of some of the little-known extra messages hiding in your equipment.

**#26:
Secret
greeting in
the Kickstart**

The Amiga developers are like most inventive people: If they see an opportunity to put their "signatures" in their software or hardware for the sake of immortality, they'll do it. For example, the insides of some Amiga cases actually have the hardware development team's signatures embossed in the case.

The internal hardware contains a greeting that you can't access directly through the Workbench.

The following BASIC program displays the hidden message after you enter the start and end addresses needed. Use the correct values for the version of Kickstart you have.

```
Addresses:
'V1.1 16653596 16653672 (early 1000's)
'V1.2 16649670 16649747 (500's and 2000's)
INPUT "Start address";Start
INPUT "End address";Finish
PRINT
FOR i = Start to Finish
  PRINT CHR$(PEEK(i));
NEXT i
```

Here we encourage you to browse through a bit of memory by entering other values. Maybe you'll find this text or a similar one in another location. If you find another message, write us with the start and end addresses: We'd like to know about your discovery.

**#27:
A love story**

Have you seen the secret text in the Preferences program of Workbench 1.2? You must execute a somewhat complicated procedure to see the message in the window's title bar.

Start Preferences 1.2 (this displays the Preferences screen). On the right you see the two mouse icons. Both mouse icons have two buttons. Move your mouse pointer to the leftmost button of the leftmost mouse icon. Click on it, and move the pointer to the next mouse button. Click on that and move the pointer to the left button of the rightmost mouse icon. Click on that button, then click on the rightmost button. Go from the left to the right a total of four times, and each time click once on each button. Once you have clicked all four buttons four times (sixteen mouse clicks), click on the Change Printer gadget. Click on the up arrow gadget by the printer window until you get to the top entry. Now click on the arrow one last time to see the love story text in the title bar.

#28:
A secret
message

Hold down both the <Shift> and <Alt> keys and any function key during a printout, and eject a disk from any drive at the same time. Another message appears on the Workbench screen.

Insert the disk again and you either get the same message again or perhaps another text. This other text only appears in older versions. When you want to see it on newer versions you must insert a disk whose disk icon is already on the Workbench screen. Then there will be enough time to display the new text.

2.
AmigaBASIC
tricks and tips

2.   AmigaBASIC tricks and tips

This chapter shows how AmigaBASIC programmers can make their programs extremely user-friendly. The days of the "user-obnoxious" home computer are long past. The earliest computers had to be rewired to perform a different program from that already set. Later computers had switches that you had to operate to enter or receive data (keyboards came still later). If you owned a C64 or other Commodore computer before buying your Amiga, you'll remember the difficulties you might have had even with that operating system as a beginner (e.g., typing LOAD"filename",8 just to load a file from disk).

There's no excuse for unfriendly user interfacing in Amiga programming. When dealing with a graphically-oriented computer like the Amiga, user-friendliness should affect every aspect of interacting with the user (i.e., all input options, selections and displays be programmed for user-friendliness).

The goal of user-friendliness can be achieved through a variety of methods. Almost all of these methods involve accessing Intuition and its graphic user interface. The use of icons, gadgets, string gadgets and requesters make a beginning user feel more comfortable with the computer, and help speed the intermediate user's productivity in the application that uses this type of interface.

Much of this chapter deals with maximizing this quality of user-friendliness, by focusing on input, selection and control. With this thought in mind, most of your programming for user response should use the mouse as the primary input device.

2.1   An Intuition window

Not everything needed for program control can be accomplished using menus, so we must look for alternatives. What are those alternatives? See the Workbench disk for some examples. Preferences is a good example of alternatives to drop-down menus. When you open Preferences all the possible options can be easily selected, and is therefore user-friendly. The Preferences program uses normal gadgets, sliders, filled gadgets and even scrolling tables to allow the user to make his selections.

Sliders control colors, key repeat delay, key repeat speed and the time between the clicks of a double-click. Filled gadgets indicate the number of characters per line and the status of Workbench interlace mode. Scrolling tables in the Change Printer section help the user select the correct printer driver. Normal gadgets on the main screen execute an action such as Save, Use or Cancel, by clicking on them.

The following programs show examples of all the above user-friendly gadgets. For openers, we need an output window to display these gadgets. AmigaBASIC usually opens a window directly after loading it. However, BASIC windows have some limitations, so we'll directly open a window using the Intuition library. The Amiga operating system libraries offer much more control than standard BASIC programming.

The first example program does nothing more than open an Intuition window on the Workbench screen. We call the file named `intuition.library` for this, which will also be used in the other example programs in this section. This program requires both `intuition.library` and `exec.library` to function. Use the `ConvertFD` BASIC program in the BASICDemos drawer on the `Extras` disk to create the `exec.library` and `intuition.library` files. When running the `ConvertFD` program be sure to correctly enter the complete disk identifier, pathname and filename at the prompt. If you don't, the `ConvertFD` program won't find the correct file. Here is an example run of the `ConvertFD` program, for Workbench 1.3 users that creates the `exec.bmap` file on a RAM disk:

```
Enter name of .fd file to read> "Extras 1.3:FD1.3/exec_lib.fd"
Enter name of .bmap file to produce > ram:exec.bmap
```

The example programs require the `exec.library` (`exec_lib.FD`), the `intuition.library` (`intuition_lib.fd`) and the `graphics.library` (`graphics_lib.fd`) to operate.

The optional disk available for this book, named T&T2:, contains the .bmap files in a drawer named bmaps, therefore the example programs that follow "look" in this drawer for the .bmap files. If your .bmap files are on a disk with a different name, or in a different drawer, alter the LIBRARY commands so the .bmap files can be opened.

The example programs that follow contain some BASIC lines that must be entered as one line in AmigaBASIC, even though they appear on two lines in this book. Formatting the program listings to fit into this book has split some long BASIC lines into two lines. An end-of-paragraph (¶) character shows where a BASIC line actually ends. When you see this character, press the <Return> key in the BASIC editor. For example, the following line appears as two lines in this book, but the ¶ marker indicates that it must be entered as one line in AmigaBASIC:

```
WinDef NWindow, 100, 50, 460, 150, 32+64+512&, 15&+4096&,
0&, Title$¶
```

The ¶ shows the actual end of the BASIC line. Here is our first example program, which opens an Intuition window on the Workbench screen:

```
'*********************************¶
'*                               *¶
'* Open Window under Intuition   *¶
'* ---------------------------   *¶
'*                               *¶
'* Author : Wolf-Gideon Bleek    *¶
'* Date   : May 22 '88           *¶
'* Version: 1.1                  *¶
'* Operating system:V1.2 & V1.3  *¶
'* Name   : Intuition-window     *¶
'*                               *¶
'*********************************¶
  OPTION BASE 1¶
  DEFLNG a-z¶
¶
' Bmaps located on disk named T&T2,yours may differ¶
  LIBRARY "T&T2:bmaps/exec.library"¶
  DECLARE FUNCTION AllocMem LIBRARY¶
  LIBRARY "T&T2:bmaps/intuition.library"¶
  DECLARE FUNCTION OpenWindow LIBRARY¶
  ¶
  MList      = 0&¶
  ¶
MainProgram:¶
  GOSUB OpenAll¶
   ¶
  ' Main part¶
  FOR i = 1 TO 10000 : NEXT i¶
  ¶
  GOSUB CloseAll¶
  ¶
END¶
OpenAll:¶
  Title$  = "My first BASIC-Window"¶
  WinDef NWindow, 100, 50, 460, 150, 32+64+512&, 15&+4096&,
0&, Title$¶
  WinBase = OpenWindow(NWindow)¶
  IF WinBase = 0 THEN ERROR 7¶
RETURN¶
CloseAll:¶
  CloseWindow(WinBase)¶
  CALL UnDef¶
RETURN¶
'-----------------------------------------------¶
SUB DefChip(Buffer, Size) STATIC¶
 SHARED MList¶
  Size=Size+8¶
```

```
    Buffer=AllocMem(Size,65538&)¶
    IF Buffer>0 THEN¶
      POKEL Buffer,MList¶
      POKEL Buffer+4,Size¶
      MList=Buffer¶
      Buffer=Buffer+8¶
    ELSE¶
      ERROR 7¶
    END IF¶
  END SUB¶
  SUB UnDef STATIC¶
   SHARED MList¶
  undef.loop:¶
    IF MList>0 THEN¶
      Address = PEEKL(MList)¶
      ListSize = PEEKL(MList+4)¶
      FreeMem MList, ListSize¶
      MList    = Address¶
      GOTO undef.loop¶
    END IF¶
  END SUB       ¶
  ¶
  SUB WinDef(bs, x%, y%, b%, h%, IDCMP, f, gad, T$) STATIC¶
    Size = 48+LEN(T$)+1¶
    DefChip bs,Size¶
    POKEW bs   ,x%       ' Left Corner¶
    POKEW bs+ 2,y%       ' Top Corner¶
    POKEW bs+ 4,b%       ' Width¶
    POKEW bs+ 6,h%       ' Height ¶
    POKEW bs+ 8,65535&   ' Detail- BlockPen¶
    POKEL bs+10,IDCMP    ' IDCMP Flags¶
    POKEL bs+14,f        ' Flags¶
    POKEL bs+18,gad      ' First Gadget¶
    POKEL bs+26,bs+48    ' Title¶
    POKEW bs+46,1        ' ScreenType ¶
    FOR i%=1 TO LEN(T$)¶
        POKE bs+47+i%,ASC(MID$(T$,i%,1))¶
    NEXT¶
  END SUB¶
```

Program description

The most important elements of the example program appear at the end of the program. Here you'll find the three subprograms which fulfill the three tasks required to open our Intuition window. DefChip() requests a memory area of the desired size. This is reserved using AllocMem(), an operating system function of exec.library. The routine stores two values in the first eight bytes (a list of the allocated memory). UnDef() releases the allocated memory. Mlist releases all memory areas one after another.

The first two subprograms are initialization routines. The WinDef() subprogram holds the most importance here, since it places the specified data in a NewWindow structure. Intuition needs this data before it can open a new window. WinDef() only places the data in a new memory area. Everything else is considered a subroutine of the main program.

Now that we know the task of the subprograms, let's look at the main program. First the `Intuition` and `Exec` libraries open. The program uses functions from both. The main section jumps to the `OpenAll` subroutine. The definition of a `NewWindow` structure using `WinDef()` is called here. This structure passes to Intuition by means of `OpenWindow()`. A correctly opened new window returns a pointer to the `Window` structure; if an error occurs it returns a 0. The new structure contains all the data necessary to create our own Intuition window.

After returning from the `OpenAll` subroutine, the program pauses using a `FOR/NEXT` loop so you can see the window for a moment. Then the BASIC interpreter jumps to another subroutine called `CloseAll`. This routine closes our window and releases the allocated memory.

Now we have a basis for our own user-friendly professional programs. Using this Intuition window, we can insert the user-friendly input facilities similar to those found in the Preferences program. Let's look at the first of these—gadgets.

2.1.1   Gadgets

The first user-friendly gadgets that we see in the Preferences program perform a direct action after the user selects them with the mouse. By moving the pointer onto one of these gadgets and pressing the left mouse button, you select different choices such as Change Printer, Edit Pointer or Cancel.

These gadgets can be accessed through BASIC programming. Amiga-BASIC pulls its gadget data from Intuition. Our new gadgets can easily be merged into the Intuition window program you read about in the preceding segment. The following subprogram defines a new gadget field (remember that the ¶ character tells you when to press the <Return> key). You can either save it as a separate BASIC program and append it later, or type it in at the end of the Intuition window program you entered previously:

```
SUB GadgetDef(bs,nx,x%,y%,b%,h%,f%,a%,T%,i,txt,si,n%)
STATIC¶
    DefChip bs,44&       ' Gadget-Structure length¶
    POKEL bs   ,nx      '*NextGadget¶
    POKEW bs+ 4,x%       ' LeftEdge¶
    POKEW bs+ 6,y%       ' TopEdge¶
```

```
        POKEW bs+ 8,b%      ' Width¶
        POKEW bs+10,h%      ' Height¶
        POKEW bs+12,f%      ' Flags¶
        POKEW bs+14,a%      ' Activation¶
        POKEW bs+16,T%      ' GadgetType¶
        POKEL bs+18,i       ' GadgetRender¶
        POKEL bs+26,txt     '*GadgetText¶
        POKEL bs+34,si      ' SpecialInfo¶
        POKEW bs+38,n%      ' GadgetID¶
    END SUB¶
```

This routine places the correct values necessary for a gadget in an area of memory. The variable bs contains the base address of our memory area. It also handles the return value of the memory allocation routine. nx marks the starting address of the next free gadget area, allowing us to use more than one gadget. We'll make use of this value later to add more gadgets to the window. x%, y%, b% and h% define the dimensions of the gadget.

Two flags, which we will discuss later, are defined with f% and a%. t% sets the gadget type (set at 1 in this first example—later on we'll add other gadget types). i and txt contain additional graphic information. i allows you to define the type of border to be displayed. txt defines the text inside the gadget. Finally, we place an identification value in n%. This value helps the program to determine which gadget was selected by the user.

Insert the GadgetDef subprogram from above at the end of the Intuition window example program, and enter the following line in the OpenAll subroutine:

```
GadgetDef Gadget,0&,50,50,90,15,0,1,1,0&,0&,0&,1
```

This call to GadgetDef defines our new gadget. This causes the following results:

- The address of the gadget structure is found after the close of the routine in Gadget

- Only one gadget is used; no more gadgets are contained in the gadget structure

- The position is 50,50

- The gadget is 90 pixels wide and 15 pixels high

- It is handled as a gadget that reacts to a mouse click

- The gadget is of boolean type and can only be activated

- There are no border graphics and no text inside the gadget (an invisible gadget)

- No additional structure is needed

- The gadget is accessed by number 1

This defined gadget structure interfaces with the new window structure using the following command sequence:

```
WinDef NWindow, 100, 50, 460, 150, 32+64+512&, 15&+4096&,
Gadget, Title$¶
```

Do not start the program yet. You <u>could</u>, but we wouldn't advise it. The program contains no routines for gadget checking. Since the gadget structure contains no graphic border the gadget is invisible. If you enter RUN now, the window appears. After doing some clicking, you might or might not find the region allocated for the gadget definition. Clicking the gadget produces no reaction. We must write another subroutine that jumps from the main program when it encounters some information.

The new program section below reads a gadget and gets a new Intuition message from the information port of the Intuition window. Then it branches to a new subroutine, IntuitionMsg, which reads and determines the result of the message:

```
      GADGETDOWN  = 32&¶
      GADGETUP    = 64&¶
      CLOSEW      = 512&¶
         ¶
      MList       = 0&¶
      Info        = 1¶
         ¶
MainProgram:¶
   GOSUB OpenAll¶
   ' Main part¶
   MainLoop:¶
      IF Info = 1 THEN¶
         IntuiMsg = GetMsg(UserPort)¶
         IF IntuiMsg > 0 THEN GOSUB IntuitionMsg¶
         GOTO MainLoop¶
      END IF    ¶
      ¶
   GOSUB CloseAll¶
      ¶
END¶
```

The GetMsg() function makes it possible to test the message port of a window for a message. This message port lies in the window structure that OpenWindow() returned to us. In this routine a new variable must be initialized to read the message port:

```
UserPort = PEEKL(WinBase+86) ¶
```

Now we can add the subroutine which controls the handling of the newly received message. It first determines the type of the message, since different actions on our window will return different messages. One message that we can handle is the `CloseWindow` message. This message returns when the user clicks on the window's close gadget. Our subroutine also displays the gadget number on the screen which was written in the gadget structure.

```
IntuitionMsg:  ¶
  MsgTyp    = PEEKL(IntuiMsg+20)¶
  Item      = PEEKL(IntuiMsg+28)¶
  GadgetNr% = PEEK(Item+39)¶
  CALL ReplyMsg(IntuiMsg)¶
  ¶
  IF (MsgTyp = GADGETDOWN) THEN¶
     'activated¶
     PRINT "DOWN Gadget-Nr.:";GadgetNr%¶
  END IF¶
  ¶
  IF (MsgTyp = GADGETUP) THEN¶
     'rel verify mode¶
     PRINT "UP   Gadget-Nr.:";GadgetNr%¶
  END IF¶
  ¶
  IF (MsgTyp = CLOSEW) THEN¶
     'System-Gadget Window closer¶
     PRINT "CLOSE WINDOW"¶
     Info = 0¶
  END IF¶
RETURN¶
```

Assemble the program sections and start the program. The Intuition window appears on the Workbench screen. Now for our first test. Click in the upper left quarter of the screen until you find the invisible gadget. It's invisible because no border or text definition exists in the Gadget structure (the gadget lies at screen location 50,50). When you click on it with the mouse, the new gadget becomes visible. After releasing the mouse button it disappears, and the gadget number appears in the AmigaBASIC Output window.

For the second test of our intuition message subroutine click on the close gadget of the window. First the text appears in the Output window, then the window closes. We have just completed the groundwork required for using gadgets.

Here is the complete program:

```
'*********************************¶
'*                               *¶
'* Gadgets with Intuition        *¶
'* ----------------------------- *¶
'*                               *¶
'* Author : Wolf-Gideon Bleek    *¶
'* Date   : May 23 '88           *¶
```

```
'* Name   : Gadget-one            *¶
'* Version: 1.2                   *¶
'* System : V1.2 & V1.3           *¶
'*                                *¶
'*********************************¶
  OPTION BASE 1¶
  DEFLNG a-z¶
  ¶
' Bmaps located on disk named T&T2,yours may differ¶
  LIBRARY "t&T2:bmaps/exec.library"¶
  DECLARE FUNCTION AllocMem LIBRARY¶
  DECLARE FUNCTION GetMsg LIBRARY¶
  LIBRARY "t&t2:bmaps/intuition.library"¶
  DECLARE FUNCTION OpenWindow LIBRARY¶
  GADGETDOWN = 32&¶
  GADGETUP   = 64&¶
  CLOSEW     = 512&¶
     ¶
  MList      = 0&¶
  Info       = 1¶
  ¶
MainProgram:¶
  GOSUB OpenAll¶
  ' Main part¶
  MainLoop:¶
    IF Info = 1 THEN¶
      IntuiMsg = GetMsg(UserPort)¶
      IF IntuiMsg > 0 THEN GOSUB IntuitionMsg¶
      GOTO MainLoop¶
    END IF    ¶
  ¶
  GOSUB CloseAll¶
  ¶
END¶
¶
OpenAll:¶
  GadgetDef Gadget, 0&, 50, 50, 90, 15, 0, 1, 1, 0&, 0&, 0&, 1¶

  Title$    = "The invisible gadget"¶
  WinDef NWindow, 100, 50, 460, 150, 32+64+512&, 15&+4096&,
Gadget, Title$¶
  WinBase   = OpenWindow(NWindow)¶
  IF WinBase = 0 THEN ERROR 7¶
  UserPort  = PEEKL(WinBase+86)¶
RETURN¶
¶
CloseAll:¶
  CALL CloseWindow(WinBase)¶
  CALL UnDef¶
RETURN¶
¶
IntuitionMsg:  ¶
  MsgTyp    = PEEKL(IntuiMsg+20)¶
  Item      = PEEKL(IntuiMsg+28)¶
```

```
      GadgetNr% = PEEK(Item+39)¶
      CALL ReplyMsg(IntuiMsg)¶
      ¶
      IF (MsgTyp = GADGETDOWN) THEN¶
         'activated¶
         PRINT "DOWN Gadget-Nr.:";GadgetNr%¶
      END IF¶
      ¶
      IF (MsgTyp = GADGETUP) THEN¶
         'rel verify mode¶
         PRINT "UP   Gadget-Nr.:";GadgetNr%¶
      END IF¶
      ¶
      IF (MsgTyp = CLOSEW) THEN¶
         'System-Gadget Window closer¶
         PRINT "CLOSE WINDOW"¶
         Info = 0¶
      END IF¶
   RETURN¶
   '-------------------------------------------¶
   ¶
   SUB DefChip(Buffer,Size)STATIC¶
    SHARED MList¶
     Size=Size+8¶
     Buffer=AllocMem(Size,65538&)¶
     IF Buffer>0 THEN¶
       POKEL Buffer,MList¶
       POKEL Buffer+4,Size¶
       MList=Buffer¶
       Buffer=Buffer+8¶
     ELSE¶
       ERROR 7¶
     END IF¶
   END SUB¶
   ¶
   SUB UnDef STATIC¶
    SHARED MList¶
   undef.loop:¶
     IF MList>0 THEN¶
       Address = PEEKL(MList)¶
       ListSize = PEEKL(MList+4)¶
       FreeMem MList, ListSize¶
       MList   = Address¶
       GOTO undef.loop¶
     END IF¶
   END SUB        ¶
   ¶
   SUB WinDef(bs, x%, y%, b%, h%, IDCMP, f, gad, T$) STATIC¶
     Size = 48+LEN(T$)+1¶
     DefChip bs,Size¶
     POKEW bs   ,x%      ' Left Corner¶
     POKEW bs+ 2,y%      ' Top Corner¶
     POKEW bs+ 4,b%      ' Width¶
     POKEW bs+ 6,h%      ' Height¶
     POKEW bs+ 8,65535&  ' Detail- BlockPen¶
     POKEL bs+10,IDCMP   ' IDCMPFlags¶
```

```
      POKEL bs+14,f          ' Flags¶
      POKEL bs+18,gad        ' First Gadget¶
      POKEL bs+26,bs+48      ' Title¶
      POKEW bs+46,1          ' Screen Type ¶

      FOR i%=1 TO LEN(T$)¶
          POKE bs+47+i%,ASC(MID$(T$,i%,1))¶
      NEXT¶
END SUB¶
¶
SUB GadgetDef(bs, nx, x%, y%, b%, h%, f%, a%, T%, i, txt, si,
n%) STATIC¶
   DefChip bs,44&        ' Gadget-Structure length¶
   POKEL bs    ,nx       '*NextGadget¶
   POKEW bs+ 4,x%        ' LeftEdge¶
   POKEW bs+ 6,y%        ' TopEdge¶
   POKEW bs+ 8,b%        ' Width¶
   POKEW bs+10,h%        ' Height¶
   POKEW bs+12,f%        ' Flags¶
   POKEW bs+14,a%        ' Activation¶
   POKEW bs+16,T%        ' GadgetType¶
   POKEL bs+18,i         ' GadgetRender¶
   POKEL bs+26,txt       '*GadgetText¶
   POKEL bs+34,si        ' SpecialInfo¶
   POKEW bs+38,n%        ' GadgetID¶
END SUB¶
¶
```

2.1.2   Gadget borders and text

A very important feature has been missing from our gadgets: visibility. You had to hunt around for this gadget, and could only see it when you clicked on it.

Let's clear up this small problem. In the description of the subprogram GadgetDef we learned about the variables txt and i. GadgetDef uses these variables to enter the basic graphic elements of Intuition. We can define an IntuiText structure for the gadget with txt, and define a graphic or line border with i.

First, let's look at the text. For this we need the IntuiText structure. It defines the position, color, character set, character size, and the text. The following subprogram allocates an area of memory and fills this allocated area with the required data:

```
SUB IntuiText(bs, cl%, x%, y%, T$, nx) STATIC¶
   Size=20+LEN(T$)+1   ' Structure length+ Text length+
Nullbyte¶
```

```
DefChip bs,Size¶
POKE  bs   ,cl%        ' FrontPen¶
POKE  bs+ 2,1          ' DrawMode¶
POKEW bs+ 4,x%         ' Left corner¶
POKEW bs+ 6,y%         ' Top corner¶
POKEL bs+12,bs+20      ' IText¶
POKEL bs+16,nx         ' NextText¶
FOR i%=1 TO LEN(T$) ¶
    POKE bs+19+i%,ASC(MID$(T$,i%,1))¶
NEXT¶
END SUB¶
```

Following the starting address of the structure we insert the character color of the text and the text's starting position in pixels. We then supply a pointer to the text. Since the pointer is allowed more text, you can supply a pointer to another `IntuiText` structure as the ending value.

The routine itself sets the drawing mode to JAM2 (i.e., foreground and background colors are "jammed" into the selected area). This ensures that the drawing mode overwrites the background, so you can clearly read the text later. You can adjust the second color to some degree by increasing a value in the parameter list and POKE the new color value into bs+1!. To insert text in the gadget, first you must put a text into the subroutine and then append the text to the `Gadget` definition routine as follows:

```
TestTxt$ = "Test-Text"¶
IntuiText Text, 2, 10, 2, TestTxt$, 0& ¶
GadgetDef Gadget, 0&, 50, 50, 90, 15, 0, 1, 1, Edge, Text,0&, 1¶
```

Next we should be concerned with border lines. Their main purpose is to create a border for the mouse click. In addition, border lines supply underlining for texts that need it. Because the edges are also passed in the gadget structure, we can create a separate structure. This structure needs a coordinate table, the color and the position, which can be treated as a normal border structure. The coordinates appear in memory following the structure.

We have developed a somewhat different subprogram for the border structure. It inserts the value into memory. Not only that; it also calculates the values of the coordinates needed by the table. This makes it very simple to define a box around a gadget. Here is the complete function:

```
SUB Border(bs, x%, y%, c%, b%, h%) STATIC¶
   DefChip bs,48&        ' Structure length+Coordinate table¶
   POKEW bs   ,x%        ' Left corner¶
   POKEW bs+2,y%         ' Top corner¶
   POKE  bs+4,c%         ' FrontPen¶
   POKE  bs+7,8          ' Count¶
   POKEL bs+8,bs+16      '*XY¶
   FOR i%=0 TO 1¶
```

```
        POKEW bs+22+i%*4,h%-1¶
        POKEW bs+24+i%*4,b%-1¶
        POKEW bs+32+i%*4,1¶
        POKEW bs+38+i%*4,h%-1¶
        POKEW bs+40+i%*4,b%-2¶
    NEXT¶
END SUB¶
```

The routine above contains the corresponding values needed to define
the border. Then we insert the base address of the structure in the definition of the gadget, as we did in the `IntuiText` structure. Now the
`Border` structure combines with the `Gadget` structure. Here is an
example:

```
Border Edge, 0, 0, 3, 90, 15¶
GadgetDef Gadget,0&, 50, 50, 90, 15, 0, 1, 1,Edge,Text,0&,1¶
```

The gadget now contains text and is surrounded by a border. This border
can be enlarged if you wish.

We would now like to show the complete listing. This program listing
contains all of the subroutines and definitions mentioned above. You
can use this to determine whether you have made any errors in putting
the modules together:

```
'*********************************¶
'*                               *¶
'* Boolean-Gadgets with Intuition *¶
'* ----------------------------- *¶
'*                               *¶
'* Author : Wolf-Gideon Bleek    *¶
'* Date   : May 23 '88           *¶
'* Name   : Gadgets              *¶
'* Version: 1.2                  *¶
'* System : V1.2 & V1.3          *¶
'*                               *¶
'*********************************¶
    OPTION BASE 1¶
    DEFLNG a-z¶
    ¶
' Bmaps located on disk named T&T2,yours may differ¶
    LIBRARY "t&T2:bmaps/exec.library"¶
    DECLARE FUNCTION AllocMem LIBRARY¶
    DECLARE FUNCTION GetMsg LIBRARY¶
    LIBRARY "t&t2:bmaps/intuition.library"¶
    DECLARE FUNCTION OpenWindow LIBRARY¶
    GADGETDOWN = 32&¶
    GADGETUP   = 64&¶
    CLOSEW     = 512&¶
        ¶
    MList      = 0&¶
    Info       = 1¶
    ¶
```

```
MainProgram:¶
  GOSUB OpenAll¶
  ' Main part¶
  MainLoop:¶
    IF Info = 1 THEN¶
      IntuiMsg = GetMsg(UserPort)¶
      IF IntuiMsg > 0 THEN GOSUB IntuitionMsg¶
      GOTO MainLoop¶
    END IF   ¶
  ¶
  GOSUB CloseAll¶
  ¶
END¶
¶
OpenAll:¶
  Border Edge, 0, 0, 3, 90, 15¶
  TestTxt$ = "Test-Text"¶
  IntuiText Text, 2, 10, 2, TestTxt$, 0& ¶
  GadgetDef Gadget, 0&, 50, 50, 90, 15, 0, 1, 1, Edge, Text, 0&,
1¶
  Title$   = "My first complete gadget"¶
  WinDef NWindow, 100, 100, 460, 100, 32+64+512&, 15&+4096&,
Gadget, Title$¶
  WinBase  = OpenWindow(NWindow)¶
  IF WinBase = 0 THEN ERROR 7¶
  RastPort = PEEKL(WinBase+50)¶
  UserPort = PEEKL(WinBase+86)¶
RETURN¶
¶
CloseAll:¶
  CALL CloseWindow(WinBase)¶
  CALL UnDef¶
RETURN¶
¶
IntuitionMsg:   ¶
  MsgTyp    = PEEKL(IntuiMsg+20)¶
  Item      = PEEKL(IntuiMsg+28)¶
  GadgetNr% = PEEK(Item+39)¶
  CALL ReplyMsg(IntuiMsg)¶
  ¶
  IF (MsgTyp = GADGETDOWN) THEN¶
    'immediately activated¶
    PRINT "DOWN Gadget-Nr.:";GadgetNr%¶
  END IF¶
  ¶
  IF (MsgTyp = GADGETUP) THEN¶
    'verify mode¶
    PRINT "UP   Gadget-Nr.:";GadgetNr%¶
  END IF¶
  ¶
  IF (MsgTyp = CLOSEW) THEN¶
    'System-Gadget Window close¶
    PRINT"CLOSE WINDOW"¶
    Info = 0¶
  END IF¶
RETURN¶
```

```
'-----------------------------------------------¶
¶
SUB DefChip(Buffer,Size)STATIC¶
 SHARED MList¶
  Size=Size+8¶
  Buffer=AllocMem(Size,65538&)¶
  IF Buffer>0 THEN¶
    POKEL Buffer,MList¶
    POKEL Buffer+4,Size¶
    MList=Buffer¶
    Buffer=Buffer+8¶
  ELSE¶
    ERROR 7¶
  END IF¶
END SUB¶
SUB UnDef STATIC¶
 SHARED MList¶
undef.loop:¶
  IF MList>0 THEN¶
    Address = PEEKL(MList)¶
    ListSize = PEEKL(MList+4)¶
    FreeMem MList, ListSize¶
    MList    = Address¶
    GOTO undef.loop¶
  END IF¶
END SUB        ¶
SUB WinDef(bs, x%, y%, b%, h%, IDCMP, f, gad, T$) STATIC¶
  Size = 48+LEN(T$)+1¶
  DefChip bs,Size¶
  POKEW bs  ,x%       ' Left Corner¶
  POKEW bs+ 2,y%      ' Top Corner¶
  POKEW bs+ 4,b%      ' Width¶
  POKEW bs+ 6,h%      ' Height¶
  POKEW bs+ 8,65535&  ' Detail- BlockPen¶
  POKEL bs+10,IDCMP   ' IDCMP Flags¶
  POKEL bs+14,f       ' Flags¶
  POKEL bs+18,gad     ' First Gadget¶
  POKEL bs+26,bs+48   ' Title¶
  POKEW bs+46,1       ' Screen Type ¶
  FOR i%=1 TO LEN(T$)¶
     POKE bs+47+i%,ASC(MID$(T$,i%,1))¶
  NEXT¶
END SUB¶
SUB GadgetDef(bs, nx, x%, y%, b%, h%, f%, a%, T%, i, txt, si,
n%) STATIC¶
  DefChip bs,44&        ' Gadget-Structure length¶
  POKEL bs  ,nx        '*NextGadget¶
  POKEW bs+ 4,x%       ' LeftEdge¶
  POKEW bs+ 6,y%       ' TopEdge¶
  POKEW bs+ 8,b%       ' Width¶
  POKEW bs+10,h%       ' Height¶
  POKEW bs+12,f%       ' Flags¶
  POKEW bs+14,a%       ' Activation¶
  POKEW bs+16,T%       ' GadgetType¶
```

```
        POKEL bs+18,i        ' GadgetRender¶
        POKEL bs+26,txt      '*GadgetText¶
        POKEL bs+34,si       ' SpecialInfo¶
        POKEW bs+38,n%       ' GadgetID¶
END SUB¶
¶
SUB IntuiText(bs, cl%, x%, y%, T$, nx) STATIC¶
     Size=20+LEN(T$)+1    ' Structure length+ Text length+
Nullbyte¶
        DefChip bs,Size¶
        POKE  bs   ,cl%      ' FrontPen¶
        POKE  bs+ 2,1        ' DrawMode¶
        POKEW bs+ 4,x%       ' Left corner¶
        POKEW bs+ 6,y%       ' Top corner¶
        POKEL bs+12,bs+20    ' IText¶
        POKEL bs+16,nx       ' NextText¶
        FOR i%=1 TO LEN(T$)¶
            POKE bs+19+i%,ASC(MID$(T$,i%,1))¶
        NEXT¶
END SUB¶
¶
SUB Border(bs, x%, y%, c%, b%, h%) STATIC¶
        DefChip bs,48&       ' Structure length+ Coordinate table¶

        POKEW bs   ,x%       ' Left corner¶
        POKEW bs+2,y%        ' Top corner¶
        POKE  bs+4,c%        ' FrontPen¶
        POKE  bs+7,8         ' Count¶
        POKEL bs+8,bs+16     '*XY¶
        FOR i%=0 TO 1¶
            POKEW bs+22+i%*4,h%-1¶
            POKEW bs+24+i%*4,b%-1¶
            POKEW bs+32+i%*4,1¶
            POKEW bs+38+i%*4,h%-1¶
            POKEW bs+40+i%*4,b%-2¶
        NEXT¶
END SUB¶
```

2.1.3   User-friendly gadgets

Let's define four gadgets that are used in many programs. The gadgets we will define are OK, Cancel, Reset, and Undo—these should all look familiar to you. OK would be used to continue a program, and Cancel would stop a function. Reset could be programmed to reset variables to their original status. Undo could be coded to reset the variable that was changed last.

We'll do this in a specific order. First we'll show you the gadget, text, and border definitions. Then we'll list the reading routines with empty subroutines. Selecting one of the four gadgets calls one of the subroutines.

The gadget definitions:

```
Border Bord, -1, -1, 1,67,14¶
IntuiText OKTxt, 1, 26, 2, "OK", 0&¶
IntuiText CancelTxt, 1, 10, 2, "Cancel", 0&¶
IntuiText ResetTxt, 1, 14, 2, "Reset", 0&¶
IntuiText UndoTxt, 1, 20, 2, "Undo", 0&¶
GadgetDef UndoGad, 0&, 380, 52, 65, 12, 0, 1, 1, Bord,
UndoTxt, 0&, 1¶
GadgetDef ResetGad, UndoGad, 380, 68, 65, 12, 0, 1, 1,
Bord, ResetTxt, 0&, 2 ¶
GadgetDef OKGad, ResetGad, 380, 84, 65, 12, 0, 1, 1, Bord,
OKTxt, 0&, 3¶
GadgetDef CancGad, OKGad, 380, 100, 65, 12, 0, 1, 1, Bord,
CancelTxt, 0&, 4 ¶
Title$ = "An example of four user friendly Gadgets"¶
WinDef NWindow, 100, 50, 460, 150, 32+64+512&, 15&+4096&,
CancGad, Title$¶
```

The reading routines:

```
'The check routines:¶
IF (MsgType = GADGETDOWN) THEN¶
 'activation¶
 PRINT "DOWN Gadget-Nr.:";GadgetNr%¶
END IF¶
¶
IF (MsgType = GADGETUP) THEN¶
 'rel verify mode¶
 PRINT "UP Gadget-Nr.:";GadgetNr%¶
 IF GadgetNr% = 1 THEN¶
  GOSUB Undo    ' put in old value¶
 END IF¶
 IF GadgetNr% = 2 THEN¶
  GOSUB ResetRoutine  'all values back to original¶
 END IF¶
 IF GadgetNr% = 3 THEN¶
  GOSUB Ok  ' end value entry¶
 END IF¶
 IF GadgetNr% = 4 THEN¶
  GOSUB Cancel  ' interrupt value entry¶
 END IF¶
END IF¶
¶
IF (MsgType = CLOSEW) THEN¶
 'close system Gadget window¶
 PRINT "CLOSE WINDOW"¶
 Info = 0¶
END IF¶
¶
RETURN¶
```

```
¶
Undo:¶
   PRINT "The UNDO gadget was selected"¶
RETURN  ¶
¶
ResetRoutine:¶
   PRINT "The RESET gadget was selected"¶
RETURN ¶
¶
Ok: ¶
   PRINT "The OK gadget was selected"¶
RETURN  ¶
¶
Cancel:¶
   PRINT "The CANCEL gadget was selected"¶
RETURN  ¶
```

Here is a listing of the complete program with the new gadget definitions added:

```
'*******************************¶
'*                             *¶
'* Friendly-Gadgets with Intuition*¶
'* --------------------------- *¶
'*                             *¶
'* Author : Wolf-Gideon Bleek   *¶
'* Date   : May 23 '88          *¶
'* Name   : Friendly-Gadgets    *¶
'* Version: 1.2                 *¶
'* System : V1.2 & V1.3         *¶
'*                             *¶
'*******************************¶
   OPTION BASE 1¶
   DEFLNG a-z¶
' Bmaps located on disk named T&T2,yours may differ¶
   LIBRARY "t&T2:bmaps/exec.library"¶
   DECLARE FUNCTION AllocMem LIBRARY¶
   DECLARE FUNCTION GetMsg LIBRARY¶
   LIBRARY "t&t2:bmaps/intuition.library"¶
   DECLARE FUNCTION OpenWindow LIBRARY¶
   GADGETDOWN = 32&¶
   GADGETUP   = 64&¶
   CLOSEW     = 512&¶
      ¶
   MList    = 0&¶
   Info     = 1¶
      ¶
MainProgramm:¶
   GOSUB OpenAll¶
   ' Main part¶
   MainLoop:¶
     IF Info = 1 THEN¶
       IntuiMsg = GetMsg(UserPort)¶
       IF IntuiMsg > 0 THEN GOSUB IntuitionMsg¶
       GOTO MainLoop¶
     END IF   ¶
```

```
   ¶
   GOSUB CloseAll¶
   ¶
END¶
¶
OpenAll:¶
¶
   Border Bord, -1, -1, 1,67,14¶
   IntuiText OKTxt, 1, 26, 2, "OK", 0&¶
   IntuiText CancelTxt, 1, 10, 2, "Cancel", 0&¶
   IntuiText ResetTxt, 1, 14, 2, "Reset", 0&¶
   IntuiText UndoTxt, 1, 20, 2, "Undo", 0&¶
   GadgetDef UndoGad, 0&, 380, 52, 65, 12, 0, 1, 1, Bord,
UndoTxt, 0&, 1¶
   GadgetDef ResetGad, UndoGad, 380, 68, 65, 12, 0, 1, 1, Bord,
ResetTxt, 0&, 2 ¶
   GadgetDef OKGad, ResetGad, 380, 84, 65, 12, 0, 1, 1, Bord,
OKTxt, 0&, 3¶
   GadgetDef CancGad, OKGad, 380, 100, 65, 12, 0, 1, 1, Bord,
CancelTxt, 0&, 4 ¶
   Title$ = "An example of four user friendly Gadgets"¶
   WinDef NWindow, 100, 50, 460, 150, 32+64+512&, 15&+4096&,
CancGad, Title$¶
   WinBase  = OpenWindow(NWindow)¶
   IF WinBase = 0 THEN ERROR 7¶
   RastPort = PEEKL(WinBase+50)¶
   UserPort = PEEKL(WinBase+86)¶
RETURN¶
¶
CloseAll:¶
   CALL CloseWindow(WinBase)¶
   CALL UnDef¶
RETURN¶
¶
IntuitionMsg:  ¶
   MsgType   = PEEKL(IntuiMsg+20)¶
   Item      = PEEKL(IntuiMsg+28)¶
   GadgetNr% = PEEK(Item+39)¶
   CALL ReplyMsg(IntuiMsg)¶
'The check routines:¶
IF (MsgType = GADGETDOWN) THEN¶
 'activation¶
 PRINT "DOWN Gadget-Nr.:";GadgetNr%¶
END IF¶
¶
IF (MsgType = GADGETUP) THEN¶
 'rel verify mode¶
 PRINT "UP Gadget-Nr.:";GadgetNr%¶
 IF GadgetNr% = 1 THEN¶
  GOSUB Undo    ' put in old value¶
 END IF¶
 IF GadgetNr% = 2 THEN¶
  GOSUB ResetRoutine  'all values back to original¶
 END IF¶
```

```
    IF GadgetNr% = 3 THEN¶
      GOSUB Ok  ' end value entry¶
    END IF¶
    IF GadgetNr% = 4 THEN¶
      GOSUB Cancel  ' interrupt value entry¶
    END IF¶
  END IF¶
¶
  IF (MsgType = CLOSEW) THEN¶
   'close system Gadget window¶
   PRINT "CLOSE WINDOW"¶
   Info = 0¶
  END IF¶
¶
RETURN¶
¶
Undo:¶
    PRINT "The UNDO gadget was selected"¶
RETURN ¶
¶
ResetRoutine:¶
    PRINT "The RESET gadget was selected"¶
RETURN ¶
¶
Ok: ¶
    PRINT "The OK gadget was selected"¶
RETURN  ¶
¶
Cancel:¶
    PRINT "The CANCEL gadget was selected"¶
RETURN  ¶
¶
'-----------------------------------------------¶
¶
SUB DefChip(Buffer,Size)STATIC¶
  SHARED MList¶
    Size=Size+8¶
    Buffer=AllocMem(Size,65538&)¶
    IF Buffer>0 THEN¶
      POKEL Buffer,MList¶
      POKEL Buffer+4,Size¶
      MList=Buffer¶
      Buffer=Buffer+8¶
    ELSE¶
      ERROR 7¶
    END IF¶
END SUB¶
SUB UnDef STATIC¶
  SHARED MList¶
undef.loop:¶
    IF MList>0 THEN¶
      Address = PEEKL(MList)¶
      ListSize = PEEKL(MList+4)¶
      FreeMem MList, ListSize¶
      MList   = Address¶
      GOTO undef.loop¶
```

```
        END IF¶
END SUB          ¶
SUB WinDef(bs, x%, y%, b%, h%, IDCMP, f, gad, T$) STATIC¶
   Size = 48+LEN(T$)+1¶
   DefChip bs,Size¶
   POKEW bs   ,x%         ' Left Corner¶
   POKEW bs+ 2,y%         ' Top Corner¶
   POKEW bs+ 4,b%         ' Width¶
   POKEW bs+ 6,h%         ' Height¶
   POKEW bs+ 8,65535&     ' Detail- BlockPen¶
   POKEL bs+10,IDCMP      ' IDCMP Flags¶
   POKEL bs+14,f          ' Flags¶
   POKEL bs+18,gad        ' First Gadget¶
   POKEL bs+26,bs+48      ' Title¶
   POKEW bs+46,1          ' Screen Type ¶
   FOR i%=1 TO LEN(T$)¶
       POKE bs+47+i%,ASC(MID$(T$,i%,1))¶
   NEXT¶
END SUB¶
SUB GadgetDef(bs, nx, x%, y%, b%, h%, f%, a%, T%, i, txt, si,
n%) STATIC¶
   DefChip bs,44&         ' Gadget-Structure length¶
   POKEL bs   ,nx         '*NextGadget¶
   POKEW bs+ 4,x%         ' LeftEdge¶
   POKEW bs+ 6,y%         ' TopEdge¶
   POKEW bs+ 8,b%         ' Width¶
   POKEW bs+10,h%         ' Height¶
   POKEW bs+12,f%         ' Flags¶
   POKEW bs+14,a%         ' Activation¶
   POKEW bs+16,T%         ' GadgetType¶
   POKEL bs+18,i          ' GadgetRender¶
   POKEL bs+26,txt        '*GadgetText¶
   POKEL bs+34,si         ' SpecialInfo¶
   POKEW bs+38,n%         ' GadgetID¶
END SUB¶
¶
SUB IntuiText(bs, cl%, x%, y%, T$, nx) STATIC¶
   Size=20+LEN(T$)+1 ' Structure length+ Text length+
Nullbyte¶
   DefChip bs,Size¶
   POKE  bs   ,cl%        ' FrontPen¶
   POKE  bs+ 2,1          ' DrawMode¶
   POKEW bs+ 4,x%         ' Left corner¶
   POKEW bs+ 6,y%         ' Top corner¶
   POKEL bs+12,bs+20      ' IText¶
   POKEL bs+16,nx         ' NextText¶
   FOR i%=1 TO LEN(T$)¶
       POKE bs+19+i%,ASC(MID$(T$,i%,1))¶
   NEXT¶
END SUB¶
¶
SUB Border(bs, x%, y%, c%, b%, h%) STATIC¶
   DefChip bs,48&         ' Structure length+ Coordinate
table¶
```

```
      POKEW bs  ,x%        ' Left corner¶
      POKEW bs+2,y%        ' Top corner¶
      POKE  bs+4,c%        ' FrontPen¶
      POKE  bs+7,8         ' Count¶
      POKEL bs+8,bs+16     '*XY¶
      FOR i%=0 TO 1¶
         POKEW bs+22+i%*4,h%-1¶
         POKEW bs+24+i%*4,b%-1¶
         POKEW bs+32+i%*4,1¶
         POKEW bs+38+i%*4,h%-1¶
         POKEW bs+40+i%*4,b%-2¶
      NEXT¶
   END SUB¶
```

2.1.4   Filled gadgets

When you create gadgets for a window, you should make it a habit to create groups of gadgets that represent specific actions and responses. Filling a window with individual gadgets is inadvisable. This ensures that only a group of gadgets can be selected. For example, let's consider the selection of a font. Only one font can be active at a time. Filled gadgets have a built-in limiting factor. When you click on the desired status, this action negates the previously clicked filled gadget (i.e., the new gadget becomes filled and the old gadget becomes "plain").

Selection tables

The programming involved in making filled gadgets is somewhat different from that required for normal gadgets. You create structures, graphics and text as usual. But after activating a gadget, the screen area occupied by the clicked gadget must change color (the filling). Intuition tests the gadget status. If the user selects a filled gadget, the background area of the gadget changes color. We use graphics.library to fill and unfill (empty) our filled gadgets. This library file contains the two commands SetDrMd (SetDrawingMode) and RectFill (RectangleFill). When calling this file, you should be sure that the line lists the correct DOS path. The following example goes into the T&T2 disk's bmaps: directory to access graphics.library:

```
LIBRARY "T&T2:bmaps/graphics.library"
```

Be sure to rename any LIBRARY call paths to suit the directories you're using.

In addition, our evaluation routine must clear (unfill) a gadget that was chosen previously. Here are our example gadgets:

```
Border Bord, -1, -1, 1, 100, 14¶
IntuiText To60, 1, 10, 2, "Topaz 60", 0&¶
IntuiText To80, 1, 10, 2, "Topaz 80", 0&¶
```

```
   IntuiText PC60, 1, 26, 2, "PC 60", 0&¶
   IntuiText PC80, 1, 26, 2, "PC 80", 0&¶
GadgetDef To60Gad, 0&, 80, 61, 98, 12, 0, 1, 1, Bord, To60, 0&,
1¶
GadgetDef To80Gad, To60Gad, 80, 74, 98, 12,0,1,1,Bord,To80,
0&, 2¶
GadgetDef PC60Gad, To80Gad, 80, 87, 98, 12,
0,1,1,Bord,PC60,0&, 3¶
GadgetDef PC80Gad, PC60Gad, 80,100, 98, 12,
0,1,1,Bord,PC80,0&,4¶
Title$ = "Font choice"¶
WinDef NWindow, 100, 50, 460, 150, 32+64+512&, 15&+4096&,
PC80Gad, Title$¶
```

All gadgets use the same `Border` structure which was used to create a table similar to the paper size table in the Preferences program. The first four texts in the program above specify four different fonts. The program then creates a pointer to the gadget list. The program places this list in the window definition area along with the window's title.

After starting the program we see a set of gadgets in the window, from which you can select the desired font. To signify the active font, we must click on the gadget box to fill it. The following new reading routine for the Intuition message will perform this change of gadget appearance (`fill.unfill`):

```
IF (MsgTyp = GADGETUP) THEN¶
 'rel verify mode¶
 PRINT "UP Gadget-Nr.:";GadgetNr%¶
 IF active THEN¶
  SetDrMd RastPort, 2¶
  RectFill RastPort, 80&, 13*active+48&, 177&,
13*active+59&¶
  SetDrMd RastPort, 1¶
 END IF¶
 active = GadgetNr%¶
 SetDrMd RastPort, 2¶
 RectFill RastPort, 80&, 13*active+48&, 177&, 13*active+59&¶

 SetDrMd RastPort, 1¶
END IF¶
```

The reading routine ensures that the program knows the variables chosen by the font. Selecting a different font fills in the current gadget and unfills the previously selected gadget.

Next we analyze the new font chosen by the user. The program calculates the border coordinates and displays the border graphically. Then the routine ends and returns to the main program.

Tables for many different purposes can be built using this method. The programmer must prepare the corresponding number of gadgets and handle the calculations involved with inverting the graphic. This should pose no problem because all of the gadgets in the table are of the same size and are easy to calculate.

Here's the complete listing, with all subprograms, library calls and variables:

```
'**********************************¶
'*                              *¶
'*  Fill-Gadgets with Intuition  *¶
'*  ----------------------------  *¶
'*                              *¶
'*  Author : Wolf-Gideon Bleek   *¶
'*  Date   : May 23 '88          *¶
'*  Name   : Fill-Gadgets        *¶
'*  Version: 1.2                 *¶
'*  System : V1.2 & V1.3         *¶
'*                              *¶
'**********************************¶
  OPTION BASE 1¶
  DEFLNG a-z¶
' Bmaps located on disk named T&T2,yours may differ¶
  LIBRARY "t&T2/bmaps/exec.library"¶
  DECLARE FUNCTION AllocMem LIBRARY¶
  DECLARE FUNCTION GetMsg LIBRARY¶
  LIBRARY "t&t2/bmaps/intuition.library"¶
  DECLARE FUNCTION OpenWindow LIBRARY¶
  LIBRARY "t&t2/bmaps/graphics.library"¶
  ¶
  GADGETDOWN = 32&¶
  GADGETUP   = 64&¶
  CLOSEW     = 512&¶
     ¶
  MList      = 0&¶
  Info       = 1¶
     ¶
MainProgramm:¶
  GOSUB OpenAll¶
  ' Main part¶
  MainLoop:¶
     IF Info = 1 THEN¶
        IntuiMsg = GetMsg(UserPort)¶
        IF IntuiMsg > 0 THEN GOSUB IntuitionMsg¶
        GOTO MainLoop¶
     END IF   ¶
     ¶
  GOSUB CloseAll¶
     ¶
END¶
  ¶
OpenAll:¶
  Border Bord, -1, -1, 1, 100, 14¶
  IntuiText To60, 1, 10, 2, "Topaz 60", 0&¶
  IntuiText To80, 1, 10, 2, "Topaz 80", 0&¶
  IntuiText PC60, 1, 26, 2, "PC 60", 0&¶
```

```
   IntuiText PC80, 1, 26, 2, "PC 80", 0&¶
   GadgetDef To60Gad, 0&, 80, 61, 98, 12, 0, 1, 1, Bord, To60,
0&, 1¶
   GadgetDef To80Gad, To60Gad, 80, 74, 98, 12, 0, 1, 1, Bord,
To80, 0&, 2¶
   GadgetDef PC60Gad, To80Gad, 80, 87, 98, 12, 0, 1, 1, Bord,
PC60, 0&, 3¶
   GadgetDef PC80Gad, PC60Gad, 80, 100, 98, 12, 0, 1, 1, Bord,
PC80, 0&, 4¶
   Title$ = "Font choice"¶
   WinDef NWindow, 100, 50, 460, 150, 32+64+512&, 15&+4096&,
PC80Gad, Title$¶
   WinBase  = OpenWindow(NWindow)¶
   IF WinBase = 0 THEN ERROR 7¶
   RastPort = PEEKL(WinBase+50)¶
   UserPort = PEEKL(WinBase+86)¶
RETURN¶
¶
CloseAll:¶
   CALL CloseWindow(WinBase)¶
   CALL UnDef¶
RETURN¶
¶
IntuitionMsg:  ¶
   MsgTyp    = PEEKL(IntuiMsg+20)¶
   Item      = PEEKL(IntuiMsg+28)¶
   GadgetNr% = PEEK(Item+39)¶
   CALL ReplyMsg(IntuiMsg)¶
   ¶
   IF (MsgTyp = GADGETDOWN) THEN¶
      'immediately activated¶
      PRINT "DOWN Gadget-Nr.:";GadgetNr%¶
   END IF¶
¶
IF (MsgTyp = GADGETUP) THEN¶
 'rel verify mode¶
 PRINT "UP Gadget-Nr.:";GadgetNr%¶
 IF active THEN¶
  SetDrMd RastPort, 2¶
  RectFill RastPort, 80&, 13*active+48&, 177&,
13*active+59&¶
  SetDrMd RastPort, 1¶
 END IF¶
 active = GadgetNr%¶
 SetDrMd RastPort, 2¶
 RectFill RastPort, 80&, 13*active+48&, 177&,
13*active+59&¶
 SetDrMd RastPort, 1¶
END IF¶
   ¶
   IF (MsgTyp = CLOSEW) THEN¶
      'System-Gadget Window close¶
      PRINT"CLOSE WINDOW"¶
      Info = 0¶
```

```
                  END IF¶
            RETURN¶
            '----------------------------------------------¶
            ¶
            SUB DefChip(Buffer,Size)STATIC¶
             SHARED MList¶
              Size=Size+8¶
              Buffer=AllocMem(Size,65538&)¶
              IF Buffer>0 THEN¶
                POKEL Buffer,MList¶
                POKEL Buffer+4,Size¶
                MList=Buffer¶
                Buffer=Buffer+8¶
              ELSE¶
                ERROR 7¶
              END IF¶
            END SUB¶
            SUB UnDef STATIC¶
             SHARED MList¶
            undef.loop:¶
              IF MList>0 THEN¶
                Address = PEEKL(MList)¶
                ListSize = PEEKL(MList+4)¶
                FreeMem MList, ListSize¶
                MList    = Address¶
                GOTO undef.loop¶
              END IF¶
            END SUB         ¶
            SUB WinDef(bs, x%, y%, b%, h%, IDCMP, f, gad, T$) STATIC¶
              Size = 48+LEN(T$)+1¶
              DefChip bs,Size¶
              POKEW bs  ,x%       ' Left Corner¶
              POKEW bs+ 2,y%       ' Top Corner¶
              POKEW bs+ 4,b%       ' Width¶
              POKEW bs+ 6,h%       ' Height¶
              POKEW bs+ 8,65535&   ' Detail- BlockPen¶
              POKEL bs+10,IDCMP    ' IDCMP Flags¶
              POKEL bs+14,f        ' Flags¶
              POKEL bs+18,gad      ' First Gadget¶
              POKEL bs+26,bs+48    ' Title¶
              POKEW bs+46,1        ' Screen Type ¶
              FOR i%=1 TO LEN(T$)¶
                  POKE bs+47+i%,ASC(MID$(T$,i%,1))¶
              NEXT¶
            END SUB¶
            SUB GadgetDef(bs, nx, x%, y%, b%, h%, f%, a%, T%, i, txt, si,
            n%) STATIC¶
              DefChip bs,44&       ' Gadget-Structure length¶
              POKEL bs   ,nx       '*NextGadget¶
              POKEW bs+ 4,x%       ' LeftEdge¶
              POKEW bs+ 6,y%       ' TopEdge¶
              POKEW bs+ 8,b%       ' Width¶
              POKEW bs+10,h%       ' Height¶
              POKEW bs+12,f%       ' Flags¶
              POKEW bs+14,a%       ' Activation¶
              POKEW bs+16,T%       ' GadgetType¶
```

```
     POKEL bs+18,i         ' GadgetRender¶
     POKEL bs+26,txt       '*GadgetText¶
     POKEL bs+34,si        ' SpecialInfo¶
     POKEW bs+38,n%        ' GadgetID¶
   END SUB¶
   ¶
   SUB IntuiText(bs, cl%, x%, y%, T$, nx) STATIC¶
     Size=20+LEN(T$)+1   ' Structure length+ Text length+
   Nullbyte¶
     DefChip bs,Size¶
     POKE  bs   ,cl%       ' FrontPen¶
     POKE  bs+ 2,1         ' DrawMode¶
     POKEW bs+ 4,x%        ' Left corner¶
     POKEW bs+ 6,y%        ' Top corner¶
     POKEL bs+12,bs+20     ' IText¶
     POKEL bs+16,nx        ' NextText¶
     FOR i%=1 TO LEN(T$)¶
        POKE bs+19+i%,ASC(MID$(T$,i%,1))¶
     NEXT¶
   END SUB¶
   ¶
   SUB Border(bs, x%, y%, c%, b%, h%) STATIC¶
     DefChip bs,48&       ' Structure length+ Coordinate table¶
     POKEW bs   ,x%       ' Left corner¶
     POKEW bs+2,y%        ' Top corner¶
     POKE  bs+4,c%        ' FrontPen¶
     POKE  bs+7,8         ' Count¶
     POKEL bs+8,bs+16     '*XY¶
     FOR i%=0 TO 1¶
        POKEW bs+22+i%*4,h%-1¶
        POKEW bs+24+i%*4,b%-1¶
        POKEW bs+32+i%*4,1¶
        POKEW bs+38+i%*4,h%-1¶
        POKEW bs+40+i%*4,b%-2¶
     NEXT¶
   END SUB
```

2.1.5   Scrolling tables

A large number of selections or an undefined number of elements can be difficult to program using filled gadgets. Scrolling tables are a logical choice. A scrolling table allows you to see only a small part of the complete table, which can be moved up or down.

You've seen scrolling tables at work if you've ever selected the Change Printer gadget in the Preferences program. When you click Change Printer, the Change Printer screen appears. This screen has a scrolling table of printer drivers in the upper right hand corner of the screen. This type of table is used because of its flexibility—it doesn't matter how many printer drivers are on a disk, you can view and select them all. You control the selection by clicking on the up and down arrows to the left of the list of printers.

Our program will need to create a table to display the possible choices and two gadgets, one for each arrow. Clicking on the arrow gadgets alters the display of possible choices. The following listing defines our scrolling table with two arrow gadgets and three display areas:

```
OpenAll:¶
  Border Bord, -1, -1, 1, 200, 14¶
  Border Box, 0, -1, 1, 50, 21¶
  GadgetDef Higher, 0&, 51, 60, 48, 18, 0, 1, 1, 0&, 0&, 0&, 1¶

  GadgetDef Lower, Higher, 51, 80, 48, 18, 0, 1, 1, 0&, 0&, 0&,
2¶
  Title$   = "Scrolling-Table"¶
  WinDef NWindow, 100, 50, 460, 150, 32+64+512&,
15&+4096&, Lower, Title$¶
  WinBase  = OpenWindow(NWindow)¶
  IF WinBase = 0 THEN ERROR 7¶
  RastPort = PEEKL(WinBase+50)¶
  UserPort = PEEKL(WinBase+86)¶
  DrawBorder RastPort, Bord, 100&, 60&¶
  DrawBorder RastPort, Bord, 100&, 73&¶
  DrawBorder RastPort, Bord, 100&, 86&¶
  DrawBorder RastPort, Box, 50&, 60&¶
  DrawBorder RastPort, Box, 50&, 79&¶
  ¶
  x = 50      : y = 60¶
  'x-          y- value¶
  x(1) =17+x  : x(2) =16+y¶
  x(3) =34+x  : x(4) =16+y¶
  x(5) =34+x  : x(6) =10+y¶
  x(7) =40+x  : x(8) =10+y¶
  x(9) =25+x  : x(10)=2+y¶
  x(11)=10+x  : x(12)=10+y¶
  x(13)=17+x  : x(14)=10+y¶
  x(15)=17+x  : x(16)=16+y¶
  ¶
  Move RastPort, 17+50&, 16+60&¶
  PolyDraw RastPort, 8&, VARPTR(x(1))¶
  ¶
  y = 62¶
  'y- Value¶
  x(2) =20+y¶
  x(4) =20+y¶
  x(6) =26+y¶
  x(8) =26+y¶
  x(10)=34+y¶
  x(12)=26+y¶
  x(14)=26+y¶
  x(16)=20+y¶
  ¶
```

```
     Move RastPort, 17+50&, 20+62&¶
     PolyDraw RastPort, 8&, VARPTR(x(1))¶
     ¶
     FOR i = 1 TO 5¶
        READ Table$(i)¶
        IntuiText ITxt(i), 1, 0, 0, Table$(i), 0&¶
     NEXT i¶
     TabOut Active¶
RETURN¶
CloseAll:¶
  CALL CloseWindow(WinBase)¶
  CALL UnDef¶
RETURN¶
```

After the window opens and the gadgets are drawn. `DrawBorder()` draws the boxes that are to contain our choices. `PolyDraw()` uses the `graphics.library` to draw a polygon. This function allows coordinate tables to be created in only a few lines of code. Here we use the `Polydraw()` routine to draw the up and down arrow graphics next to the scrolling table.

Following that, `OpenAll` reads five texts from `DATA` statements, which will later be used in our table. The `TabOut` subroutine handles the output of our choices.

Below we've printed the entire program with this new output routine and the `DATA` statements:

```
'*************************************¶
'*                                   *¶
'* Scrolling-Table-Gadgets           *¶
'* -----------------------           *¶
'*                                   *¶
'* Author  : Wolf-Gideon Bleek       *¶
'* Date    : May 31 '88              *¶
'* Name    : Scroll-Gadgets          *¶
'* Version: 1.2                      *¶
'* System : V1.2 & V1.3              *¶
'*                                   *¶
'*************************************¶
  OPTION BASE 1¶
  DEFLNG a-w¶
  DEFINT x¶
' Bmaps located on disk named T&T2,yours may differ¶
  LIBRARY "t&t2:bmaps/exec.library"¶
  DECLARE FUNCTION AllocMem LIBRARY¶
  DECLARE FUNCTION GetMsg LIBRARY¶
  LIBRARY "t&t2:bmaps/intuition.library"¶
  DECLARE FUNCTION OpenWindow LIBRARY¶
  LIBRARY "t&t2:bmaps/graphics.library"¶
  ¶
  GADGETDOWN = 32&¶
  GADGETUP   = 64&¶
```

```
        CLOSEW    = 512&¶
        ¶
        MList     = 0&¶
        Info      = 1¶
        Active    = 2¶
        ¶
        DIM x(16)¶
        DIM SHARED Table$(5), ITxt(5)¶
        ¶
MainProgramm:¶
    GOSUB OpenAll¶
    ' Main part¶
    MainLoop:¶
        IF Info = 1 THEN¶
            IntuiMsg = GetMsg(UserPort)¶
            IF IntuiMsg > 0 THEN GOSUB IntuitionMsg¶
            GOTO MainLoop¶
        END IF   ¶
    ¶
    GOSUB CloseAll¶
    ¶
END¶
OpenAll:¶
    Border Bord, -1, -1, 1, 200, 14¶
    Border Box, 0, -1, 1, 50, 21¶
    GadgetDef Higher, 0&, 51, 60, 48, 18, 0, 1, 1, 0&, 0&, 0&, 1¶

    GadgetDef Lower, Higher, 51, 80, 48, 18, 0, 1, 1, 0&, 0&, 0&,
2¶
    Title$    = "Scrolling-Table"¶
    WinDef NWindow, 100, 50, 460, 150, 32+64+512&, 15&+4096&,
Lower, Title$¶
    WinBase   = OpenWindow(NWindow)¶
    IF WinBase = 0 THEN ERROR 7¶
    RastPort  = PEEKL(WinBase+50)¶
    UserPort  = PEEKL(WinBase+86)¶
    DrawBorder RastPort, Bord, 100&, 60&¶
    DrawBorder RastPort, Bord, 100&, 73&¶
    DrawBorder RastPort, Bord, 100&, 86&¶
    DrawBorder RastPort, Box, 50&, 60&¶
    DrawBorder RastPort, Box, 50&, 79&¶
    ¶
    x = 50      : y = 60¶
    'x-          y- value¶
    x(1) =17+x : x(2) =16+y¶
    x(3) =34+x : x(4) =16+y¶
    x(5) =34+x : x(6) =10+y¶
    x(7) =40+x : x(8) =10+y¶
    x(9) =25+x : x(10)=2+y¶
    x(11)=10+x : x(12)=10+y¶
    x(13)=17+x : x(14)=10+y¶
    x(15)=17+x : x(16)=16+y¶
    ¶
    Move RastPort, 17+50&, 16+60&¶
    PolyDraw RastPort, 8&, VARPTR(x(1))¶
    ¶
```

```
    y = 62¶
   'y- Value¶
    x(2) =20+y¶
    x(4) =20+y¶
    x(6) =26+y¶
    x(8) =26+y¶
    x(10)=34+y¶
    x(12)=26+y¶
    x(14)=26+y¶
    x(16)=20+y¶
    ¶
    Move RastPort, 17+50&, 20+62&¶
    PolyDraw RastPort, 8&, VARPTR(x(1))¶
    ¶
    FOR i = 1 TO 5¶
       READ Table$(i)¶
       IntuiText ITxt(i), 1, 0, 0, Table$(i), 0&¶
    NEXT i¶
    TabOut Active¶
RETURN¶
CloseAll:¶
   CALL CloseWindow(WinBase)¶
   CALL UnDef¶
RETURN¶
IntuitionMsg:  ¶
   MsgTyp    = PEEKL(IntuiMsg+20)¶
   Item      = PEEKL(IntuiMsg+28)¶
   GadgetNr% = PEEK(Item+39)¶
   CALL ReplyMsg(IntuiMsg)¶
   ¶
   IF (MsgTyp = GADGETDOWN) THEN¶
      'activated¶
      PRINT "DOWN Gadget-Nr.:";GadgetNr%¶
   END IF¶
   ¶
   IF (MsgTyp = GADGETUP) THEN¶
      'verify mode¶
      PRINT "UP   Gadget-Nr.:";GadgetNr%¶
      IF GadgetNr% = 1 AND Active<>4 THEN Active=Active+1
: TabOut(Active)¶
      IF GadgetNr% = 2 AND Active<>1 THEN Active=Active-1
: TabOut(Active)¶
   END IF¶
   ¶
   IF (MsgTyp = CLOSEW) THEN¶
      'System-Gadget Window closer¶
      PRINT "CLOSE WINDOW"¶
      Info = 0¶
   END IF¶
RETURN¶
'--------------------------------------------¶
SUB DefChip(Buffer,Size)STATIC¶
 SHARED MList¶
   Size=Size+8¶
```

```
    Buffer=AllocMem(Size,65538&)¶
    IF Buffer>0 THEN¶
      POKEL Buffer,MList¶
      POKEL Buffer+4,Size¶
      MList=Buffer¶
      Buffer=Buffer+8¶
    ELSE¶
      ERROR 7¶
    END IF¶
END SUB¶
SUB UnDef STATIC¶
 SHARED MList¶
undef.loop:¶
    IF MList>0 THEN¶
      Address = PEEKL(MList)¶
      ListSize = PEEKL(MList+4)¶
      FreeMem MList, ListSize¶
      MList    = Address¶
      GOTO undef.loop¶
    END IF¶
END SUB        ¶
SUB WinDef(bs, x%, y%, b%, h%, IDCMP, f, Gad, T$) STATIC¶
  Size = 48+LEN(T$)+1¶
  DefChip bs,Size¶
  POKEW bs   ,x%       ' LeftEdge¶
  POKEW bs+ 2,y%       ' TopEdge¶
  POKEW bs+ 4,b%       ' Width¶
  POKEW bs+ 6,h%       ' Height¶
  POKEW bs+ 8,65535&   ' Detail- BlockPen¶
  POKEL bs+10,IDCMP    ' IDCMPFlags¶
  POKEL bs+14,f        ' Flags¶
  POKEL bs+18,Gad      ' FirstGadget¶
  POKEL bs+26,bs+48    ' Title¶
  POKEW bs+46,1        ' ScreenType ¶
  FOR i%=1 TO LEN(T$)¶
      POKE bs+47+i%,ASC(MID$(T$,i%,1))¶
  NEXT¶
END SUB¶
SUB GadgetDef(bs, nx, x%, y%, b%, h%, f%, a%, T%, i, txt, si,
n%) STATIC¶
  DefChip bs,44&      ' Gadget-Structure length¶
  POKEL bs   ,nx      '*NextGadget¶
  POKEW bs+ 4,x%      ' LeftEdge¶
  POKEW bs+ 6,y%      ' TopEdge¶
  POKEW bs+ 8,b%      ' Width¶
  POKEW bs+10,h%      ' Height¶
  POKEW bs+12,f%      ' Flags¶
  POKEW bs+14,a%      ' Activation¶
  POKEW bs+16,T%      ' GadgetType¶
  POKEL bs+18,i       ' GadgetRender¶
  POKEL bs+26,txt     '*GadgetText¶
  POKEL bs+34,si      ' SpecialInfo¶
  POKEW bs+38,n%      ' GadgetID¶
END SUB¶
SUB IntuiText(bs, cl%, x%, y%, T$, nx) STATIC¶
```

```
        Size=20+LEN(T$)+1      ' Structure length+ Text length+
    Nullbyte¶
      DefChip bs,Size¶
      POKE  bs    ,cl%      ' FrontPen¶
      POKE  bs+ 2,1         ' DrawMode¶
      POKEW bs+ 4,x%        ' LeftEdge¶
      POKEW bs+ 6,y%        ' TopEdge¶
      POKEL bs+12,bs+20     ' IText¶
      POKEL bs+16,nx        ' NextText¶
      FOR i%=1 TO LEN(T$)¶
          POKE bs+19+i%,ASC(MID$(T$,i%,1))¶
      NEXT¶
    END SUB¶
    SUB Border(bs, x%, y%, C%, b%, h%) STATIC¶
      DefChip bs,48&         ' Structure length+ coordinate table¶
      POKEW bs    ,x%        ' LeftEdge¶
      POKEW bs+2,y%          ' TopEdge¶
      POKE  bs+4,C%          ' FrontPen¶
      POKE  bs+7,8           ' Count¶
      POKEL bs+8,bs+16       '*XY¶
      FOR i%=0 TO 1¶
          POKEW bs+22+i%*4,h%-1¶
          POKEW bs+24+i%*4,b%-1¶
          POKEW bs+32+i%*4,1¶
          POKEW bs+38+i%*4,h%-1¶
          POKEW bs+40+i%*4,b%-2¶
      NEXT¶
    END SUB¶
    'exchange returned in PropInfo¶
    SUB STRINGINFO(bs,max%,buff$) STATIC¶
      IF LEN(buff$)>max% THEN¶
          nmax%=LEN(buff$)¶
      ELSE¶
          nmax%=max%¶
      END IF¶
      IF (nmax% AND 1) THEN nmax%=nmax%+1¶
      Size=36+2*(nmax%+4)¶
      DefChip bs,Size¶
      POKEL bs,bs+36¶
      POKEL bs+4,bs+40+nmax%¶
      POKEW bs+10,max%+1¶
      IF buff$<>""THEN¶
        FOR i%=1 TO LEN(buff$)¶
          POKE bs+35+i%,ASC(MID$(buff$,i%,1))¶
        NEXT¶
      END IF¶
    END SUB      ¶
    SUB TabOut(Active) STATIC¶
    SHARED RastPort¶
      COLOR 0,0¶
      FOR i = 0 TO 2¶
        SetAPen RastPort, 0¶
        RectFill RastPort, 101&, 13*i+60&, 296&, 13*i+71&¶
      NEXT i¶
```

```
            COLOR 1,0¶
            FOR i = Active-1 TO Active+1¶
               IF i>0 AND i<5 THEN¶
                   POKEW ITxt(i)+6, 62+(i-Active+1)*13¶
                   PrintIText RastPort, ITxt(i), 110&, 0&¶
               END IF¶
            NEXT i¶
            SetDrMd RastPort, 2¶
            RectFill RastPort, 101&, 73&, 296&, 84&¶
            SetDrMd RastPort, 1¶
        END SUB¶
        DATA Scroll-Table¶
        DATA Closer¶
        DATA Table¶
        DATA Gadget¶
        DATA System gadgets¶
```

2.1.6   Proportional gadgets

Proportional gadgets (also called sliders) allow the user to enter values that change in a proportional manner. Setting screen colors in the Preferences program is a good example of proportional gadgetry. Each controller can accept a value between 0 and 15, with each number representing the intensity of a color from no intensity (0) to high intensity (15).

You could also add three string gadgets into which a number may be entered, but for this kind of selection a proportional gadget is much more convenient than a string gadget. You can change the red, green and blue values by selecting the knob in the desired proportional gadget and moving the mouse pointer to the left or right, thus moving the knob.

The intuition.library file provides help in programming proportional gadgets. The container in a proportional gadget is the region containing the knob. This container sets the borders in which the proportional gadget's knob may be moved. This movement can be in the horizontal direction, vertical direction, or in both directions at the same time. The user defines the knob graphic, or the proportional gadget routine uses the default Intuition knob graphic. The container usually has a visible border to allow easy selection by the user.

The Gadget structure must be enlarged to contain a PropInfo structure. This structure has connections to the SpecialInfo pointer. For this we have a subprogram which places the parameters in memory.

```
SUB PropInfo(bs, Flags%, HPot%, VPot%, HBody%, VBody%)
STATIC¶
  DefChip bs,22&¶
  POKEW bs   ,Flags%¶
  POKEW bs+ 2,HPot%¶
  POKEW bs+ 4,VPot%¶
  POKEW bs+ 6,HBody%¶
  POKEW bs+ 8,VBody%¶
END SUB¶
```

We should address the values we added to the `Info` structure first. Flags here define whether the knob should move horizontally (2) or vertically (4). The `autoknob` (1) flag informs Intuition that no graphic exists for the knob, and that Intuition should use the default knob graphic available from Intuition. `HPot` and `VPot` define the knob's position. 0 indicates the lower right axis while &HFFFF indicates the upper left axis. After the user moves the knob he can read the new position from here. `HBody` and `VBody` return the step increment of the knob. Both values are calculated as part of the whole (&HFFFF). Intuition inserts all further values found in the structure—these values don't have to be defined by the program.

`Autoknob` graphically defines the knob. `Autoknob` requires an eight-byte memory area which contains the knob's position (X and Y coordinates) and width. If all four values are unset, the initialization routine sets them. We still need two more structures to complete our proportional gadget:

```
PropInfo PropI, 1+2, 0, 0, &HFFF, 0¶
IntuiText, Text, 2, -80, 2, "Mover:", 0&¶
DefChip Buffer, 8&¶
GadgetDef Gadget, 0&, 150, 30, 100, 10, 0, 1+2, 3, Buffer,
Text, PropI, 1¶
```

We can construct complete proportional gadgets from these few pieces of data. As an example, we have a listing that uses three such gadgets in a window. These three proportional gadgets allow the user to change the value of the corresponding color register when selected with the mouse.

```
'**********************************¶
'*                               *¶
'* Proportional-Gadgets          *¶
'* --------------------          *¶
'*                               *¶
'* Author : Wolf-Gideon Bleek    *¶
'* Date   :May 23 '88            *¶
'* Name   :Proportional-Gadgets  *¶
'* Version: 1.2                  *¶
'* System : V1.2 & V1.3          *¶
'*                               *¶
'**********************************¶
```

```
                    OPTION BASE 1¶
                    DEFLNG a-z¶
                    ¶
                    LIBRARY "T&T2:bmaps/exec.library"¶
                    DECLARE FUNCTION AllocMem LIBRARY¶
                    DECLARE FUNCTION GetMsg LIBRARY¶
                    LIBRARY "T&T2:bmaps/intuition.library"¶
                    DECLARE FUNCTION OpenWindow LIBRARY¶
                    GADGETDOWN = 32&¶
                    GADGETUP   = 64&¶
                    CLOSEW     = 512&¶
                       ¶
                    MList      = 0&¶
                    Info       = 1¶
                    ¶
              MainProgramm:¶
                 GOSUB OpenAll¶
                 ' Main part¶
              MainLoop:¶
                    IF Info = 1 THEN¶
                       IntuiMsg = GetMsg(UserPort)¶
                       IF IntuiMsg > 0 THEN GOSUB IntuitionMsg¶
                       GOTO MainLoop¶
                    END IF    ¶
                 ¶
                 GOSUB CloseAll¶
                 ¶
              END¶
              OpenAll:¶
                 IntuiText RedTxt, 2, -80, 2, "Red", 0& ¶
                 IntuiText GrnTxt, 2, -80, 2, "Green", 0& ¶
                 IntuiText BluTxt, 2, -80, 2, "Blue", 0& ¶
                 PropInfo Prop1, 1+2, 0, 0, &HFFF, 0¶
                 PropInfo Prop2, 1+2, 0, 0, &HFFF, 0¶
                 PropInfo Prop3, 1+2, 0, 0, &HFFF, 0¶
                 DefChip Buffer(1), 8&¶
                 DefChip Buffer(2), 8&¶
                 DefChip Buffer(3), 8&¶
                 GadgetDef RedGad, 0&, 150, 30, 114, 10, 0, 1+2, 3,
              Buffer(1), RedTxt, Prop1, 1¶
                 GadgetDef GrnGad, RedGad, 150, 45, 114, 10, 0, 1+2, 3,
              Buffer(2), GrnTxt, Prop2, 2¶
                 GadgetDef BluGad, GrnGad, 150, 60, 114, 10, 0, 1+2, 3,
              Buffer(3), BluTxt, Prop3, 3¶
                 Title$   = "Color initialization"¶
                 WinDef NWindow, 100, 50, 460, 150, 32+64+512&,
              15&+4096&, BluGad, Title$¶
                 WinBase  = OpenWindow(NWindow)¶
                 IF WinBase = 0 THEN ERROR 7¶
                 RastPort = PEEKL(WinBase+50)¶
                 UserPort = PEEKL(WinBase+86)¶
              RETURN¶
              ¶
              CloseAll:¶
                 CALL CloseWindow(WinBase)¶
                 CALL UnDef¶
```

```
RETURN¶
¶
IntuitionMsg:  ¶
  MsgTyp    = PEEKL(IntuiMsg+20)¶
  Item      = PEEKL(IntuiMsg+28)¶
  GadgetNr% = PEEK(Item+39)¶
  CALL ReplyMsg(IntuiMsg)¶
  ¶
  IF (MsgTyp = GADGETDOWN) THEN¶
    'activated¶
    PRINT "DOWN Gadget-Nr.:";GadgetNr%¶
  END IF¶
  ¶
  IF (MsgTyp = GADGETUP) THEN¶
    'verify mpode¶
    PRINT "UP   Gadget-Nr.:";GadgetNr%;¶
    PRINT " Pos:";PEEKW(Buffer(GadgetNr%))¶
    Red = PEEKW(Buffer(1))¶
    Grn = PEEKW(Buffer(2))¶
    Blu = PEEKW(Buffer(3))¶
    PALETTE 1, Red/100, Grn/100, Blu/100¶
  END IF¶
  ¶
  IF (MsgTyp = CLOSEW) THEN¶
    'System-Gadget Window closer¶
    PRINT "CLOSE WINDOW"¶
    Info = 0¶
  END IF¶
RETURN¶
'---------------------------------------------¶
SUB DefChip(Buffer,Size)STATIC¶
 SHARED MList¶
  Size=Size+8¶
  Buffer=AllocMem(Size,65538&)¶
  IF Buffer>0 THEN¶
    POKEL Buffer,MList¶
    POKEL Buffer+4,Size¶
    MList=Buffer¶
    Buffer=Buffer+8¶
  ELSE¶
    ERROR 7¶
  END IF¶
END SUB¶
SUB UnDef STATIC¶
 SHARED MList¶
undef.loop:¶
  IF MList>0 THEN¶
    Address = PEEKL(MList)¶
    ListSize = PEEKL(MList+4)¶
    FreeMem MList, ListSize¶
    MList    = Address¶
    GOTO undef.loop¶
  END IF¶
END SUB         ¶
```

```
SUB WinDef(bs, x%, y%, b%, h%, IDCMP, f, Gad, T$) STATIC¶
  Size = 48+LEN(T$)+1¶
  DefChip bs,Size¶
  POKEW bs   ,x%         ' Left corner¶
  POKEW bs+ 2,y%         ' Top corner¶
  POKEW bs+ 4,b%         ' Width¶
  POKEW bs+ 6,h%         ' Height¶
  POKEW bs+ 8,65535&     ' Detail- BlockPen¶
  POKEL bs+10,IDCMP      ' IDCMP Flags¶
  POKEL bs+14,f          ' Flags¶
  POKEL bs+18,Gad        ' First Gadget¶
  POKEL bs+26,bs+48      ' Title¶
  POKEW bs+46,1          ' Screen Type ¶
  FOR i%=1 TO LEN(T$)¶
     POKE bs+47+i%,ASC(MID$(T$,i%,1))¶
  NEXT¶
END SUB¶
SUB GadgetDef(bs, nx, x%, y%, b%, h%, f%, a%, T%, i, Txt, si,
n%) STATIC¶
  DefChip bs,44&         ' Gadget-Structure length¶
  POKEL bs   ,nx         '*NextGadget¶
  POKEW bs+ 4,x%         ' Left corner¶
  POKEW bs+ 6,y%         ' Top corner¶
  POKEW bs+ 8,b%         ' Width¶
  POKEW bs+10,h%         ' Height¶
  POKEW bs+12,f%         ' Flags¶
  POKEW bs+14,a%         ' Activation¶
  POKEW bs+16,T%         ' GadgetType¶
  POKEL bs+18,i          ' GadgetRender¶
  POKEL bs+26,Txt        '*GadgetText¶
  POKEL bs+34,si         ' SpecialInfo¶
  POKEW bs+38,n%         ' GadgetID¶
END SUB¶
SUB IntuiText(bs, cl%, x%, y%, T$, nx) STATIC¶
  Size=20+LEN(T$)+1  ' IntuiText-Structure length + Text
length+ Nullbyte¶
  DefChip bs,Size¶
  POKE  bs   ,cl%        ' FrontPen¶
  POKE  bs+ 2,1          ' DrawMode¶
  POKEW bs+ 4,x%         ' Left corner¶
  POKEW bs+ 6,y%         ' Top corner¶
  POKEL bs+12,bs+20      ' IText¶
  POKEL bs+16,nx         ' NextText¶
  FOR i%=1 TO LEN(T$)¶
     POKE bs+19+i%,ASC(MID$(T$,i%,1))¶
  NEXT¶
END SUB¶
SUB Border(bs, x%, y%, c%, b%, h%) STATIC¶
  DefChip bs,48&         'Border-Structure length+
coordinates¶
  POKEW bs   ,x%         ' Left corner¶
  POKEW bs+2,y%          ' Top corner¶
  POKE  bs+4,c%          ' FrontPen¶
  POKE  bs+7,8           ' Count¶
  POKEL bs+8,bs+16       '*XY¶
  FOR i%=0 TO 1¶
```

```
            POKEW bs+22+i%*4,h%-1¶
            POKEW bs+24+i%*4,b%-1¶
            POKEW bs+32+i%*4,1¶
            POKEW bs+38+i%*4,h%-1¶
            POKEW bs+40+i%*4,b%-2¶
    NEXT¶
END SUB¶
SUB PropInfo(bs, Flags%, HPot%, VPot%, HBody%, VBody%)
STATIC¶
    DefChip bs,22&¶
    POKEW bs   ,Flags%¶
    POKEW bs+ 2,HPot%¶
    POKEW bs+ 4,VPot%¶
    POKEW bs+ 6,HBody%¶
    POKEW bs+ 8,VBody%¶
END SUB¶
    ¶
```

Looking toward the future

You should be able to develop many user-friendly programs from all of the information in this section. We have tried to develop procedures that allow easy access to the operating system, especially Intuition. All the programs presented here are in modular form, and make it possible to easily add these modules to your own programs. This is done the following way:

Write each subprogram in a one directory as an ASCII file (`save "program_name",A`). Put comments listing the required parameters before each routine. When you need to use an Intuition call, then load the subprogram using `Merge` and put the Intuition call in the `OpenAll` subroutine.

2.2   A file monitor

Now that we know the fundamentals of programming gadgets and accessing Intuition, we'd like to show you a program that uses even more Intuition calls. Accessing the screen displays using the operating system is 10 times faster than in BASIC. Not only that, displaying data on the screen through the operating system is many times faster than in BASIC.

The file monitor in this section permits you to view any disk file in hexadecimal and ASCII text formats. It also allows you to change or edit the file. The file monitor uses an Intuition screen so gadgets control the program.

The example program that follows contain a few BASIC lines that must be entered on one line in AmigaBASIC, even though they appear on two lines in this book. Formatting the program listings to fit into this book has split some long BASIC lines into two lines of text. To show where a BASIC line actually ends, we added an end-of-paragraph marker (¶). This character shows when you should press the <Return> key at the end of a line. For example, the following line appears as two lines below but must be entered as one line in AmigaBASIC:

```
WinDef NWindow, 100, 50, 460, 150, 32+64+512&, 15&+4096&, 0&,
Title$¶
```

The ¶ shows the actual end of the BASIC line.

Here is the file monitor program listing:

```
'REM DISKMON¶
  OPTION BASE 1¶
  DEFLNG a-z¶
'   ON ERROR GOTO FAILED   ;REM remove after testing¶
  DECLARE FUNCTION ALLOCMEM LIBRARY¶
  DECLARE FUNCTION GETMSG LIBRARY¶
  LIBRARY"T&T2:bmaps/exec.library"¶
  LIBRARY"T&T2:bmaps/graphics.library"¶
  DECLARE FUNCTION OPENSCREEN LIBRARY¶
  DECLARE FUNCTION OPENWINDOW LIBRARY¶
  LIBRARY"T&T2:bmaps/intuition.library"¶
  DECLARE FUNCTION LOCK LIBRARY¶
  DECLARE FUNCTION EXAMINE LIBRARY¶
  DECLARE FUNCTION EXNEXT LIBRARY¶
  DECLARE FUNCTION IOERR LIBRARY¶
  DECLARE FUNCTION XOPEN LIBRARY¶
  DECLARE FUNCTION XREAD LIBRARY¶
  DECLARE FUNCTION XWRITE LIBRARY¶
  DECLARE FUNCTION SEEK LIBRARY¶
```

```
        LIBRARY"T&T2:bmaps/dos.library"¶
   '  LPRINT :REM used to load printer driver at startup¶
        PRINT"----------FILE MONITOR-V1.0----------"¶
        PRINT") '88 by DATA BECKER (w)'88 by S. M."¶
        PRINT ¶
        PRINT"Program starts in a few seconds."¶
        PRINT"Please stand by...(no Multitasking"¶
        PRINT"during initialization!)"¶
        DIM SHARED borders(14),itxt(25),gadgets(24),sinfo(2)¶
        bfec01=12577793&¶
        clearentry$=SPACE$(30)¶
        clearstring$=STRING$(80,0)¶
        INITIALIZE¶
        DIRECTORY¶
        start%=-1¶
        blocked%=0¶
        WHILE (-1)¶
          qualifier%=PEEK(bfec01)¶
          IF (qualifier%>&H60)AND(qualifier%<&H68)THEN¶
            IF qualifier%AND 1 THEN GOSUB keypressed¶
          END IF  ¶
          intuimsg=GETMSG(userport)¶
          IF intuimsg>0 THEN GOSUB IntuitionMsg¶
        WEND  ¶
IntuitionMsg:¶
  MsgTyp=PEEKL(intuimsg+20)¶
  IF MsgTyp=2097152& THEN¶
    IF start% THEN RETURN¶
    ascii.i%=PEEKW(intuimsg+24)¶
    IF ascii.i%>0 GOTO keypressed¶
  END IF¶
  Item=PEEKL(intuimsg+28)¶
  GadgetNr%=PEEK(Item+39)¶
  IF MsgTyp=32 THEN¶
    IF(GadgetNr%=10)OR(GadgetNr%=14)THEN blocked%=-1¶
    RETURN¶
  END IF        ¶
  IF MsgTyp<>64 THEN RETURN¶
  blocked%=0¶
  IF GadgetNr%<0 THEN ERROR 255¶
  IF GadgetNr%<5 THEN¶
    COPYMEM SADD(clearstring$),sinfo(1)+36,80¶
    POKEL sinfo(1)+36,CVL("DF"+CHR$(47+GadgetNr%)+":")¶
    lasttype%=0¶
    DIRECTORY¶
  ELSEIF GadgetNr%<10 THEN¶
    SETFILEACTDIR¶
    IF lasttype%=1 THEN¶
      STATUS "Loading Block"¶
      OPENFILE¶
      IF oldhandle>0 THEN :STATUS "Edit"¶
      RETURN¶
    END IF¶
    DIRECTORY¶
  ELSEIF GadgetNr%=10 THEN¶
    blocked%=0¶
```

```
              DIRECTORY¶
              RETURN¶
          ELSEIF GadgetNr%=11 THEN¶
              IF dirstart%>4 THEN dirstart%=dirstart%-5:DISPLAYDIR¶
          ELSEIF GadgetNr%=12 THEN¶
              IF number%>dirstart%+5 THEN¶
                 dirstart%=dirstart%+5¶
                 DISPLAYDIR¶
              END IF    ¶
          ELSEIF GadgetNr%=13 THEN¶
              DIRECTORY¶
          ELSEIF GadgetNr%=14 THEN¶
              blocked%=0¶
              newoffset=PEEKL(sinfo(2)+28)*488¶
              IF (newoffset>=newflen)OR(newoffset<0) THEN¶
                 POKEL sinfo(2)+36,CVL("0"+MKI$(0)+CHR$(0))¶
                 STATUS "illegal Input"¶
                 DISPLAYBEEP scrbase¶
                 RETURN¶
              END IF¶
              oldpos=SEEK(oldhandle,newoffset,-1)¶
              currentoffset=newoffset¶
              STATUS "reading Block"¶
              READBLOCK¶
              RETURN¶
          ELSEIF oldhandle=0 THEN¶
              POKEL sinfo(2)+36,CVL("0"+MKI$(0)+CHR$(0))¶
              STATUS "no File selected"¶
              DISPLAYBEEP scrbase¶
              RETURN¶
          ELSEIF GadgetNr%=15 THEN¶
              COPYMEM fundo,fbuffer,488¶
              DISPLAYBUFFER¶
          ELSEIF GadgetNr%=16 THEN¶
              STATUS "reading again"¶
              oldpos=SEEK(oldhandle,-amtread,0)¶
              READBLOCK¶
          ELSEIF GadgetNr%=17 THEN¶
             IF currentoffset<newflen-488 THEN¶
                STATUS "reading next Sec"¶
                currentoffset=currentoffset+488¶
                READBLOCK¶
             END IF¶
          ELSEIF GadgetNr%=18 THEN¶
             IF currentoffset>487 THEN¶
                STATUS "reading last Sec"¶
                currentoffset=currentoffset-488¶
                oldpos=SEEK(oldhandle,-amtread-488,0)¶
                READBLOCK¶
             END IF¶
          ELSEIF GadgetNr%=19 THEN¶
             STATUS "writing Buffer"¶
             oldpos=SEEK(oldhandle,-amtread,0)¶
             wr=XWRITE(oldhandle,fbuffer,amtread)¶
          ELSEIF GadgetNr%=20 THEN¶
             DUMPFILE                    ¶
```

```
       ELSEIF GadgetNr%=21 THEN¶
         DUMPBUFFER¶
       ELSEIF GadgetNr%=22 THEN¶
         edmode%=0¶
         STATUS "switched to HEX"¶
         DISPLAYBUFFER¶
       ELSEIF GadgetNr%=23 THEN¶
         edmode%=1¶
         STATUS "switched to ASCII"¶
         DISPLAYBUFFER¶
       ELSEIF GadgetNr%=24 THEN¶
         STATUS "ARE YOU SURE? Y/N"¶
         t%=0¶
         WHILE (t%<>&HD4)AND(t%<>&H93)¶
           t%=PEEK(bfec01)¶
         WEND¶
         IF t%=&HD4 THEN  ¶
           STATUS "You ARE sure! BYE"¶
           GOTO FAILED¶
         END IF         ¶
       END IF¶
       STATUS "OKAY"¶
       RETURN¶
  keypressed:¶
     ascii$=UCASE$(CHR$(ascii.i%))¶
     IF edmode%=1 GOTO ASCIImode¶
     value%=INSTR("0123456789ABCDEF",ascii$)-1¶
     IF qualifier%=&H67 THEN¶
       offset%=offset%-32  :'REM PAL uses 24¶
       IF offset%<0 THEN offset%=amtread-1:nibble%=1¶
       CURSOROFF¶
       CURSORON¶
       RETURN¶
     ELSEIF qualifier%=&H65 THEN¶
       offset%=offset%+32   : REM PAL uses 24¶
       IF offset%>=amtread THEN offset%=0:nibble%=0¶
       CURSOROFF¶
       CURSORON¶
       RETURN¶
     ELSEIF qualifier%=&H63 THEN¶
       IF nibble%=0 THEN¶
         nibble%=1¶
       ELSE¶
         nibble%=0¶
         offset%=offset%+1¶
         IF offset%>=amtread THEN offset%=0¶
       END IF¶
       CURSOROFF¶
       CURSORON¶
       RETURN¶
     ELSEIF qualifier%=&H61 THEN¶
       IF nibble%=1 THEN¶
         nibble%=0             ¶
       ELSE¶
         nibble%=1¶
         offset%=offset%-1¶
```

```
             IF offset%<0 THEN offset%=amtread-1¶
          END IF¶
          CURSOROFF¶
          CURSORON¶
          RETURN¶
       END IF  ¶
      IF value%>=0 THEN¶
          IF nibble%=0 THEN andi%=15:muls%=16:GOTO mk¶
          andi%=240¶
          muls%=1¶
mk:      a%=(PEEK(fbuffer+offset%)AND andi%)+value%*muls%¶
         POKE fbuffer+offset%,a%¶
         CURSOROFF¶
         MOVE rastport,o.x%,o.y%+6¶
         SETAPEN rastport,1¶
         SETBPEN rastport,0¶
         TEXT rastport,SADD("0123456789ABCDEF")+value%,1¶
¶
' PAL systems can display both ascii and hex¶
'        MOVE rastport,(o.b%+54)*8,o.y%+6¶
'        SETAPEN rastport,0¶
'        SETBPEN rastport,1¶
'        TEXT rastport,fbuffer+offset%,1¶
  ¶
         IF nibble%=0 THEN nibble%=1:GOTO mk2¶
         nibble%=0¶
         offset%=offset%+1¶
         IF offset%>=amtread THEN offset%=0¶
mk2:¶
         CURSORON¶
         RETURN¶
       END IF¶
      RETURN  ¶
ASCIImode:¶
     IF qualifier%=&H67 THEN¶
        offset%=offset%-32 :'PAL uses  24¶
        IF offset%<0 THEN offset%=amtread-1:nibble%=1¶
        CURSOROFF¶
        CURSORON¶
        RETURN¶
     ELSEIF qualifier%=&H65 THEN¶
        offset%=offset%+32 :'PAL uses 24¶
        IF offset%>=amtread THEN offset%=0:nibble%=0¶
        CURSOROFF¶
        CURSORON¶
        RETURN¶
     ELSEIF qualifier%=&H63 THEN¶
        offset%=offset%+1:IF offset%>=amtread THEN offset%=0¶
        CURSOROFF¶
        CURSORON¶
        RETURN¶
     ELSEIF qualifier%=&H61 THEN¶
        offset%=offset%-1¶
        IF offset%<0 THEN offset%=amtread-1¶
        CURSOROFF¶
        CURSORON¶
```

```
          RETURN¶
        END IF   ¶
        IF ascii$<>CHR$(0) THEN¶
          value%=ascii.i%¶
          POKE fbuffer+offset%,value%¶
          CURSOROFF¶
            ¶
' PAL Systems can be adapted to display both ASCII and hex¶
'       MOVE rastport,o.x%+(o.m%=0)*nibble%,o.y%+6¶
'       SETAPEN rastport,1¶
'       SETBPEN rastport,0¶
'       TEXT rastport,SADD(RIGHT$("0"+HEX$(value%),2)),2¶
            ¶
          SETAPEN rastport,0¶
          SETBPEN rastport,1¶
'REM PAL orginal:  MOVE rastport,(o.b%+54)*8,o.y%+6¶
          MOVE rastport,o.b%*8,o.y%+6¶
          TEXT rastport,fbuffer+offset%,1¶
            ¶
            ¶
          offset%=offset%+1¶
          IF offset%>=amtread THEN offset%=0¶
          CURSORON¶
          RETURN¶
        END IF¶
        RETURN   ¶
          ¶
FAILED:¶
        UNDEF¶
        IF scrbase>0 THEN¶
          IF winbase>0 THEN¶
            CLOSEWINDOW winbase¶
            IF oldhandle>0 THEN :XCLOSE oldhandle¶
          END IF¶
          CLOSESCREEN scrbase¶
        END IF¶
        LIBRARY CLOSE¶
        END¶
'     SYSTEM ¶
  ¶
SUB DUMPBUFFER STATIC¶
  SHARED fbuffer,HEXBUFF,currentlongs,currentoffset¶
  outstring$=SPACE$(1134)¶
  HEXBUFF currentlongs-1,fbuffer,SADD(outstring$)¶
  STATUS "printing"¶
  FOR i%=0 TO 20¶
    LPRINT RIGHT$("
"+STR$(currentoffset+i%*20),8);": ";¶
    LPRINT MID$(outstring$,i%*54+1,54)¶
  NEXT¶
  LPRINT¶
END SUB¶
SUB DUMPFILE STATIC¶
  SHARED amtread,oldhandle,currentoffset¶
    savedoffset=currentoffset¶
    oldpos=SEEK(oldhandle,0,-1)¶
```

```
                                currentoffset=0¶
df.loop:¶
  READBLOCK¶
  DUMPBUFFER¶
  currentoffset=currentoffset+488¶
  IF amtread=488 GOTO df.loop¶
  currentoffset=savedoffset¶
  oldpos=SEEK(oldhandle,currentoffset,-1)¶
  READBLOCK¶
END SUB¶
   ¶
SUB CURSORON STATIC¶
 SHARED o.x%,o.y%,edmode%,o.m%,rastport,offset%,nibble%¶
 SHARED o.b%¶
   z%=INT(offset%/32)¶
   o.b%=offset%-z%*32¶
   l%=INT(o.b%/4)¶
   o.x%=(o.b%*2+l%-(edmode%=0)*nibble%)*8¶
   o.y%=z%*8+2¶
   SETAPEN rastport,3¶
   SETDRMD rastport,3¶
   ¶
 IF edmode%=0 THEN  RECTFILL rastport,o.x%,o.y%,o.x%+7-
(edmode%=1)*8,o.y%+7¶
'REM orginal PAL :RECTFILL rastport,o.x%,o.y%,o.x%+7-
(edmode%=1)*8,o.y%+7¶
   ¶
   IF edmode%=1 THEN RECTFILL
rastport,(o.b%)*8,o.y%,(o.b%)*8+7,o.y%+7¶
'REM orginal PAL: RECTFILL
rastport,(o.b%)*8,o.y%,(o.b%)*8+7,o.y%+7¶
   ¶
   SETDRMD rastport,1¶
   o.m%=edmode%¶
END SUB¶
 ¶
SUB CURSOROFF STATIC¶
 SHARED o.x%,o.y%,o.m%,o.b%,rastport¶
   SETAPEN rastport,3¶
   SETDRMD rastport,3¶
   ¶
   IF o.m%=0 THEN  RECTFILL rastport,o.x%,o.y%,o.x%+7-
(o.m%=1)*8,o.y%+7¶
'REM orginal PAL: RECTFILL rastport,o.x%,o.y%,o.x%+7-
(o.m%=1)*8,o.y%+7¶
 ¶
   IF o.m%=1  THEN  RECTFILL
rastport,(o.b%)*8,o.y%,(o.b%)*8+7,o.y%+7¶
'REM orginal PAL: RECTFILL
rastport,(o.b%+54)*8,o.y%,(o.b%+54)*8+7,o.y%+7¶
 ¶
   SETDRMD rastport,1¶
END SUB    ¶
 ¶
SUB OPENFILE STATIC¶
 SHARED oldhandle,scrbase,currentoffset,actdir,newflen ¶
```

```
       SHARED numblocks¶
        IF oldhandle>0 THEN :XCLOSE oldhandle¶
        oldhandle=XOPEN(actdir,1005)¶
        IF oldhandle=0 THEN¶
          STATUS "File Open Error"¶
          DISPLAYBEEP scrbase¶
          EXIT SUB¶
        END IF¶
        numblocks=newflen/488¶
        w=CVL(RIGHT$("   "+STR$(numblocks),4))¶
        POKEL itxt(12)+20,w¶
        currentoffset=0¶
        READBLOCK¶
      END SUB¶
      SUB READBLOCK STATIC¶
       SHARED oldhandle,fbuffer,fundo,amtread,currentlongs¶
       SHARED currentoffset¶
        amtread=XREAD(oldhandle,fbuffer,488)¶
        IF amtread<488 THEN¶
          v$=STRING$(488-amtread,0)¶
          COPYMEM SADD(v$),fbuffer+amtread,LEN(v$)¶
        END IF¶
        x=currentoffset/488¶
        w=CVL(LEFT$(MID$(STR$(x),2)+MKL$(0),4))¶
        POKEL sinfo(2)+36,w¶
        currentlongs=(amtread+3)/4¶
        COPYMEM fbuffer,fundo,488   ¶
        DISPLAYBUFFER¶
      END SUB  ¶
      SUB DISPLAYBUFFER STATIC¶
       SHARED HEXBUFF,currentlongs,fbuffer,rastport,amtread¶
       SHARED start%,offset%,nibble%,edmode%¶
        ASCIIbuffer$=SPACE$(1134)¶
        HEXBUFF currentlongs-1,fbuffer,SADD(ASCIIbuffer$)¶
        SETAPEN rastport,0¶
        RECTFILL rastport,0,0,639,140¶
        SETAPEN rastport,1¶
        SETBPEN rastport,0¶
        IF edmode%=0 THEN¶
        l%=72¶
        FOR i%=0 TO 15¶
          MOVE rastport,0,i%*8+8¶
          IF i%=15 THEN l%=17¶
          TEXT rastport,SADD(ASCIIbuffer$)+i%*72,l%¶
        NEXT¶
        END IF¶
        SETAPEN rastport,0¶
        SETBPEN rastport,1¶
        l%=32¶
        IF edmode%=1 THEN¶
        FOR i%=0 TO 15¶
          MOVE rastport,0,i%*8+8¶
          IF i%=15 THEN l%=8¶
          TEXT rastport,fbuffer+i%*32,l%¶
        NEXT¶
        END IF¶
```

```
                     start%=0¶
                     offset%=0¶
                     nibble%=0¶
                     CURSORON¶
              END SUB  ¶
              SUB SETFILEACTDIR STATIC¶
               SHARED GadgetNr%,actdir,scrbase,clearstring$,newflen¶
               SHARED dirstart%,dirbuff,lasttype%¶
                compare1$=STRING$(31,0)¶
                compare2$=STRING$(80,0)¶
                COPYMEM actdir,SADD(compare2$),79¶
                COPYMEM itxt(GadgetNr%)+20,SADD(compare1$),30¶
                l2%=INSTR(compare2$,CHR$(0))-1¶
                l1%=INSTR(compare1$,CHR$(0))-1¶
                IF lasttype%=1 THEN¶
                   l2%=INSTR(compare2$,":")¶
              path.loop:¶
                   l3%=INSTR(l2%+1,compare2$,"/")¶
                   IF l3%>l2% THEN l2%=l3%:GOTO path.loop¶
                END IF  ¶
                IF(l1%+l2%)>78 THEN¶
                   STATUS "FileName Too Long"¶
                   DISPLAYBEEP scrbase¶
                   EXIT SUB¶
                END IF¶
                v$=LEFT$(compare2$,l2%)¶
                IF(lasttype%>1)AND(RIGHT$(v$,1)<>":")THEN v$=v$+"/"¶
                lasttype%=PEEK(dirbuff+(dirstart%+GadgetNr%-5)*36+31)¶
                v$=LEFT$(v$+compare1$+clearstring$,79)¶
                COPYMEM SADD(v$),actdir,79¶
                newflen=PEEKL(dirbuff+(dirstart%+GadgetNr%-5)*36+32)¶
              END SUB     ¶
              SUB DISPLAYDIR STATIC¶
               SHARED dirstart%,number%,clearentry$,dirbuff,winbase¶
                FOR i%=5 TO 9¶
                   COPYMEM SADD(clearentry$),itxt(i%)+20,30¶
                NEXT¶
                i%=0¶
                IF number%<=dirstart% GOTO displaydir.show¶
                REFRESHGADGETS gadgets(23),winbase,0¶
              displaydir.loop:¶
                a=dirbuff+(i%+dirstart%)*36¶
                COPYMEM a,itxt(i%+5)+20,30¶
                POKE itxt(i%+5),PEEK(a+31)¶
                i%=i%+1¶
                IF (i%<5)AND(number%>(dirstart%+i%))GOTO displaydir.loop¶

              displaydir.show:    ¶
                REFRESHGADGETS gadgets(23),winbase,0¶
              END SUB¶
              SUB DIRECTORY STATIC¶
               SHARED number%,dirstart%,actdir,lasttype%¶
               SHARED fileinfo,clearentry$,dirbuff,newflen¶
                STATUS "Examining Entry"¶
                dirlock=LOCK(actdir,-2)¶
                IF dirlock=0 THEN¶
```

```
         STATUS "File not found"¶
         EXIT SUB¶
      END IF¶
      e=EXAMINE(dirlock,fileinfo)¶
      IF e=0 THEN¶
         UNLOCK dirlock¶
         STATUS "Examine Error"¶
         EXIT SUB¶
      END IF¶
      IF PEEKL(fileinfo+120)<0 THEN¶
         newflen=PEEKL(fileinfo+124)¶
         UNLOCK dirlock¶
         OPENFILE¶
         lasttype%=1¶
         EXIT SUB¶
      END IF¶
      lasttype%=3¶
      number%=0¶
      dirstart%=0¶
      FOR i%=5 TO 9¶
         COPYMEM SADD(clearentry$),itxt(i%)+20,30¶
      NEXT¶
      STATUS "reading Directory"  ¶
   directory.loop:¶
      e=EXNEXT(dirlock,fileinfo)¶
      IF e=0 THEN¶
         e=IOERR¶
         IF e<>232 THEN¶
           STATUS "Directory invalid"¶
           number%=0¶
         ELSE¶
           STATUS "Okay"¶
         END IF¶
         UNLOCK dirlock¶
         DISPLAYDIR¶
         EXIT SUB¶
      END IF¶
      a=dirbuff+number%*36¶
      COPYMEM fileinfo+8,a,30¶
      IF PEEKL(fileinfo+120)<0 THEN c%=1 ELSE c%=3¶
      POKE a+31,c%¶
      POKEL a+32,PEEKL(fileinfo+124)¶
      number%=number%+1¶
      IF number%<72 GOTO directory.loop¶
      UNLOCK dirlock¶
      STATUS "Okay"¶
      DISPLAYDIR¶
   END SUB¶
   SUB INITIALIZE STATIC¶
    SHARED HEXBUFF,fbuffer,fundo,nscreen,dirbuff,fileinfo¶
    SHARED actdir,scrbase,winbase,viewport,rastport¶
    SHARED userport¶
    FORBID¶
    DEFCHIP HEXBUFF,60&¶
    DEFCHIP fbuffer,488&¶
    DEFCHIP fundo,488&¶
```

```
DEFCHIP nscreen,88&¶
DEFCHIP dirbuff,2592&¶
DEFCHIP fileinfo,252&¶
DEFCHIP shows,68&¶
borders(13)=shows+28¶
borders(14)=shows+48¶
FOR i%=0 TO 14¶
  READ i$¶
  POKEW HEXBUFF+i%*4,VAL("&H"+LEFT$(i$,4))¶
  POKEW HEXBUFF+i%*4+2,VAL("&H"+RIGHT$(i$,4))¶
NEXT¶
FOR i%=0 TO 6¶
  READ i$¶
  POKEW shows+i%*4,VAL("&H"+LEFT$(i$,4))¶
  POKEW shows+i%*4+2,VAL("&H"+RIGHT$(i$,4))¶
NEXT¶
POKE shows+29,10¶
POKE shows+31,3¶
POKE shows+33,7¶
POKE shows+35,7¶
POKE shows+37,1¶
POKEW shows+42,256¶
COPYMEM shows+28,shows+48,20¶
FOR i%=0 TO 1¶
  POKEL shows+i%*20+38,shows+i%*14¶
NEXT¶
FOR i%=1 TO 12¶
  READ a%,b%,c%,d%,e%,f%¶
  BORDER borders(i%),a%,b%,c%,d%,e%¶
  IF f%>0 THEN POKEL borders(i%)+12,borders(f%)¶
NEXT¶
FOR i%=1 TO 4¶
  INTUITEXT itxt(i%),1,6,3,"DF"+CHR$(47+i%)+":",0&¶
NEXT¶
FOR i%=5 TO 9¶
  INTUITEXT itxt(i%),1,8,0,SPACE$(30),0&¶
NEXT¶
FOR i%=10 TO 25¶
  READ a%,b%,c%,d$,e%¶
  IF e%>0 THEN f=itxt(e%) ELSE f=0¶
  INTUITEXT itxt(i%),a%,b%,c%,d$,f¶
NEXT¶
STRINGINFO sinfo(1),79,"DF0:"¶
STRINGINFO sinfo(2),4,"0"+STRING$(15,0)¶
actdir=sinfo(1)+36¶
d=0¶
FOR i%=1 TO 24¶
  READ e%,f%,G%,h%,j%,k%,l%,m%,n%,o%¶
¶
  f%=f%-56 :REM NTSC FIX ***************************¶
¶
  IF o%>0 THEN a=sinfo(o%) ELSE a=0¶
  IF n%>0 THEN b=itxt(n%) ELSE b=0¶
  IF m%>0 THEN c=borders(m%) ELSE c=0¶
  GADGET gadgets(i%),d,e%,f%,G%,h%,j%,k%,l%,c,b,a,i%¶
  d=gadgets(i%)¶
```

```
      NEXT¶
      POKEL nscreen+4,41943296&¶
      POKE nscreen+9,2¶
      POKE nscreen+12,192¶
      POKEW nscreen+14,&H10F¶
      nwindow=nscreen+32¶
      POKEL nwindow+4,41943296&¶
      POKEW nwindow+8,259¶
      POKE nwindow+11,32¶
      POKE nwindow+13,96¶
      POKE nwindow+15,1¶
      POKE nwindow+16,24¶
      POKEL nwindow+18,d¶
      POKE nwindow+47,15¶
      POKEW nscreen+82,&HFFF¶
      POKE nscreen+84,15¶
      POKEW nscreen+86,&HFD0¶
      PERMIT¶
      scrbase=OPENSCREEN(nscreen)¶
      IF scrbase=0 THEN ERROR 7¶
      POKEL nwindow+30,scrbase¶
      winbase=OPENWINDOW(nwindow)¶
      IF winbase=0 THEN ERROR 7¶
      rastport=PEEKL(winbase+50)¶
      viewport=scrbase+44¶
      userport=PEEKL(winbase+86)¶
      LOADRGB4 viewport,nscreen+80,4¶
END SUB¶
SUB STATUS(t$)STATIC¶
 SHARED winbase¶
  t$=LEFT$(t$+SPACE$(17),17)¶
  COPYMEM SADD(t$),itxt(22)+20,17¶
  REFRESHGADGETS gadgets(23),winbase,0¶
END SUB    ¶
SUB DEFCHIP(Buffer,size)STATIC¶
 SHARED MList¶
  size=size+8¶
  Buffer=ALLOCMEM(size,65538&)¶
  IF Buffer>0 THEN¶
    POKEL Buffer,MList¶
    POKEL Buffer+4,size¶
    MList=Buffer¶
    Buffer=Buffer+8¶
  ELSE¶
    ERROR 7¶
  END IF¶
END SUB¶
SUB UNDEF STATIC¶
 SHARED MList¶
undef.loop:¶
  IF MList>0 THEN¶
    Buffer=PEEKL(MList)¶
    size=PEEKL(MList+4)¶
    FREEMEM MList,size¶
    MList=Buffer¶
    GOTO undef.loop¶
```

```
      END IF¶
END SUB        ¶
SUB GADGET(bs,nx,x%,y%,b%,h%,f%,a%,t%,i,txt,si,n%)STATIC¶
   DEFCHIP bs,44&¶
   POKEL bs,nx¶
   POKEW bs+4,x%¶
   POKEW bs+6,y%¶
   POKEW bs+8,b%¶
   POKEW bs+10,h%¶
   POKEW bs+12,f%¶
   POKEW bs+14,a%¶
   POKEW bs+16,t%¶
   POKEL bs+18,i¶
   POKEL bs+26,txt¶
   POKEL bs+34,si¶
   POKEW bs+38,n%¶
END SUB¶
SUB INTUITEXT(bs,c1%,x%,y%,t$,nx)STATIC¶
   size=20+LEN(t$)+1¶
   DEFCHIP bs,size¶
   POKE bs,c1%¶
   POKE bs+2,1¶
   POKEW bs+4,x%¶
   POKEW bs+6,y%¶
   POKEL bs+12,bs+20¶
   POKEL bs+16,nx¶
   COPYMEM SADD(t$),bs+20,LEN(t$)¶
END SUB¶
SUB BORDER(bs,x%,y%,c%,b%,h%)STATIC¶
   DEFCHIP bs,48&¶
   POKEW bs,x%¶
   POKEW bs+2,y%¶
   POKE bs+4,c%¶
   POKE bs+7,8¶
   POKEL bs+8,bs+16¶
   FOR i%=0 TO 1¶
      POKEW bs+22+i%*4,h%-1¶
      POKEW bs+24+i%*4,b%-1¶
      POKEW bs+32+i%*4,1¶
      POKEW bs+38+i%*4,h%-1¶
      POKEW bs+40+i%*4,b%-2¶
   NEXT¶
END SUB¶
SUB STRINGINFO(bs,max%,buff$)STATIC¶
   IF LEN(buff$)>max% THEN nmax%=LEN(buff$) ELSE nmax%=max%¶
   IF(nmax%AND 1)THEN nmax%=nmax%+1¶
   size=36+2*(nmax%+4)¶
   DEFCHIP bs,size¶
   POKEL bs,bs+36¶
   POKEL bs+4,bs+40+nmax%¶
   POKEW bs+10,max%+1¶
   IF buff$<>""THEN¶
      COPYMEM SADD(buff$),bs+36,LEN(buff$)¶
   END IF¶
END SUB        ¶
```

```
DATA 48E7F0C0,4CEF0308,001C5303,22187407,E9991001,
0200000F¶
DATA 06000030,0C00003A,65040600,000712C0,51CAFFE6,
12FC0020¶
DATA 51CBFFDA,4CDF030F,4E750000,10003800,7C00FE00,
38003800¶
DATA 38003800,38003800,FE007C00,38001000¶
DATA 0,0,2,43,13,0,-6,-3,2,268,45,0,-6,-3,3,268,13,0¶
DATA 0,0,2,28,13,0,0,-45,2,28,13,4,0,-15,2,28,13,5¶
DATA -62,-3,2,172,13,0,0,0,2,65,13,0,0,0,2,109,13,0¶
DATA 0,15,2,218,13,9,0,0,2,60,13,0,0,0,2,43,28,0¶
DATA 3,-56,0,"Block:",0,3,40,0,"of:",10,1,72,0,"    0",11¶
DATA 3,6,3,"OK",0,1,6,3,"UNDO",0,1,6,3,"PRINT BUFFER",0¶
DATA 1,6,3," PRINT FILE",0,1,17,3,"READ",0,1,17,3,
"NEXT",0¶
DATA 1,17,3,"BACK",0,1,13,3,"WRITE",0,3,6,18,
"Status:",15¶
DATA 1,70,18,"reading Directory",21,1,9,3,"ASCII",0¶
DATA 1,9,3," HEX",0,1,6,10,"QUIT",0¶
DATA 0,198,43,13,0,3,1,1,1,0,0,213,43,13,0,3,1,1,2,0¶
DATA 0,228,43,13,0,3,1,1,3,0,0,243,43,13,0,3,1,1,4,0¶
DATA 52,201,256,8,0,3,1,2,5,0,52,209,256,8,0,3,1,0,6,0¶
DATA 52,217,256,8,0,3,1,0,7,0,52,225,256,8,0,3,1,0,8,0¶
DATA 52,233,256,8,0,3,1,0,9,0,52,246,256,8,0,3,4,3,0,1¶
DATA 317,198,28,13,4,3,1,13,0,0¶
DATA 317,228,28,13,4,3,1,14,0,0¶
DATA 317,243,28,13,0,3,1,6,13,0¶
DATA 416,201,40,8,0,2051,4,7,12,2¶
DATA 529,198,43,13,1,3,1,1,14,0¶
DATA 575,198,65,13,0,3,1,8,17,0¶
DATA575,213,65,13,0,3,1,8,18,0¶
DATA 575,228,65,13,0,3,1,8,19,0¶
DATA575,243,65,13,0,3,1,8,20,0¶
DATA 354,213,109,13,0,3,1,9,16,0¶
DATA 354,228,109,13,0,3,1,10,22,0¶
DATA 466,213,60,13,0,3,1,11,24,0¶
DATA 466,228,60,13,0,3,1,11,23,0¶
DATA 529,213,43,28,128,3,1,12,25,0¶
```

2.2.1   Using the file monitor

This monitor uses a large amount of chip RAM. This means that you should only run one task when on a monitor session—the file monitor. If you run a second program while the file monitor is running, you may run out of chip RAM. The LPRINT at the beginning of the program ensures that the printer driver loads into memory before the program's memory allocation takes place. If you aren't using a printer you may delete this line.

The four gadgets which list the most frequently accessed drives may be changed by editing the corresponding DATA statements. These gadgets are used by the directory routine. To select a drive simply click on the proper gadget.

The default drives for the program range from drive DF0: through drive DF3:. If you want to enter other drives in the gadgets, change the DATA statements with the corresponding names, and make sure that the name is no longer than four characters (including the ending colon). You can also assign the desired drives with the drive labels DF0: through DF3: by using Assign before loading this monitor.

Using the gadgets

The four gadgets on the left border of the screen help speed up the selection of the drive and directories. Simply click on the DF0: gadget to see the main directory of the internal drive.

The file list displays up to five directory entries. Files and programs appear in white text and directories are shown as yellow text. Clicking on a directory name opens and displays the contents of that directory. When you click on a file, the first data block of the desired file loads into memory and then appears on the screen. This data block can be edited in hexadecimal or ASCII form.

The string gadget under the file list displays the current directory or filename. When you click on it a cursor appears. You can now enter your own paths/filenames from the keyboard. This is useful when you want to enter a long path, or if you want to access a drive not listed in the four disk drive gadgets.

The scroll arrows to the right of the file list let you scroll up and down the file list and view all the available names. The directories scroll by five entries at a time.

The OK gadget updates the entry in the string gadget (this is the same as pressing the <Return> key when you're done editing the string gadget).

The line `Block #### of: ####` shows you the current data block number on display of the active file, and the total number of blocks in that file. The first block number is handled as an integer gadget, which allows you to enter the desired data block number by clicking on the gadget. This displays the desired block.

Both Print gadgets allow you to output either the editor buffer or the entire file on a printer in hexadecimal format. After the printing process ends, the last block edited reappears on the screen. The Status display shows all of the errors and the current operations. If all is well, the Status display says OK.

The ASCII and HEX gadgets make it possible to select hexadecimal display or ASCII display. This is a valuable option for changing text (e.g., customizing the AmigaBASIC menus). The Quit gadget, with a confirming requester, ends this program.

The READ, NEXT and BACK gadgets let you read the current block, next block and previous block of the file. The Write gadget writes the editor's buffer to the disk. No requester appears (this speeds up the operation). If you write a block by mistake, select the Undo gadget and select the Write gadget again.

The Undo buffer contains the original contents of the data currently on display. The Undo gadget takes the contents of the Undo buffer and places it in the editor buffer (the buffer containing the data currently displayed).

The editor accepts any characters that can be entered from the keyboard, including the cursor keys. PAL system users can display both hexadecimal and ASCII modes on the screen at once, since the PAL screen has a larger display. The program code above contains comments on what must be changed to run the full display on a PAL system.

The program can multitask, although we don't recommend it (see the beginning of this segment). The key combinations left <Amiga><M> and left <Amiga><N> toggle between the file monitor and Workbench screen.

One last item: The file monitor can only read disk paths up to two directory levels deep. Should you desire more flexibility here, you must dimension the directory buffer correspondingly and adjust the directory subprogram. You can access each file with direct input into the string gadget.

2.2.2   Patching files with the monitor

Patching means changing an existing program by manipulating certain bytes of that program. This makes it possible to customize any program to suit your own needs.

There is one thing you should bear in mind, however: Changing copyright messages or copying commercial programs, patched or otherwise, is <u>against</u> <u>the</u> <u>law</u>. To stay on the side of law and order, patch any commercial programs for your own use. Don't alter copyright messages or use this file monitor for illegal purposes.

2.2.3   Patching AmigaBASIC

Using the file monitor you can customize your copy of AmigaBASIC. You can change the menus and error messages to give your AmigaBASIC interpreter a personal touch.

Warning: Whenever you patch any program or edit any file using the file monitor, make sure you patch a copy of a program or file. Never patch the original program or file!

To patch AmigaBASIC, start by copying AmigaBASIC to another disk. Run the file monitor program and select the ASCII mode. Next insert the disk that contains the copy of AmigaBASIC (NOT the original!). Select AmigaBASIC and press the <Return> key.

Once the file is done loading, click on the Block gadget, enter 28 and press <Return>. Now use the Next and Back gadgets to page through AmigaBASIC until you find the menus. Use the cursor keys to position the cursor, then edit the file to customize AmigaBASIC. Click on the Write gadget to save your changes. If you made a mistake, click Undo, fix the problem and click the Write gadget again. Click on the Quit gadget and press <Y> to quit the program.

You may need a few clues on what to do to change your menus. Here are some examples of what we did to change our AmigaBASIC menus using the file monitor program:

Original menus:

Project	Edit	Run	Windows
New	Cut	Start	Show List
Open	Copy	Stop	Show Output
Save	Paste	Continue	
Save as		Suspend	
Quit		Trace on	
		Step	

Edited menus:

Stuff	Edit	Run	Screens
Oops it	Cut	Go	List
Load it	Copy	Break	BASIC
Save it	Paste	Keep on	
Save as		Whoa	
System		Trace on	
		Step	

2.3   Accessing AmigaDOS from AmigaBASIC

The Amiga operating system consists of many small functions which combine to perform larger tasks. One of the most important tasks is disk access. Every time you perform any disk management, the Amiga accesses disk routines in the operating system. This also occurs in AmigaBASIC; when AmigaBASIC performs disk access, the end result stems from the operating system routines.

Few users realize how easily they can use these disk routines in AmigaBASIC. The first step is to open the `dos.library` file, which makes the Device Operating System available to the user. To use any of the programs in this section, you'll need to convert the `dos_lib.fd` file stored in the FD directory of your Extras disk into a `.bmap` file. The `FDConvert` program (in the `BasicDemos` directory of the Extras disk) converts `_lib.fd` files into `dos.bmap` files. The operating system can read the `dos_lib.fd` file as is, but AmigaBASIC cannot read the information in that form. However, the converted `.bmap` file converts the DOS function data into a form that AmigaBASIC can understand.

Note: We used version 1.3 of the operating system for selecting our `.bmap` files; you may be able to use version 1.2, but we recommend that you purchase Workbench 1.3 and Extras 1.3 if you don't have them.

The command sequence for accessing this file from AmigaBASIC is:

```
LIBRARY "dos.library"
```

Notice the name. The file stored on the disk for access should be `dos.bmap`, the filename used for AmigaBASIC access must be `dos.library`.

Let's take a closer look at the `dos.library` file's contents before we begin programming. Here's a listing of the most important commands:

File access
```
xOpen(name, accessMode)
Close(file)
xRead(file, buffer, length)
Write(file, buffer, length)
Seek(file, position, offset)
Lock(name, type)
UnLock(lock)
DupLock(lock)
```

File control
```
DeleteFile(name)
Rename(oldName,newName)
Examine(lock, fileInfoBlock)
ExNext(lock, fileinfoBlock)
Info(lock, parameterblock)
CreateDir(name)
CurrentDir(lock)
SetComment(name, comment)
SetProtection(name, mask)
DateStamp(date)
ParentDir(lock)
```

**Process
handling**
```
CreateProc(name, pri, segList, stackSize)

Exit(returnCode)
LoadSeg(fileName)
UnLoadSeg(segment)
IsInteractive(file)
Execute(string, file, file)
DeviceProc(name)
Delay(timeout)
```

The above list is far from complete—these are the ones of most interest to us as BASIC programmers. Also, the process handling functions aren't really that easy to access from BASIC. Thus, we shall pay most attention to the first two groups.

The file access group lists the commands used when AmigaBASIC accesses either sequential or relative files. This group seems to have more functions than BASIC actually uses—we'll be accessing some of these functions soon.

The file control group lists functions for maintaining disk structure. This structure includes directories, file data and file changes.

2.3.1   File access through AmigaDOS

Look carefully at the file access group of dos.library functions. You'll see that AmigaDOS has functions named Open() and Close(). However, these apparently normal functions use a completely different set of arguments. Let's take a closer look at how they work.

The following program uses the first three (and most important) AmigaDOS functions in dos.library. It loads the first 200 bytes of any ASCII file into a buffer and displays the data as ASCII text. Enter the program and save it in ASCII format as follows:

```
SAVE "xopendemo",a
```

Run the program. It will read itself and display the first 200 bytes of itself on the screen. Here's the listing:

```
'*********************************¶
'*    xOpendemo              *¶
'*    xOpen() function test  *¶
'* ------------------------- *¶
'*                           *¶
'* Author : Wolf-Gideon Bleek *¶
'* Date   : July 9, 1988     *¶
'* Version: 1.0              *¶
'* Operating system:V1.2 & V1.3 *¶
'*                           *¶
'*********************************¶
' libraries located on T&T2 disk , your may differ¶
LIBRARY "T&T2:bmaps/dos.library"¶
¶
DECLARE FUNCTION xOpen& LIBRARY¶
DECLARE FUNCTION xRead& LIBRARY¶
'               xClose¶
¶
DIM Memory%(100)¶
¶
WIDTH 70¶
¶
File$ = "xOpendemo"+CHR$(0)¶
Handle& = xOpen&(SADD(File$), 1005)¶
Amount& = xRead&(Handle&, VARPTR(Memory%(0)), 200&)¶
¶
CALL xClose(Handle&)¶
¶
FOR i = 0 TO 200¶
    PRINT CHR$(PEEK(VARPTR(Memory%(0))+i));¶
NEXT i¶
¶
LIBRARY CLOSE¶
```

Command description

The xOpen() function corresponds to the AmigaBASIC OPEN statement. However, the functions have two different names to keep the programmer from confusing them. xOpen() requires an argument of a pointer to a string consisting of the filename and the mode number. This supplies us with the file handle needed for file access. If an error occurs, the function returns a null value.

With the help of the handle we can access the open file using the xRead() function. Again, this function is named differently in the .bmap file to avoid confusing it with the READ function in BASIC. xRead() waits for the handle passed by the xOpen() function. This handle tells xRead() which file to access, since more than one file can be open at a time. This is similar to the logical file numbers used in AmigaBASIC.

Next we must pass the address of a buffer into which the data can be read. We dimensioned a simple array that can hold 200 bytes. This array can accept 100 integer variables of two bytes apiece. The last argument represents the number of bytes to be read. This value should be no larger than the size of the buffer, otherwise the data could be placed in memory being used for other tasks, possibly resulting in a system crash.

Once the function executes, it places the first 200 bytes of the open file into the buffer. The xClose() function closes the file, and the program ends by displaying these 200 bytes on the screen.

You may still be wondering what these three file functions can do for you. Here's an example. A program handles many algorithms as one group. An array containing 100 x 100 elements is used to store these algorithms. We should be able to save this algorithmic data for later recall, since calculation time could take up to five hours. Therefore, you must design a save routine to store the algorithms on disk. You can either write single numbers using PRINT#, or save the memory address of the array in question for saving to disk using the xWrite() function. This latter method lets you reload all the values using the xRead() command.

The following sample program handles a 10 x 10 numerical array and demonstrates the procedures listed above:

```
'*********************************¶
'*                               *¶
'* xwritedemo                    *¶
'* Saving data with xWrite()     *¶
'* ---------------------------   *¶
'*                               *¶
'* Author : Wolf-Gideon Bleek    *¶
'* Date    : July 10,1988        *¶
'* Version: 1.0                  *¶
'* Operating system: V1.2 & V1.3 *¶
'*                               *¶
'*********************************¶
¶
OPTION BASE 1¶
'libraries on T&T2 disk , your may differ¶
LIBRARY "T&T2:bmaps/dos.library"¶
¶
DECLARE FUNCTION xOpen& LIBRARY¶
DECLARE FUNCTION xRead& LIBRARY¶
DECLARE FUNCTION xWrite& LIBRARY¶
'               xClose¶
¶
DIM Matrix%(10,10)¶
¶
WIDTH 70¶
¶
FOR i = 1 TO 10¶
  FOR j = 1 TO 10¶
     Matrix%(i,j) = RND*10¶
     PRINT Matrix%(i,j);" ";¶
```

```
              NEXT j¶
              PRINT¶
            NEXT i¶
            PRINT¶
            ¶
            File$ = "Matrix"+CHR$(0)¶
            Handle& = xOpen&(SADD(File$), 1006)¶
            Amount& = xWrite&(Handle&, VARPTR(Matrix%(1,1)), 200&)¶
            ¶
            CALL xClose(Handle&)¶
            ¶
            FOR i = 1 TO 10¶
              FOR j = 1 TO 10¶
                Matrix%(i,j) = 0¶
              NEXT j¶
            NEXT i¶
            ¶
            Handle& = xOpen&(SADD(File$), 1005)¶
            Amount& = xRead&(Handle&, VARPTR(Matrix%(1,1)), 200&)¶
            CALL xClose(Handle&)¶
            ¶
            FOR i = 1 TO 10¶
              FOR j = 1 TO 10¶
                PRINT Matrix%(i,j);" ";¶
              NEXT j¶
              PRINT¶
            NEXT i¶
            PRINT¶
```

Program description

The program fills a 10 x 10 array with random numbers. The xWrite& function writes this data to disk. The number 1006 in the first xOpen() function line opens the file Matrix for writing (1005 opens files for reading).

The program clears the array. Next the xRead() function reads the file and places the file contents in the Matrix array. The contents of the array appear on the screen and the program ends.

If you have the time and the inclination, experiment with an array that has many more elements. Determine the number of bytes to be read and written, and insert this value in place of the value 200&. Change the values in the loop to the new values and test the modified program. If you're still curious, you can program the entire saving process using BASIC commands in conjunction with xRead() and xWrite().

Both of the programs presented, involve data storage in sequential format. AmgaDOS supports both sequential and random (relative) file access. Random files involve commands that send the file pointer to a specfic position in a file. If we compute this position, the pointer moves to that point in the file and reads the data.

Let's take a closer look at random file access. Enter the following program and run it. It takes random file information from the DATA statements and writes this data to a file named addresses.obj:

```
'*********************************¶
'*              randomgen         *¶
'*                                *¶
'* generates random file for use  *¶
'* with seekdemo program          *¶
'* from Abacus' MORE TRICKS AND   *¶
'* TIPS for the Amiga             *¶
'*                                *¶
'*********************************¶
¶
OPEN "r",#1,"df1:Addresses.obj",100¶
FIELD #1,30 AS nam$,30 AS address$,20 AS city$,12 AS
phone$,8 AS comment$¶
CLS¶
PRINT:PRINT "Now reading data and creating random file."¶
PRINT:PRINT "Please be patient...."¶
¶
viewandwrite:¶
    ¶
  READ
xvalue,namedata$,addrdata$,citydata$,phondata$,cmmtdata$
¶
IF xvalue>-1 THEN¶
¶
 LSET      nam$=namedata$¶
 LSET      address$=addrdata$¶
 LSET      city$=citydata$¶
 LSET      phone$=phondata$¶
 LSET      comment$=cmmtdata$  ¶
          x=xvalue¶
     PUT #1,x¶
¶
 PRINT "Record "x" ("nam$") stored."¶
GOTO viewandwrite:¶
END IF¶
¶
CLOSE 1¶
PRINT:PRINT "   File generated and closed. Now use the
seekdemo"¶
      PRINT "   program to read each record."¶
END¶
¶
DATA 1,Jim Oldfield Jr.,5370 52nd Street SE, Grand Rapids
MI, 555-1212,printers¶
DATA 2 ,Doug D.R. Cotton,P.O. Box 2800,Sparta MI,459-
1212,good bbs¶
DATA 3,Jim D'Haem,5370 52nd Street SE,Grand Rapids
MI,957-4488,landlord¶
DATA 4 ,Dick Droste,P.O. Box 9999,Youpie MI,555-
1414,graphix¶
DATA 5 ,Gene Traas,RFD 2000,Hastings MI,999-1119,proofer¶
DATA -1,,,,,¶
```

The record length of the generated test file measures 100 bytes. Enter and run the next program. It opens the addresses.obj file and prompts the user for a record number. When the user enters a number from 1 to 5 and presses the <Return> key, the file pointer moves to the number of the file record requested, and displays the record in the screen. The Seek() function determines the position of the file pointer.

```
'****************************************¶
'*                                      *¶
'* seekdemo                             *¶
'* Direct access to relative files      *¶
'*           using Seek                 *¶
'*------------------------------------- *¶
'*                                      *¶
'* Author : Wolf-Gideon Bleek           *¶
'* Date   : July 10, 1988               *¶
'* Version: 1.0                         *¶
'* Operating systems: V1.2 & V1.3       *¶
'*                                      *¶
'****************************************¶
¶
'libraries on T&T2 disk, yours may differ¶
LIBRARY "T&T2:bmap/dos.library"¶
¶
DECLARE FUNCTION xOpen& LIBRARY¶
DECLARE FUNCTION xRead& LIBRARY¶
DECLARE FUNCTION Seek&  LIBRARY¶
'                 xClose¶
¶
DIM Memory%(100)¶
¶
WIDTH 30¶
¶
PRINT "Record no."¶
INPUT "(1-5):";no&¶
¶
File$ = "df1:Addresses.obj"+CHR$(0)¶
¶
Handle& = xOpen&(SADD(File$), 1005)¶
¶
  Position& = Seek&(Handle&, (no&-1)*100&, 0&)¶
  Amount& = xRead&(Handle&, VARPTR(Memory%(0)), 100&)¶
¶
CALL xClose(Handle&)¶
¶
FOR i = 0 TO 99¶
   PRINT CHR$(PEEK(VARPTR(Memory%(0))+i));¶
NEXT i¶
LIBRARY CLOSE¶
```

**DOS lock
access**

Now we come to another form of file access. The abovementioned methods showed how to read data from files. However, file data can be transferred as well. AmigaDOS has two commands available for this task.

The Lock() function selects the filename and the access mode. This access mode equals -2 if a read access is intended, and -1 if a write access was intended. Reading allows multiple tasks to be performed on the open file. However, writing allows only one task per access.

Unlock() serves the same purpose as xClose(): Both file access and reserved memory are released.

Look at the following program. It accesses any file, selects the access mode and releases it. We'll need this information for later testing in this section.

```
'********************************¶
'*                              *¶
'* lockdemo                     *¶
'* File access through Lock     *¶
'* ---------------------------- *¶

'*                              *¶
'* Author : Wolf-Gideon Bleek   *¶
'* Date   : July 11, 1988       *¶
'* Version: 1.0                 *¶
'* Operating systems: V1.2 & V1.3 *¶
'*                              *¶
'********************************¶
¶
¶
LIBRARY "libs/dos.library"¶
¶
DECLARE FUNCTION Lock& LIBRARY¶
¶
¶
  PRINT "Please enter a filename."¶
  PRINT¶
  INPUT "Filename:";File$¶
  PRINT¶
  ¶
  File$  = File$ + CHR$(0)¶
  FileL& = Lock&(SADD(File$), -2&)¶
  ¶
  IF FileL& <> 0 THEN¶
    PRINT "File found, Lock set!"¶
    UnLock(FileL&)¶
  ELSE¶
    PRINT "File not found, No lock possible!"¶
  END IF¶
```

2.3.2   File, directory and disk information

Lock can do more than access the file handle. We can access directories and disks using Lock as well.

Once you have control of the Lock function, you have control of many other functions which execute in conjunction with Lock. The first one we'll look at together is Examine(). This function takes information from the file identified by a Lock, as you may have seen in CLI commands. Examine() requires an area of buffer memory into which the data can be transferred. This task is performed by AllocMem(), a memory creation function of the exec.bmap file.

The following program examines file data using Lock and Examine():

```
'*****************************************¶
'*                                       *¶
'* examdemo                              *¶
'* File Informationen through Examine    *¶
'*'------------------------------------- *¶
'*                                       *¶
'* Author : Wolf-Gideon Bleek            *¶
'* Date   : July 11, 1988                *¶
'* Version: 1.0                          *¶
'* Operating system: V1.2 & V1.3         *¶
'*                                       *¶
'*****************************************¶
¶
'libraries located in T&T disk, yours may differ¶
LIBRARY "T&T2:bmaps/dos.library"¶
¶
DECLARE FUNCTION Lock& LIBRARY¶
DECLARE FUNCTION Examine LIBRARY¶
¶
LIBRARY "T&T2:bmaps/exec.library"¶
¶
DECLARE FUNCTION AllocMem& LIBRARY¶
¶
Typ& = 2^16¶
¶
InfoBlock& = AllocMem&(300&, Typ&)¶
¶
IF InfoBlock& <> 0 THEN¶
¶
  PRINT "Please enter a filename."¶
  PRINT¶
  INPUT "Filename:";File$¶
  PRINT¶
  ¶
  File$  = File$ + CHR$(0)¶
```

```
      FileL& = Lock&(SADD(File$), -2&)¶
      ¶
      IF FileL& <> 0 THEN¶
        PRINT "Lock set!"¶
        Status = Examine(FileL&, InfoBlock&)¶
        PRINT "DiskKey ";PEEKL(InfoBlock&)¶
        PRINT "DirType ";PEEKL(InfoBlock&+4)¶
        PRINT "Name      ";¶
        FOR i = 8 TO 38¶
          IF PEEK(InfoBlock&+i)<>0 THEN¶
          PRINT CHR$(PEEK(InfoBlock&+i));¶
          END IF¶
        NEXT i¶
        ¶
        UnLock(FileL&)¶
      ELSE¶
        PRINT "No lock possible!"¶
      END IF¶
  ¶
      CALL FreeMem(InfoBlock&, 300&)¶
      ¶
  ELSE¶
  ¶
      PRINT "No free memory--sorry!"¶
  ¶
  END IF
```

Program description

After both libraries open, our program first looks for a free block of memory for the later data storage. Next the program prompts the user for a filename to which he wants the lock assigned. If everything works so far, `Examine()` receives the file info block and places this block in a segment of buffer memory. Then the program displays some information and the filename and all open channels and libraries are closed and the program ends.

The `ExNext()` function can analyze the next entry of a directory, and even be used to display a directory listing. The lock's name must match the name of a directory (e.g., `libs`, `df1:`, etc.). The program displays directory entries until the `Status` variable contains a zero.

```
'***********************************¶
'*                                 *¶
'* exnextdemo                      *¶
'* Directory display thru ExNext() *¶
'*   -   - -----     -- -    --    *¶
'*                                 *¶
'* Author : Wolf Gideon Bleek      *¶
'* Date   : July 11, 1988          *¶
'* Version: 1.0                    *¶
'* Operating system: V1.2 & V1.3   *¶
'*                                 *¶
'***********************************¶
¶
' libraries on T&T disk, your may differ¶
LIBRARY "T&T2:bmaps/dos.library"¶
```

```
¶
DECLARE FUNCTION Lock& LIBRARY¶
DECLARE FUNCTION Examine LIBRARY¶
DECLARE FUNCTION ExNext LIBRARY¶
¶
LIBRARY "T&T2:bmaps/exec.library"¶
¶
DECLARE FUNCTION AllocMem& LIBRARY¶
¶
Typ& = 2^16¶
¶
InfoBlock& = AllocMem&(300&, Typ&)¶
¶
¶
IF InfoBlock& <> 0 THEN¶
¶
  PRINT "Please enter the directory name."¶
  PRINT¶
  INPUT "Filename:";Dir$¶
  PRINT¶
  ¶
  Dir$ = Dir$ + CHR$(0)¶
  DirL& = Lock&(SADD(Dir$), -2&)¶
  ¶
  IF DirL& <> 0 THEN¶
    Status = Examine(DirL&, InfoBlock&)¶
    ¶
    WHILE(Status<>0)¶
    ¶
      i = 8¶
      ¶
      WHILE(PEEK(InfoBlock&+i)<>0)¶
      ¶
        PRINT CHR$(PEEK(InfoBlock&+i));¶
        i = i + 1¶
        ¶
      WEND¶
      ¶
      PRINT¶
      Status = ExNext(DirL&, InfoBlock&)¶
      ¶
    WEND¶
    ¶
    UnLock(DirL&)¶
    ¶
  ELSE¶
  ¶
    PRINT "No lock possible!"¶
    ¶
  END IF¶
¶
  CALL FreeMem(InfoBlock&, 300&)¶
ELSE¶
  PRINT "No free memory--sorry!"¶
¶
END IF¶
```

**Program
description**

This program's operation is similar to the preceding program, except that this program has a more elaborate main loop. This loop makes it easy to read the first entry of the directory using `Examine`. After entering the directory name, the program enables the lock.

Next the program looks for further entries using the `ExNext()` function. It displays the next directory name on record and repeats the loop as long as the `Status` variable returns a value unequal to zero. If the program finds a null value in the `Status` variable, the program signals the error NO_MORE_ENTRIES and stops.

AmigaDOS has three more functions in the field of directory handling. The `ParentDir()` function determines whether a subdirectory exists in a particular directory. This requires a lock on the current directory, and returns either a lock to the subdirectory or null (if the program is already in the root directory). The following program makes use of this function and displays the current level in the directory tree.

```
'*******************************¶
'* parentdir                   *¶
'*      List Directory Level   *¶
'* --------------------------- *¶
'*                             *¶
'* Author : Wolf-Gideon Bleek  *¶
'* Date   : July 11,1988       *¶
'* Version: 1.0                *¶
'* Operating system: V1.2 & V1.3*¶
'*                             *¶
'*******************************¶
¶
' libraries are in the T&T2 disk, yours may differ¶
LIBRARY "T&T2:bmaps/dos.library"¶
¶
DECLARE FUNCTION Lock& LIBRARY¶
DECLARE FUNCTION ParentDir& LIBRARY¶
¶
¶
  PRINT "Please enter the directory name."¶
  PRINT¶
  INPUT "Name:";Dir$¶
  PRINT¶
  ¶
  Level = 0¶
  ¶
  Dir$ = Dir$ + CHR$(0)¶
  DirL& = Lock&(SADD(Dir$), -2&)¶
  ¶
  IF DirL& <> 0 THEN¶
¶
    WHILE(DirL& <> 0)¶
      ¶
      DirL& = ParentDir&(DirL&)¶
      Level = Level + 1¶
      ¶
```

```
               WEND¶
               ¶
               UnLock(DirL&)¶
            ¶
               IF Level = 1 THEN¶
                 PRINT ">> Main directory! <<"¶
               END IF¶
               ¶
               PRINT "Level: ";Level¶
                  ¶
            ELSE¶
            ¶
               PRINT "No lock possible!"¶
               ¶
            END IF¶
```

Program description

The program searches the directory levels until a null is returned, when it is at the main directory. The call to `ParentDir()` returns the directory level. You may enter multiple directories in the path to find different levels.

Two functions remain which directly apply to directories. The first, `CurrentDir()`, is similar to the AmigaBASIC `CHDIR` command. The user sets a lock on the directory and accesses this function. The old lock is returned until the current directory is given. Using this you can reset directory paths anytime.

Directories can also be accessed from `dos.library`. The last function just needs the name of the new directory. The directory will be treated as a subdirectory of the current directory. Therefore, you must first use `CurrentDir()` before accessing any directory. The result is equal to the lock of the new directory.

Now that we've seen how to access directories and get information from directory files, let's do some more detailed reading of this disk data. AmigaDOS has a third directory function named `Info()`. It loads information about a disk and places this information in a buffer. We can then read this easily and display important disk information:

```
'*********************************¶
'*                               *¶
'* info                          *¶
'* Disk information through Info  *¶
'* ----------------------------- *¶
'*                               *¶
'* Author : Wolf-Gideon Bleek    *¶
'* Date   : July 11,1988         *¶
'* Version: 1.0                  *¶
'* Operating system: V1.2 & V1.3 *¶
'*                               *¶
'*********************************¶
        ¶
        ¶
LIBRARY "T&T2:bmaps/dos.library"¶
```

```
¶
DECLARE FUNCTION Lock& LIBRARY¶
DECLARE FUNCTION Info LIBRARY¶
¶
LIBRARY "T&T2:bmapsexec.library"¶
¶
DECLARE FUNCTION AllocMem& LIBRARY¶
¶
typ& = 2^16¶
¶
Info& = AllocMem&(300&, typ&)¶
¶
IF Info& <> 0 THEN¶
¶
  PRINT "Please enter a device name."¶
  PRINT¶
  INPUT "Name:";Dev$¶
  PRINT¶
  ¶
  Dev$  = Dev$ + CHR$(0)¶
  DevL& = Lock&(SADD(Dev$), -2&)¶
  ¶
  IF DevL& <> 0 THEN¶
    ¶
    Status = Info(DevL&, Info&)¶
    ¶
    i = 8¶
    WHILE(PEEK(Info&+i)<>0)¶
      PRINT CHR$(PEEK(Info&+i));¶
    WEND¶
    ¶
    PRINT¶
    ¶
    PRINT "Soft Errors: ";PEEKL(Info&)¶
    PRINT "Unit Number: ";PEEKL(Info&+4)¶
    PRINT "Disk Status: "; : st& = PEEKL(Info&+8)¶
    IF st& = 80 THEN PRINT "Write protected"¶
    IF st& = 81 THEN PRINT "Validated"¶
    IF st& = 82 THEN PRINT "Disk ready"¶
    ¶
    PRINT¶
    PRINT "NumBlocks   : ";PEEKL(Info&+12)¶
    PRINT "NumUsed     : ";PEEKL(Info&+16)¶
    PRINT "BytespBlock: ";PEEKL(Info&+20)¶
    PRINT "DiskType    : "; : typ& = PEEKL(Info&+24)¶
    FOR i = 3 TO 0 STEP -1 ¶
      PRINT CHR$((typ& / 256^i) AND 255);¶
    NEXT i¶
    ¶
    PRINT¶
    ¶
    UnLock(DevL&)¶
    ¶
  ELSE¶
    ¶
    PRINT "Not found, No lock possible!"¶
```

```
     ¶
     END IF¶
¶
     CALL FreeMem(Info&, 300&)¶
     ¶
ELSE¶
¶
     PRINT "No free memory--sorry!"¶
¶
END IF¶
```

Program description

After placing the lock on a disk entry, the `Info()` function reads the disk information. This information is then displayed on the screen. Then disk access ends and the program releases the memory it allocated.

2.3.3   Direct file control

You'll recognize three out of the next four functions from the `CLI`. This segment describes how you can make use of these functions from AmigaBASIC.

Start by creating three simple test programs in AmigaBASIC and saving them to the same directory (just a `REM` or `PRINT` statement will do). Name these test files `DeleteTest`, `My_Old_Name` and `Protect_Me`. Enter the three demo programs below and save them to the same directory as the three programs you just entered (preferably the main directory).

The `DeleteFile()` function is completely compatible with the `CLI` `Delete` command. Entering the filename as a string deletes the file. Notice that `DeleteFile()` does not automatically delete a file's matching `.info` file—the `.info` file must be deleted separately. Here's a short demonstration program which deletes the BASIC program named `DeleteTest` and the `DeleteTest.info` file:

```
' Demo of DeleteFile()¶
' Deletes existing BASIC file named DeleteTest¶
' and its .info file¶
¶
LIBRARY "T&T2:bmaps/dos.library"¶
¶
DECLARE FUNCTION DeleteFile LIBRARY¶
¶
file$ = "DeleteTest" + CHR$(0)¶
status = DeleteFile(SADD(file$))¶
¶
file$ = "DeleteTest.info" + CHR$(0)¶
status = DeleteFile(SADD(file$))¶
```

The Rename() function is completely compatible with the CLI
Rename command. The user enters two texts—one representing the
old name and one representing the new name. Here's a brief
demonstration program which renames the program My_Old_Name
and its .info file to The_New_Stuff:

```
' Demo of Rename¶
' Renames existing BASIC program¶
' named My_Old_Name to The_New_Stuff¶
' and its info file¶
¶
LIBRARY "T&T2:bmaps/dos.library"¶
¶
DECLARE FUNCTION Rename LIBRARY¶
¶
OldFile$ = "My_Old_Name" + CHR$(0)¶
NewFile$ = "The_New_Stuff" + CHR$(0)¶
OldInfo$ = "My_Old_Name.info" + CHR$(0)¶
NewInfo$ = "The_New_Stuff.info" + CHR$(0)¶
¶
Status = Rename(SADD(OldFile$), SADD(NewFile$))¶
Status = Rename(SADD(OldInfo$), SADD(NewInfo$))¶
```

The last file control function is named SetProtection(). This
function sets and unsets the protection bits on files in Version 1.2
(which has four protection bits) and in Version 1.3 (which has eight
protection bits). These bits lie in a particular order following a file.
Thus, you can protect some files from being deleted. Here's a short
program to demonstrate (change the filename to suit your own needs):

```
' Demo of SetProtection¶
' Sets protection bits on the file named Protect_Me¶
LIBRARY "T&T2:bmaps/dos.library"¶
DECLARE FUNCTION SetProtection LIBRARY¶
¶
File$ = "Protect_Me"+CHR$(0)¶
Mask& = 4+8¶
status = SetProtection(SADD(File$), Mask&)¶
```

The mask& variable can be divided into the following bits:

Bit #   Meaning when bit is set

Bit #	Meaning when bit is set
0	File cannot be deleted
1	File cannot be executed (not implemented)
2	File cannot be overwritten (not implemented)
3	File cannot be read (not implemented)
4	File stays unchanged after a copy procedure
5	Program file can be made resident
6	File is a script file, and cannot be run using Execute
7	File cannot be listed (not implemented on 1.2)

2.4   Libraries and applications

So far you've seen brief examples of DOS functions accessed from AmigaBASIC. These programs were enough to demonstrate the functions, and give you a little knowledge on the subject. We will conclude this chapter with a larger program that might be of great use to the BASIC programmer.

You should be able to find many uses for this program. It allows you to make archival listings of disk directories. It starts by letting you create directory lists for printing. Once you generate a directory listing, you can display it and manipulate it to some degree, and even sort the list in alphabetical order.

2.4.1   Directory manager

This program, which lets you perform directory management, lets you read a directory and display it in tabular form. This list can be sorted alphabetically in order of directories and files.

This system works well for program or text disks consisting of many files, which are normally difficult to read from a normal directory command because the listing scrolls by so quickly (e.g., `files` from AmigaBASIC). Compiling the directory into a list makes it easier to find a file, and converting the directory to a file lets you read the directory from a word processor.

```
'*****************************************¶
'* dirmanager                         *¶
'*    Directory manager in AmigaBASIC  *¶
'* ------------------------------------ *¶
'*                                     *¶
'* Author : Wolf-Gideon Bleek          *¶
'* Date   : July 11, 1988              *¶
'* Version: 1.0                        *¶
'* Operating system: V1.2 & V1.3       *¶
'*                                     *¶
'*****************************************¶
¶
¶
LIBRARY "T&T2:bmaps/dos.library"¶
¶
DECLARE FUNCTION Lock& LIBRARY¶
DECLARE FUNCTION Examine LIBRARY¶
```

```
DECLARE FUNCTION ExNext LIBRARY¶
¶
¶
LIBRARY "T&T2:bmaps/exec.library"¶
¶
DECLARE FUNCTION AllocMem& LIBRARY¶
¶
Info&    = 0¶
¶
Typ&     = 2^16¶
MaxSize& = 300¶
¶
Suffix$  = "no ending"¶
¶
DIM Dir$(200), File$(200), Size$(200)¶
¶
Info& = AllocMem&(MaxSize&, Typ&)¶
OPEN "ram:temporary" FOR OUTPUT AS 255¶
¶
OPEN "RAM:dir-list" FOR APPEND AS 1¶
CLOSE 1¶
¶
MENU 1,0,1,"Data      "¶
MENU 1,1,1,"Load      "¶
MENU 1,2,1,"Save      "¶
MENU 1,3,1,"Quit      "¶
¶
MENU 2,0,1,"Directory  "¶
MENU 2,1,1,"Complete  "¶
MENU 2,2,1,"Sort      "¶
MENU 2,3,1,"Display   "¶
MENU 2,4,1,"Delete    "¶
¶
MENU 3,0,1,"Settings"¶
MENU 3,1,1,"Filter extensions"¶
¶
¶
MENU 4,0,0,""¶
¶
ON MENU GOSUB Selects¶
MENU ON¶
¶
WHILE 1¶
    IF FileMemory& <> 0 THEN¶
    FreeMem(FileMemory&, Length&)¶
  END IF¶
  ¶
SLEEP¶
WEND¶
¶
¶
Selects:¶
  HM = MENU(0)¶
  MP = MENU(1)¶
  ¶
  FOR i = 1 TO 3¶
```

```
      MENU i, 0, 0¶
   NEXT i¶
   ¶
   IF HM = 1 AND MP = 3 THEN¶
     MENU RESET¶
     CALL FreeMem(Info&, MaxSize&)¶
     CLOSE 255¶
     LIBRARY CLOSE¶
     END        ¶
   END IF¶
   ¶
   IF HM = 1 AND MP = 1 THEN GOSUB LoadIt  ¶
   IF HM = 1 AND MP = 2 THEN GOSUB SaveData¶
   ¶
   IF HM = 2 AND MP = 1 THEN GOSUB GetDir¶
   IF HM = 2 AND MP = 2 THEN GOSUB Sort¶
   IF HM = 2 AND MP = 3 THEN GOSUB DisplayIt¶
   IF HM = 2 AND MP = 4 THEN GOSUB DeleteIt¶
                                         ¶
   IF HM = 3 AND MP = 1 THEN GOSUB NewSuffix¶
   ¶
   PRINT¶
   PRINT "OK"¶
   PRINT¶
   ¶
   FOR i = 1 TO 3¶
     MENU i,0,1¶
   NEXT i¶
   ¶
   RETURN¶
   ¶
¶
LoadIt:¶
   PRINT "LOAD file created by dirmanager"¶
   PRINT¶
             ¶
   PRINT "Please enter the filename."¶
   PRINT¶
   INPUT "Filename:";SourceFile$¶
                          ¶
   IF SourceFile$ = "" THEN RETURN¶
   ¶
   PRINT¶
   PRINT "Loading file..."¶
¶
   OPEN "RAM:dir-list" FOR OUTPUT AS 2¶
   OPEN SourceFile$ FOR INPUT AS 1¶
   ¶
   WHILE(EOF(1)=0)¶
      ¶
     INPUT#1, Dir$, File$, Size$¶
     PRINT#2, Dir$¶
     PRINT#2, File$¶
     PRINT#2, Size$¶
     ¶
   WEND¶
```

```
    ¶
    CLOSE 1¶
    CLOSE 2¶
¶
    RETURN¶
    ¶
    ¶
SaveData:¶
    PRINT "SAVE file created by dirmanager"¶
    PRINT¶
                                    ¶
    PRINT "Please enter the filename."¶
    PRINT¶
    INPUT "Filename:";DestFile$¶
    ¶
    IF DestFile$ = "" THEN RETURN¶
    ¶
    PRINT¶
    PRINT "Saving file..."¶
¶
    OPEN "RAM:dir-list" FOR INPUT AS 1¶
    OPEN DestFile$ FOR OUTPUT AS 2¶
    ¶
    WHILE(EOF(1)=0)¶
        ¶
        INPUT#1, Dir$, File$, Size$¶
        PRINT#2, Dir$¶
        PRINT#2, File$¶
        PRINT#2, Size$¶
    ¶
    WEND¶
    ¶
    CLOSE 1¶
    CLOSE 2¶
    ¶
    RETURN¶
    ¶
¶
GetDir:¶
    PRINT "Load directory"¶
    PRINT¶
    ¶
    PRINT "Please enter the directory path."¶
    PRINT¶
    INPUT "Directory name:";Dir$¶
    ¶
    IF Dir$ = "" THEN RETURN¶
¶
    PRINT¶
    PRINT "Reading directory..."¶
    PRINT¶
    ¶
    Dir$  = Dir$ + CHR$(0)¶
    DirLk& = Lock&(SADD(Dir$), -2&)¶
    ¶
    IF DirLk& <> 0 THEN¶
```

```
¶
  OPEN "RAM:dir-list" FOR APPEND AS 1¶
  ¶
  Status = Examine(DirLk&, Info&)¶
  PRINT "Directory: ";¶
  CALL Display(Info&, 255, "")¶
  Directories$ = File$¶
  ¶
  Status = ExNext(DirLk&, Info&)¶
  ¶
  WHILE(Status<>0)¶
  ¶
    CALL Display(Info&, 1, Directories$)¶
    Status = ExNext(DirLk&, Info&)¶
    ¶
  WEND¶
¶
  CLOSE 1¶
  ¶
ELSE¶
¶
  PRINT "Directory not found!"¶
  ¶
END IF¶
¶
RETURN¶
¶
¶
Sort:¶
¶
  PRINT "Sorting directory"¶
  PRINT¶
  ¶
  OPEN "ram:dir-list" FOR INPUT AS 1¶
¶
  z = 0¶
  ¶
  WHILE(EOF(1)=0)¶
    ¶
    INPUT#1, Dir$(z), File$(z), Size$(z)¶
    z = z + 1¶
    ¶
  WEND¶
  ¶
  CLOSE 1¶
  ¶
  FOR i = 0 TO z - 2
    k = i¶
    FOR j = i TO z - 1¶
      IF Dir$(j)+File$(j)<Dir$(k)+File$(k) THEN k = j¶
    NEXT j¶
    SWAP Dir$(i), Dir$(k)¶
    SWAP File$(i), File$(k)¶
    SWAP Size$(i), Size$(k)¶
  NEXT i¶
  ¶
```

```
      OPEN "ram:dir-list" FOR OUTPUT AS 1¶
      ¶
      FOR i = 0 TO z - 1¶
        PRINT#1, Dir$(i)¶
        PRINT#1, File$(i)¶
        PRINT#1, Size$(i)¶
      NEXT i¶
      ¶
      CLOSE 1¶
      ¶
      RETURN¶
   ¶
   ¶
DisplayIt:¶
   ¶
      PRINT "Listing directory"¶
      PRINT¶
      ¶
      OPEN "ram:dir-list" FOR INPUT AS 1¶
   ¶
      WHILE(EOF(1)=0)¶
        ¶
        INPUT#1, Dir$, File$, Size$¶
        PRINT Dir$;TAB(40);File$;TAB(70);Size$¶
      ¶
      WEND¶
      ¶
      CLOSE 1¶
      ¶
      RETURN¶
   ¶
   ¶
DeleteIt:¶
      ¶
      PRINT "Delete dir-list from RAM"¶
      PRINT¶
      PRINT "Do you really want to delete all data?"¶
      ¶
      INPUT "Y/N<Return>: ";a$¶
      ¶
      IF a$<>"Y" THEN RETURN¶
      ¶
      KILL "ram:dir-list"¶
   ¶
      PRINT                                  ¶
      PRINT "Directory deleted"¶
                                       ¶
      OPEN "ram:dir-list" FOR APPEND AS 1¶
      CLOSE 1¶
      ¶
      RETURN¶
         ¶
   ¶
NewSuffix:¶
   ¶
      PRINT "User-defined file extension filter"¶
```

```
      PRINT¶
      ¶
      PRINT "Please enter an extension (e.g., .ext)"¶
      PRINT "or press <Return> to display all files."¶
      PRINT¶
      ¶
      INPUT "Extension: ";Suffix$¶
      ¶
      IF Suffix$ = "" THEN Suffix$ = "No ending"¶
      ¶
      RETURN¶
      ¶
        ¶
SUB Display(Mem&, Ch%, Dir$) STATIC¶
SHARED File$, Suffix$¶
¶
  i = 8 : File$=""¶
¶
  WHILE(PEEK(Mem&+i)<>0)¶
    File$ = File$ + CHR$(PEEK(Mem&+i))¶
    i = i + 1                       ¶
      ¶
  WEND¶
    ¶
  IF RIGHT$(UCASE$(File$), LEN(Suffix$)) =
UCASE$(Suffix$) THEN EXIT SUB¶
    ¶
  PRINT File$;TAB(35);¶
  PRINT#Ch%, Dir$¶
  PRINT#Ch%, File$¶
        ¶
  IF PEEKL(Mem&+4)<0 THEN¶
    PRINT PEEKL(Mem&+124);TAB(45);¶
    PRINT#Ch%, PEEKL(Mem&+124)¶
  ELSE¶
    PRINT " DIR";TAB(45);¶
    PRINT#Ch%, "DIR"¶
  END IF¶
¶
  PRINT¶
¶
END SUB¶
¶
```

Program description

After starting the program, press the right mouse button. Three menu titles appear in the menu bar—File, Directory and Settings. The File menu lets the user save directory data to disk, or load previously saved directory data. If the user selects either item, the program asks for the name of the file to be saved or loaded. Selecting the Quit item ends the program.

The Directory menu supplies options for managing directory data. The Complete item gets the complete directory from disk. The program prompts the user for the directory name or device number. Enter this and press the <Return> key to load the directory.

The Sort item sorts the directory currently in memory into alphabetical order.

The Display item displays the list of data loaded so far. The program divides this list into three columns—the disk name, the file/directory name and the number of bytes used/DIR (for directory).

The Delete item deletes the directory list from the RAM disk. The only response the computer accepts to delete the RAM file is <Y><Return>. If you enter a lower case <y>, or any other key, the function aborts.

The Settings menu has only one item—the Filter extensions item. This can be implemented when you have too many files of one particular extension on a disk, and these files make the directory hard to read. For example, if you want to see a directory of BASIC programs without seeing their .info files, select the Filter extensions item. Enter the text .info at the prompt and press <Return>. Now if you select the Complete item from the Directory menu, the program suppresses the .info filenames from the list.

2.4.2   Program documentation

The program starts by opening the two .bmap files needed: dos.library, which loads the directories, and exec.library, which handles memory management. Next the program initializes variables and pointers, arrays for the Sort routine and memory for the Examine() function.

A temporary file opens for storing later output (i.e., its data doesn't go to the screen). Also, the dir-list file opens for appending data (e.g., more than one disk directory). If dir-list doesn't exist during program execution, errors can occur. Directory data is kept as a file in the RAM disk instead of in variable arrays. This offers a good demonstration of RAM disk usage, as well as keeping more memory free for the program itself. So the RAM disk always opens for appending when other data is read. It keeps appending data until no more memory exists.

The next routine creates the three menus and their items, and removes them when the program ends. You'll find the menu reading loop in this same area, which allows you to select a menu item. If the user selects a menu item, the program jumps to the Selects routine, which contains the menu numbers and item numbers required.

If a menu item was selected, first the program disables all the menus to avoid accidentally selecting a second item during execution of the current item. This routine then branches to the respective subprogram and executes the task. Once execution of the item ends, a short delay loop executes and the menus are re-activated.

Here are detailed descriptions of the important routines as they appear in program order:

The LoadIt routine requests the name of an existing directory file (created by the SaveData routine). The program adds a lock, opens the RAM file and adds the new data to the RAM file. First the routine loads the directory name with path using Examine(). The display of this file uses an extra SUB program which filters output and transmits the data to different devices (more on this later). The end of the directory file causes the exit from the subroutine.

The SaveData routine prompts the user for a filename. If the user presses <Return> without any other input, the routine ends. Entering a filename and pressing <Return> generates two files: a RAM file for reading and a written file for later data transfer. The data in the RAM disk matches that data in the written file, until no new data can be read. This ends the saving process.

The GetDir subroutine loads a directory. The user enters a directory name or path and presses <Return>. The program checks for an existing name. It loads the directory if the name exists, and exits the routine if not. This will result in an error message—you may want to add error trapping to this program.

The Sort routine alphabetically sorts directory entries contained in the RAM disk by filename.

The DisplayIt routine controls all screen display. This assigns a pointer to the memory range into which the directory data was placed. This information includes the number of the data channel, which controls the data output, as well as the disk path itself. First the routine reads the name of the entry and places it in the File$ variable. Then it tests whether the filename extension matches the saved extension. If so, the routine exits without displaying data, since these files and entries should be skipped.

The DisplayIt routine checks the file and displays all three file items as a single-line entry (disk name, filename, bytes/DIR). This routine lists the directory until no more data exists. The end of the routine jumps back to the main program.

The first two data items appear on the screen: The directory path and the filename. Next the program lists the sizes of the files. These values are read as a FileInfo structure. If the value is less than zero, the program displays the abbreviation DIR. In any case, the file output appears on the screen.

The `DeleteIt` routine deletes the `dir-list` RAM file and opens an empty file of the same name. The INPUT statement that determines whether you want to delete the contents of the RAM file only accepts a capital Y as a positive response. Any other selection (including a lower case y) aborts the function.

The `NewSuffix` routine prompts the user for an extension name for files you don't want to appear in the list. If the user presses <Return> without entering an extension, the routine ensures the display of all filenames.

We hope that these programs offer you a good demonstration of using libraries for file control in AmigaBASIC.

3.
Machine language

3.   Machine language

AmigaBASIC is a good programming language, but it's definitely not the fastest. The best language to program in is machine language. The reason for this is that machine language instructions run a thousand times faster than BASIC commands. Every feature of the computer can be accessed from machine language, some that may not be available in BASIC—system routines can be called at almost any time. True, machine language is hard to learn, but programming on the Amiga with a good assembler can be learned relatively quickly. AssemPro from Abacus is a very good assembler for the beginner.

Let's talk for a moment about the C programming language, which executes at about a tenth the speed of machine language. You can do many of the same things in C that you can in machine language. Unfortunately, many of the unusual routines you might want to call in C require fairly extensive programming. For all that trouble, you might as well program in machine language.

You may not know anything about machine language. That's fine—this chapter doesn't demand that much knowledge from you. However, for the most effective Amiga programming, we recommend that you start learning 68000 machine language. Get an elementary book on the subject (*Amiga Machine Language* from Abacus is a good text on 68000 machine code on the Amiga) and study. We repeat: You won't need that knowledge for this chapter—we'll explain the code as carefully as we can.

This chapter contains many useful machine language programs and routines. You'll find BASIC extensions and unusual demonstrations of what you can do with the mouse. We've even included a program designed for zapping viruses (a problem in the Amiga community).

The routines below were written using Abacus' *AssemPro* assembler. For those of you who don't have access to an assembler, we've included BASIC loaders for each program whenever possible.

3.1   Division by zero handler

Dividing a value by zero may be one of the biggest causes of Guru Meditations. Let's start by looking at what happens during and after a division by zero, so we can think about how we can solve this problem.

The processor itself creates an exception. The Status register from the 68000 passes to a buffer. The processor automatically switches to supervisor mode. The Trace bit is erased to disable single-step mode. Now the program counter (PC), Status register, Instruction register (and its condition when the error occurred), access address and the Superstate word (which explains the processor's condition) are placed on the Supervisor stack.

After an Exception routine the processor continues working with the program, which releases the error, the RTE (ReTurn from Exception) instruction executes. The Exception vector appears at RTE. You can find a variation on this in the CLI SetAlert command, which waits for error flag settings, then determines from the Superstate word whether RTE or a Guru follows.

We'd like to clarify the following: When you have a program that has such a small denominator that it can no longer be represented by a word (The 68000 commands DIVU and DIVS process words only), the denominator is rounded off to zero. Here's where the problem crops up: the 68000 can't divide by zero.

RTE returns us to the program. This return goes to the address after the command that releases the error. This is good, right? Wrong. Think about this: What usually happens when you divide by a very small number, for example .00001? You could get a fairly large number as a result.

The register which held the result now contains a very small value. The result is that all subsequent calculations must also be wrong as soon the next Exception is released. The program only returns nonsense, which is of no help to the user. We can assume that the denominator was infinitely small instead of just zero. This allows division once again. We can write the following in place of "infinitely small":

```
                        1
-------------------------------------------
    Denominator = infinitely_large
```

For division by this denominator, we get help from the old rule: When dividing by a fraction, multiply by the inverse:

```
Counter = x
Inverse denominator = infinitely_large

Result = Counter * Inverse denominator
       = x * infinitely_large
       = infinitely_large
```

We insert the largest possible value for `infinitely_large` which the commands `DIVS` and `DIVU` can process, and the computation is correct in spite of Exception. We write an Exception routine which stores the correct values in the corresponding registers before you return with `RTE`.

For this reason, you must know which command releases the Exception because the highest possible value for `DIVU` is $FFFF, and for `DIVS`, $FFF. Furthermore, we must determine in which data register this value must be transferred. The number of the data register is found directly in the opcode, as the following table shows:

Command	Command code bits															
	15	14	13	12	11	10	9	8	7	6	5	4	3	2	1	0
DIVU	1	0	0	0	x	x	x	0	1	1	y	y	y	y	y	y
DIVS	1	0	0	0	x	x	x	1	1	1	y	y	y	y	y	y

Bits 9-11 (x) return the number of the data register where the result is stored. Bits 0-5 give the addressing type, which you don't need to know about here. Here's the machine language version of the program:

```
;Division by Zero - Handler; by SM'88

Init_Trap:                      ;Install handler
  Move.l 4,A6                   ;ExecBase to A6
  Move.l #Div_End-Div,D0        ;Handler-Length to D0

  MoveQ  #1,D1                  ;MEMF_Public
  Jsr    -198(a6)               ;call AllocMem
  Move.l  D0,New_Trap           ;get address

  Beq.s  Init_End               ;End, when error
  Move.l D0,A1                  ;Address to A1
  Lea    Div,A0                 ;CodeStart-Address

  MoveQ  #(Div_End-Div)-1,D0    ;CodeLength-1
Copy_Code:                      ;Handler copy
  Move.b (A0)+,(A1)+            ;Byte copy
  DBra   D0,Copy_Code           ;Next Byte
  Move.l New_Trap,20            ;New Trap-Vector


Init_End:                       ;Adieu
  MoveQ  #0,D0                  ;No = 0 !!!
  Divu   D0,D1                  ;Go Ahead, Make My Day
  rts                          ;End
```

```
New_Trap:                       ;New Trap-Vector
   dc.l   0                     ;1 LongWord

Div:                            ;DivisionByZeroHandler
   MoveM.l D0-A6,-(sp)          ;All Register (s.u.)
   Move.l  62(sp),A0            ;get PC from Stack
   Move.w  -2(A0),D0            ;get last command
   Move.l  #$ffff,D1            ;large value for Divu

   Btst    #8,D0                ;Was it Divu-instruction?
   Beq.s   GoOn                 ;then continue
   Move.l  #$7fff,D1            ;Else Divs-Value

GoOn:                           ;Data register transfer
   Lsr.w   #7,D0                ;Scroll command bitwise
   AndI.l  #28,D0               ;Ignore register

   Move.l  D1,0(sp,d0.l)        ;Register and Stack ndern
   MoveM.l (sp)+,D0-A6          ;Genderte Register laden
   Rte                          ;Return from Exception
Div_End:                        ;Label: SizeOf

   End
```

You may have been wondering how the new result value arrives in the data register. After storing the entire register on the stack, which always stores the highest address register first, the other registers are used in descending order (see the third line of the program). They are simply used with four multiplied register numbers as an offset for the stack access. Should something not function properly, the system does a Guru.

We released a division by zero Exception after installing the new Trap vector (division by zero occurs in line 20).

Here is a short BASIC routine that stores the program as a CLI command (you should call this command using your startup sequence):

```
OPEN "sys:c/DIVZERO" FOR OUTPUT AS 1
FOR i=1 TO 176
 READ a$
 a%=VAL("&H"+a$)
 PRINT #1,CHR$(a%);
NEXT
CLOSE 1
KILL "sys:c/DIVZERO.info"
datas:
DATA 0,0,3,F3,0,0,0,0,0,0,0,1,0,0,0,0,0,0,0,0
DATA 40,0,0,1B,0,0,3,E9,0,0,0,1B,2C,78,0,4,20,3C,0,0
DATA 0,30,72,1,4E,AE,FF,3A,23,C0,0,0,0,36,67,18,22,40,41,F9
DATA 0,0,0,3A,70,2F,12,D8,51,C8,FF,FC,21,F9,0,0,0,36,0,14
DATA 70,0,82,C0,4E,75,0,0,0,0,48,E7,FF,FE,20,6F,0,3E,30,28
DATA FF,FE,22,3C,0,0,FF,FF,8,0,0,8,67,6,22,3C,0,0,7F,FF
DATA EE,48,2,80,0,0,0,0,1C,2F,81,8,0,4C,DF,7F,FF,4E,73,0,0
DATA 0,0,3,EC,0,0,0,3,0,0,0,0,0,0,12,0,0,0,1C
DATA 0,0,0,2A,0,0,0,0,0,0,3,F2,0,0,3,F2
```

3.2   Attention: Virus alarm!

Computer viruses are a major topic of discussion wherever you hear computer users talking shop. Some people say that there are no such things as computer viruses—that it's all media hype, and that viruses don't really exist. We'll leave the debate up to others. However, we personally believe in viruses.

Computer viruses spread with amazing speed. The most common viruses seen on the Amiga are the SCA virus and the Byte Bandit virus. Once you could simply say, "You're safe as long as you use commercial software." This is no longer true today: We have a problem that cannot be taken seriously enough.

Who's responsible?

When viruses come under debate, the first question that crops up is, "Who's responsible for these programs?" Viruses came from the world of the software pirate, who cracks the protection on a commercial program, and perhaps adds a virus to it. The pirated copies spread viruses even further, and may even return to the manufacturers from whence the original programs came. Suddenly original games from the factory have viruses on them! This has happened to a few game manufacturers. One highly respected manufacturer of software for another 68000-based computer was shocked by the fact that a pair of magazine executives had planted a virus on a fairly expensive and powerful piece of illustration software.

How does a virus propagate? Generally the virus program hides in the boot block of a disk. When you boot using this disk, the operating system loads the boot sectors (the first two sectors of a disk). Usually these sectors contain the initialization routine for the DOS library. The `Install` command writes this routine to disks to make them bootable. The operating system jumps directly to the boot routine, which is exactly what the virus wants.

The virus copies itself to an area of memory, changes system vectors and goes through the DOS initialization. This places them in the system unnoticed. If you place another boot disk in a drive, one virus writes itself to the boot block. Another type of virus does this during a reset.

Unfortunately, many programs start with a loader in the boot block, which the virus simply overwrites, destroying the disk. Moreover, infected computers suffer different interruptions caused by the virus. This is first noticeable when the virus decides that enough disks have been infected (it keeps track of the number of disks it's infected).

109

The sole enemy of Amiga viruses at the time of this writing is the
`Install` command, which simply overwrites the infected boot block.
Some known viruses can recognize the use of `Install`. When the
`Install` command starts writing to the boot block, the virus sets a
flag somewhere during the write procedure and reformats the disk. A
system infected in such a manner is usually beyond help.

3.2.1   The ultimate virus killer

The following program should be stored in the startup sequence of
every boot disk you have. It examines the system vectors that can be
used by the viruses, and deletes these vectors. The entire boot disk must
be reconfigured using the `Install` command. By disabling the virus
program in memory this cannot be written back to the disk after
`Install`.

```
;VIRUS-KILLER V1.0; by SM'87

start:
  move.l 4,a6              ;EXECBASE at a6
  moveq #0,d1             ;Flags: no Virus here
  tst.l 46(a6)            ;Test, for distorted Cool-Capture
  beq.s noSCA            ;Wasn't SCA-Virus
  clr.l 46(a6)           ;Cool-Capture clear
  addq.b #1,d1           ;Bit 0 set
noSCA:
   cmpi.w #$FC,148(a6)   ;Vertical Blank Interrupt normal?
   beq.s noVBI           ;no?
   addq.b #2,d1          ;Bit 1 set
   bra.s ClearTag        ;KickTag-Pointer clear
noVBI:
   tst.l 550(a6)         ;KickTag-Pointer changed?
   beq.s GoOn            ;no?
   addq.b #4,d1          ;Bit 2 set
ClearTag:
   clr.l 550(a6)         ;Pointer cleared
   clr.l 554(a6)         ;Pointer cleared
GoOn:
   move.b d1,Virusflag   ;Flag reserved
   lea dosname,a1        ;Address of Lib names
   moveq #0,d0           ;Version is the same
   jsr -552(a6)          ;OpenLibrary
   move.l d0,dosbase     ;Reserve Library-Base
   beq errfix            ;Branch on Error
   move.l d0,a6          ;Prepare for DOS call
   jsr -60(a6)           ;Get Output-handle
   move.l d0,Outputhandle ;and store
   beq errfix            ;Branch when error
   move.l #title,d2      ;Title at d2
   move.l #titleend-title,d3 ;Text-Length
```

```
        jsr writeout                    ;Text output
        tst.b Virusflag                 ;Virusflag test
        bne.s Virusfound                ;Branch on Virus
        move.l #clean,d2                ;Clear message
        move.l #cleanend-clean,d3       ;Length
        jsr writeout                    ;Text output
        bra errfix                      ;Program end
Virusfound:                             ;Virus is active
        btst #0,Virusflag               ;Cool-Capture?
        beq.s notsca                    ;No
        move.l #scaV,d2                 ;Message
        move.l #scaVend-scaV,d3         ;Length
        jsr writeout                    ;Text output
notsca:
        btst #1,Virusflag               ;VB-Interrupt?
        beq.s notvbi                    ;No
        move.l #bbVvbi,d2               ;Message
        move.l #bbVvbiend-bbVvbi,d3     ;Length
        jsr writeout                    ;output
        bra.s bbfound                   ;next Message
notvbi:
        btst #2,Virusflag               ;Kicktag?
        beq.s errfix                    ;No
        move.l #bbVtag,d2               ;Message
        move.l #bbVtagend-bbVtag,d3     ;Length
        jsr writeout                    ;output
bbfound:
        move.l #bbv,d2                  ;message
        move.l #bbvend-bbv,d3           ;Length
        jsr writeout                    ;output
errfix:
        move.l 4,a6
        move.l dosbase,d0
        beq.s quit
        move.l d0,a1
        jsr -414(a6)
quit:
        moveq #0,d0
        rts
writeout:
        move.l outputhandle,d1
        jmp -48(a6)
dosname:dc.b "dos.library",0
title:dc.b $c,$9b,"1;31;42m - Virus-Killer"
        dc.b " V1.0 - ",10,13
        dc.b "(c)  1988 by S. Maelger",10,13,10
        dc.b $9b,"0;31;40m"
titleend:align
clean:dc.b "No symptoms for Virus"
        dc.b "-Infection found !",10,13,10
cleanend:align
scaV:dc.b "Reset-Vector Cool-Capture has"
        dc.b " been used!",10,13
        dc.b "SCA-Virus suspected !",10,13
        dc.b "Virus in memory destroyed.",10,13,10
scaVend:align
```

```
bbVvbi:dc.b "Vertical Blank Interrupt has "
        dc.b "been used!",10,13
bbVvbiend:align
bbV:dc.b "Byte-Bandit-Virus suspected!",10,13
    dc.b "Virus in memory destroyed.",10,13,10
bbVend:align
bbVtag:dc.b "KickTagPointer is no longer"
        dc.b " in operating system!",10,13
bbVtagend:align
dosbase:dc.l 0
outputhandle:dc.l 0
Virusflag:dc.b 0
    end
```

Here is the BASIC loader version of the Virus check program listed above:

```
OPEN "sys:c/Virus_chk" FOR OUTPUT AS 1
FOR i=1 TO  800
  READ a$
  a%=VAL("&H"+a$)
  PRINT #1,CHR$(a%);
NEXT
CLOSE 1
KILL "sys:c/Virus_chk.info"
datas:
DATA 0,0,3,F3,0,0,0,0,0,0,0,1,0,0,0,0,0,0,0,0
DATA 0,0,0,A4,0,0,3,E9,0,0,0,A4,2C,78,0,4,72,0,4A,AE
DATA 0,2E,67,6,42,AE,0,2E,52,1,C,6E,0,FC,0,94,67,4,54,1
DATA 60,8,4A,AE,2,26,67,A,58,1,42,AE,2,26,42,AE,2,2A,13,C1
DATA 0,0,2,8C,43,F9,0,0,1,12,70,0,4E,AE,FD,D8,23,C0,0,0
DATA 2,84,67,0,0,AA,2C,40,4E,AE,FF,C4,23,C0,0,0,2,88,67,0
DATA 0,9A,24,3C,0,0,1,1E,26,3C,0,0,0,46,4E,B9,0,0,1,8
DATA 4A,39,0,0,2,8C,66,16,24,3C,0,0,1,64,26,3C,0,0,0,2A
DATA 4E,B9,0,0,1,8,60,0,0,6A,8,39,0,0,0,0,2,8C,67,12
DATA 24,3C,0,0,1,8E,26,3C,0,0,0,5E,4E,B9,0,0,1,8,8,39
DATA 0,1,0,0,2,8C,67,14,24,3C,0,0,1,EC,26,3C,0,0,0,29
DATA 4E,B9,0,0,1,8,60,1C,8,39,0,2,0,0,2,8C,67,24,24,3C
DATA 0,0,2,52,26,3C,0,0,0,32,4E,B9,0,0,1,8,24,3C,0,0
DATA 2,16,26,3C,0,0,0,3B,4E,B9,0,0,1,8,2C,78,0,4,20,39
DATA 0,0,2,84,67,6,22,40,4E,AE,FE,62,70,0,4E,75,22,39,0,0
DATA 2,88,4E,EE,FF,D0,64,6F,73,2E,6C,69,62,72,61,72,79,0,C,9B
DATA 31,3B,33,31,3B,34,32,6D,20,2D,20,56,69,72,75,73,2D,4B,69,6C
DATA 6C,65,72,20,56,31,2E,30,20,2D,20,A,D,28,63,29,20,20,31,39
DATA 38,38,20,62,79,20,53,2E,20,4D,61,65,6C,67,65,72,2A,D,A,9B
DATA 30,3B,33,31,3B,34,30,6D,4E,6F,20,73,79,6D,70,74,6F,6D,73,20
DATA 66,6F,72,20,56,69,72,75,73,2D,49,6E,66,65,63,74,69,6F,6E,20
DATA 66,6F,75,6E,64,20,21,A,D,A,52,65,73,65,74,2D,56,65,65,74
DATA 6F,72,20,43,6F,6F,6C,2D,43,61,70,74,75,72,65,20,68,61,73,20
DATA 62,65,65,6E,20,75,73,65,64,21,A,D,53,43,41,2D,56,69,72,75
DATA 73,20,73,75,73,70,65,63,74,65,64,20,21,A,D,56,69,72,75,73
DATA 20,69,6E,20,6D,65,6D,6F,72,79,20,64,65,73,74,72,6F,79,72,64
DATA 2E,A,D,A,56,65,72,74,69,63,61,6C,20,42,6C,61,6E,6B,20,49
DATA 6E,74,65,72,72,75,70,74,20,68,61,73,20,62,65,65,6E,20,75,73
DATA 65,64,21,A,D,0,42,79,74,65,2D,42,61,6E,64,69,74,2D,56,69
DATA 72,75,73,20,73,75,73,70,65,63,74,65,64,21,A,D,56,69,72,75
```

```
DATA 73,20,69,6E,20,6D,65,6D,6F,72,79,20,64,65,73,74,72,6F,79,65
DATA 64,2E,A,D,A,0,4B,69,63,6B,54,61,67,50,6F,69,6E,74,65,72
DATA 20,69,73,20,6E,6F,20,6C,6F,6E,67,65,72,20,69,6E,20,6F,70,65
DATA 72,61,74,69,6E,67,20,73,79,73,74,65,6D,21,A,D,0,0,0,0
DATA 0,0,0,0,0,0,0,0,0,0,3,EC,0,0,0,16,0,0,0,0
DATA 0,0,0,30,0,0,0,36,0,0,0,42,0,0,0,52,0,0,0,5C
DATA 0,0,0,68,0,0,0,6E,0,0,0,76,0,0,0,82,0,0,0,8E
DATA 0,0,0,96,0,0,0,A2,0,0,0,AA,0,0,0,B2,0,0,0,BE
DATA 0,0,0,C8,0,0,0,D0,0,0,0,DC,0,0,0,E2,0,0,0,EE
DATA 0,0,0,F8,0,0,1,A,0,0,0,0,0,0,3,F2,0,0,3,F2
```

3.3   Machine language and BASIC

To call machine language routines in BASIC, a long variable must transfer the starting address of the routine. We demonstrate this on the operating system's Reset routine, which begins at memory location $FC0000. Unfortunately, BASIC always causes difficulties when handling long variables. The BASIC interpreter almost exclusively computes with floating point variables, and later converts the number into long values.

The error frequently encountered is that the normal floating point variables are accurate to only a couple of decimal places. When calculating in long values, the converted result is low by a value between 1 and 5. To get around this you must either use machine language routines which are more accurate in long value arithmetic, or use strings:

```
SMreset&=CVL(CHR$(0)+CHR$(&HFC)+MKI$(0))
```

For frequent use of system routines and machine language programs, you have the option of declaring all variables that have no label as long:

```
DEFLNG a-z
SMreset=CVL(CHR$(0)+CHR$(&HFC)+MKI(0))
SMreset
```

Note: Be careful! When you enter the above example and start it, the BASIC interpreter jumps to the Reset routine. This is only an example of jumping into a machine language routine, the routine happens to reset the computer. If you want to perform a reset in a BASIC program, there is a much better and faster method available:

```
POKEL 32,CVL(CHR$(0)+CHR$(&HFC)+MKI$(0))
```

But we digress—we're supposed to be talking about machine language. To take the next step in the direction of adding BASIC command enhancements, we write a short routine which switches the Power LED on and off. You may remember that this is what the Amiga does when you reset it (or when it resets on its own). The essential routine looks like this:

```
Code                  Mnemonic
089000100BFE001       BCHG #1, $BFE001   ;switch brightness
4E5                   RTS                ;that is all
```

Now comes the question of where we can put the code. That's not as easy as it sounds because the address where the code begins must always be even, otherwise a Guru #3 occurs (addressing error). The

68000 processor can only process commands at even addresses, so each command must be found at an even address. Here BASIC doesn't tell you what's going on, and places its variables bytewise in the variable buffer, when enough memory exists. To be absolutely certain that the address is even, the memory location should be allocated by the system. That can be done with the Exec routine AllocMem. The following routine uses AllocMem:

```
' LED-FLICKER.BAS¶
DEFLNG a-z¶
DECLARE FUNCTION AllocMem LIBRARY¶
LIBRARY"t&t2:bmaps/exec.library"¶
SMmagic=AllocMem(10,1) '10 bytes, memory area public RAM¶
FOR i%=0 TO 4¶
 READ Power$¶
 POKEW SMmagic+i%*2,VAL("&H"+Power$)¶
NEXT¶
DATA 879, 1, BF, E001, 4E75¶
PRINT "Watch the power LED flicker"¶
FOR i%=1 TO 20 'switch 20 times¶
 a!=TIMER+.5 'delay 0,5 seconds¶
 WHILE a!>TIMER:WEND 'wait¶
 SMmagic 'call Assembler routine¶
NEXT¶
FreeMem SMmagic,10 'free memory location¶
LIBRARY CLOSE 'close SYS¶
```

We have no problem with the simple routine, which uses none of its own registers. Any assembler on the market will accept the following example:

```
MOVE.L DO,Dataregister0
...
Dataregister0:dc.1 0
```

This routine defines a label within a program, onto which the data register D0 should be placed. When corresponding codes like those in the Power LED program are poked into memory, the Guru Meditation is guaranteed to appear in a hurry. The reason is the addressing method that was used in the above MOVE.L. It is addressed absolutely.

The absolute addressing cannot be used because we never know where the program will end up in memory once it loads.

The code must first approximate the respective beginning address, which we want to use. A good assembler has an option for letting the programmer create program counter relative code (PC realative). In every case you must write:

```
LEA dataregister0(PC),A0
MOVE.L DO,(A0)
...
```

If you only programmed using PC Realtive code your program could not use all assembler instruction, and the programming would be very extensive. We want to show you a way you can use every machine language instruction, completely avoiding any memory allocations, bypassing any fancy load routines, and finally, allowing function calls to C programs.

3.3.1   Assembler and C programs from BASIC

We could just give you the facts about this kind of access. Instead, let's look at the entire (non-BASIC) program. Whether it's a favorite game, word processor or BASIC interpreter, programs are absolute addressed, yet the 68000 requires relative addressing so the program can be placed anywhere in memory. If you stop to think about this for a while, you may come to the conclusion that the addresses in the program can be present only as offsets. Shortly after loading the program the operating system must calculate the correct addresses so the program can adjust itself to the addresses it will be loaded at.

The problem: How to anticipate it. The operating system knows which commands must be coded. This is saved with a Link module, which contains this information, from the assembler. Usually a saved assembler program consists of a code segment (your program), a data segment, and a BSS segment (which reserves free memory locations for the program directly after loading), as well as one or more link segments.

You can examine what the operating system does by using the load routine to start the program (your program should not start by itself). This is contained in the `dos.library` and can be called from BASIC with no problem This routine is called `LoadSeg` and needs the name of the program ending with a null byte. Memory allocation and all other work is done from `LoadSeg`. The syntax looks like this:

```
MainSegment=LoadSeg ( SADD( "Filename" + CHR$(0)))
```

You need the `UnloadSeg` routine to release the reserved memory locations, which must be given the return value from `LoadSeg`:

```
UnloadSeg MainSegment
```

There are difficulties with the value that was received from `LoagSeg`. Because AmigaDOS is written in BCPL (a compiler language), the value is handled as a BCPL value. The BCPL language refers to this value as the Main or Code segment. For your own use, you must convert this to an address. DOS does so as if the memory consists of only long values placed one after another. Consequently, it handles the number of the long value from the start of memory as the return value.

To get a correct address, this value must be multiplied by four (four bytes per long value). This address is not exactly given in the program. The BCPL pointer to the next segment is stored in the first long value of the main segment. This segment begins with another BCPL pointer to another segment, and so on. The program appears following this pointer, so use the following routine to access a machine routine:

```
DEFLNG a-z¶
DECLARE FUNCTION loadseg LIBRARY¶
LIBRARY"dos.library"¶
'change the file name for your machine language program¶
bcpl.segstart=loadseg(SADD("df1:asm.prg"+prg"+CHR$(0)))¶
Segment=bcpl.segstart*4¶
Routine=Segment+4¶
Routine¶
unloadseg bcpl.segstart¶
LIBRARY CLOSE¶
```

Here's another item. To see the start addresses of the individual segments, insert the following code preceding the call to `Routine`:

```
PRINT "Main program begins at address";Routine
i%=1
WHILE Segment<>0
 PRINT i%;". Segment begins at address";Segment+4
 Segment=PEEKL(Segment)*4
WEND
```

Now we come to the parameter statement. BASIC deals with assembler routines in the same way that the C language deals with program sections. The parameters are stored in long value form on the stack, so in the following example parameter `P3` goes onto the stack first, then `P2` and finally `P1`. So, parameter `P1` becomes the first parameter taken from the stack in the called program. After the parameters, the routine jump with `JSR` (Jump to SubRoutine) takes the code to the last return jump address on the stack:

```
Routine P1,P2,P3
```

The return jump address of the routine is on the stack:

```
Stackpointer + 12 = P3 (Long)
Stackpointer +  8 = P2 (Long)
Stackpointer +  4 = P1 (Long)
Stackpointer +  0 = return jump address (using JSR)
```

When you load a C routine with the above program, you can call it exactly as you would call an assembler program. When you can, you should always use machine language because machine code generated from C is actually slower than "real" machine language. Some BASIC compilers create code that executes faster than C because the operating system routines are called exactly the way you write BASIC commands.

Portions of the operating system are programmed in C, which is why the Amiga is so slow. C requires large amounts of memory for execution. Only a small percentage of the operating system is written in C, which comprises the largest section of the memory needed by the operating system. This explains why the operating system gets smaller and faster: The developers gradually replace the C routines more and more with machine language routines as they get the chance to upgrade the system.

In a C program, the parameters are in the brackets in the same order as they are given in BASIC. How do you get from machine language to C? We should start by mentioning that you cannot change any of the registers without first saving their current values These values should be be stored at the beginning of the program:

```
START: MOVEMEM.L D0-A6,-(A7)   ;save registers: with that
                               ;you find 15 registers and
                               ;the return jump address on
                               ;the stack.
                               ;the first parameter is
                               ;at SP+(16*4) = 64(SP)
       MOVEM.L 64(SP),D0-D2    ;pick up the three
                               ;parameters
...
END: MOVEM.L (A7)+,D0-A6       ;register taken from stack
     RTS
```

You may be wondering how the values returned to the BASIC program are accessed. With this in mind, we give the address of a variable as a parameter and access the return values using the VARPTR or Sadd function. The address is taken from the stack in the machine language program and written to the return value. When you return multiple values, an address is given to an array variable (be careful with strings there you get the address of the string descriptor, which consists of 5 bytes).

3.3.2   BASIC enhancement: ColorCycle

To illustrate parameter transfer in a machine language program, here's an enhancement to AmigaBASIC. It allows you to rotate the colors as is allowed in *DPaint®*:

```
;----------------------------------------;
; BASIC-Extension  ColorCycle SMmagic'88 ;
;----------------------------------------;
; Syntax: AddressRoutine WINDOW(7),from,to ;
; from=Start  color; tos=End color       ;
; Color always "from" --> "to"           ;
; from < to: Rotation up                 ;
```

```
              ; from > to: Rotation down                    ;
              ;-------------------------------------------;
Cycle:        MOVEM.L D0-A6,-(SP)   ;Reserve register on Stack
              MOVE.L 4,A6           ;get ExecBase from A6
              LEA GFXNAME,A1        ;Library-Name at A1
              MOVEQ #0,D0           ;Version is same
              JSR -552(A6)          ;OpenLibrary call
              TST.L D0              ;Test, is Base available
              BEQ.S Exit            ;When not, thend End
              MOVE.L D0,A6          ;GfxBase at A6
              MOVE.L 64(SP),A0      ;WindowBase attended to
              MOVE.L 46(A0),A0      ;ScreenBase determined
              ADD.L #44,A0          ;ViewPort of Screens in A0
              MOVE.L 4(A0),A1       ;ColorTable to A1
              MOVE.L 4(A1),A1       ;ColorMap determined
              LEA CTab,A2           ;User Buffer to A2
              MOVEQ #15,D0          ;15 Longs (32 Words)
CopyCT:       MOVE.L (A1)+,(A2)+    ;ColorMap copied
              DBRA D0,CopyCT        ;(when not changed else
              MOVEM.L 68(SP),D0-D1  ;get start- and End color
              ANDI.W #31,D0         ;should it be more than 31
              ANDI.W #31,D1         ;ditto
              LSL.B #1,D0           ;*2 (use as offset)
              LSL.B #1,D1           ;ditto
              LEA CTab,A1           ;Address of our buffer
              MOVE.W (A1,D1.W),D2   ;reserve last color
              CMP.B D0,D1           ;determine rotation dir.
              BEQ.S ClLib           ;both colors same ???
              BGT.S Up              ;colors rotate up
Down:         MOVE.W 2(A1,D1.W),(A1,D1.W) ;colors then down
              ADDQ.B #2,D1          ;increment Offset
              CMP.B D0,D1           ;End reached?
              BNE.S Down            ;no? then next color
              BRA.S SetLC           ;close
Up:           MOVE.W -2(A1,D1.W),(A1,D1.W) ;color downward
              SUBQ.B #2,D1          ;decrement  Offset
              CMP.B D0,D1           ;bottom reached?
              BNE.S Up              ;no? then next color
SetLC:        MOVE.W D2,(A1,D1.W)   ;color reserved
              MOVEQ #32,D0          ;32 cloors set
              JSR -192(A6)          ;LoadRGB4 (a0=VP,a1=Ctab,d0)
ClLib:        MOVE.L A6,A1          ;GfxBase at A1
              MOVE.L 4,A6           ;get  ExecBase
              JSR -414(A6)          ;Library closed
Exit:         MOVEM.L (SP)+,D0-A6   ;Register from Stack
              RTS                   ;end
GFXNAME:      DC.B "graphics.library",0,0 ;Library-Name
CTab:         DS.W 32                    ;32 Words buffer
              END
```

The code is configured so that you can either assemble it in PC relative
or normal mode. The following BASIC program calls and demonstrates
the ColorCycle routine:

```
'Load first routine:¶
```

```
DEFLNG a-z¶
DECLARE FUNCTION loadseg LIBRARY¶
LIBRARY"T&T2:bmaps/dos.library"¶
a=loadseg(SADD("T&T2:ColorCycle"+CHR$(0)))¶
prg=a*4+4¶
'A little grafic¶
FOR i%=0 TO 3¶
 LINE (0,i%*40)-STEP(80,40),i%,bf¶
NEXT¶
'Demo: Rotate colors forward and backward¶
FOR i%=0 TO 50¶
 t!=TIMER+.2¶
 WHILE t!>TIMER¶
 WEND¶
 prg WINDOW(7),1,3¶
NEXT¶
FOR i%=0 TO 50¶
 t!=TIMER+.2¶
 WHILE t!>TIMER¶
 WEND¶
 prg WINDOW(7),3,1¶
NEXT¶
'Release memory¶
unloadseg a¶
LIBRARY CLOSE¶
```

The following BASIC loader generates the ColorCycle file on disk:

```
OPEN "COLORCYCLE" FOR OUTPUT AS 1
FOR i=1 TO  300
 READ a$
 a$="&H"+a$
 PRINT#1,CHR$(VAL(a$));
NEXT
CLOSE 1
DATA 0,0,3,F3,0,0,0,0,0,0,0,1,0,0,0,0,0,0,0,0,40,0,0,3A,0,0
DATA 3,E9,0,0,0,3A,48,E7,FF,FE,2C,78,0,4,43,F9,0,0,0,94,70,0
DATA 4E,AE,FD,D8,4A,80,67,76,2C,40,20,6F,0,40,20,68,0,2E,D1
DATA FC,0,0,0,2C,22,68,0,4,22,69,0,4,45,F9,0,0,0,A6,70,F,24
DATA D9,51,C8,FF,FC,4C,EF,0,3,0,44,2,40,0,1F,2,41,0,1F,E3,8
DATA E3,9,43,F9,0,0,0,A6,34,31,10,0,B2,0,67,26,6E,E,33,B1,10
DATA 2,10,0,54,1,B2,0,66,F4,60,C,33,B1,10,FE,10,0,55,1,B2,0
DATA 66,F4,33,82,10,0,70,20,4E,AE,FF,40,22,4E,2C,78,0,4,4E
DATA AE,FE,62,4C,DF,7F,FF,4E,75,67,72,61,70,68,69,63,73,2E
DATA 6C,69,62,72,61,72,79,0,0,0,0,0,0,0,0,0,0,0,0,0,0,0,0,0
DATA 0,0,0,0,0,0,0,0,0,0,0,0,0,0,0,0,0,0,0,0,0,0,0,0,0,0,0,0
DATA 0,0,0,0,0,0,0,0,0,0,0,0,0,0,0,0,0,0,0,0,0,0,0,0,0,3,EC
DATA 0,0,0,3,0,0,0,0,0,0,A,0,0,0,32,0,0,0,52,0,0,0,0,0,0,3
DATA F2,0,0,3,F2
DATA BECKER
```

3.3.3   Putting the mouse to sleep

When the Amiga executes any disk operation, the wait pointer appears (the cloud graphic with the two Zs drawn inside it). Professional programs have different shaped mouse pointers. We also want to disable the mouse in BASIC. This would be useful for disk operations or reading data. The following program is an enhancement to do this:

```
;---------------------------------------------------------;
;BASIC-Extension Zzz                           SMmagic'88;
;---------------------------------------------------------;
;Syntax: Zzz WINDOW(7),OnOff                              ;
;OnOff  even or 0   :    Mouse is slepping                ;
;OnOff  odd    (1) :    Mouse is normal                   ;
;---------------------------------------------------------;
ZZZ:       MOVEM.L D0-A6,-(SP)   ;Reserve register
           MOVE.L 4,A6           ;Get Base address of Exec
           LEA INTNAME,A1        ;Address of Library-Names
           MOVEQ #0,D0           ;Version is same
           JSR -552(A6)          ;OpenLibrary
           TST.L D0              ;No, what's happening?
           BEQ.S ENDE            ;No? then end
           MOVE.L D0,A6          ;IntuitionBase loaded
           MOVE.L 64(SP),A0      ;get WindowBase
           MOVE.L 68(SP),D0      ;get OnOff-Flag
           BTST #0,D0            ;Bit 0 test
           BEQ.S SLEEP           ;Even number? Good night
           JSR -60(A6)           ;ClearPointer called
           BRA.S EXIT            ;and end
SLEEP:     LEA MOUSE,A1          ;Addess the Pointer data
           MOVEQ #22,D0          ;Height in d0
           MOVEQ #16,D1          ;Width in d1
           MOVEQ #0,D2           ;xoffset clear
           MOVE.L D2,D3          ;yoffset clear
           JSR -270(A6)          ;SetPointer called
EXIT:      MOVE.L A6,A1          ;IntuitionBase to a1
           MOVE.L 4,A6           ;ExecBase
           JSR -414(A6)          ;CloseLibrary call
ENDE:      MOVEM.L (SP)+,D0-A6   ;Register from Stack
           RTS                   ;return to BASIC-Program
INTNAME: DC.B "intuition.library",0 ;Library-Name
MOUSE:     DC.L 0,$3000300,$7A007A0,$1FF01FF0,$3FF03FF0
           DC.L $30F83FF8,$3DFC3FFC,$7BFC7FFC,$30FE3FFE
           DC.L $3F863FFE,$1FEF1FFF,$3FDE3FFE,$1F861FFE
           DC.L $FFC0FFC,$3F803F8,$E000E0,$3800380,$7E007E0
           DC.L $3400340,0,$600060,$700070,$200020,0
           END                   ;End the data
;One typical call in BASIC:
;ZZZ WINDOW(7),0      'sleeping
;ZZZ WINDOW(7),1      'normal
```

The following BASIC generator creates the machine code for this routine:

```
OPEN "ZZZ" FOR OUTPUT AS 1
FOR i=1 TO  260
 READ a$
 a$="&H"+a$
 PRINT#1,CHR$(VAL(a$));
NEXT
CLOSE 1
DATA 0,0,3,F3,0,0,0,0,0,0,0,1,0,0,0,0,0,0,0,0,40,0,0,31,0,0,3
DATA E9,0,0,0,31,48,E7,FF,FE,2C,78,0,4,43,F9,0,0,0,50,70,0,4E
DATA AE,FD,D8,4A,80,67,32,2C,40,20,6F,0,40,20,2F,0,44,8,0,0,0
DATA 67,6,4E,AE,FF,C4,60,12,43,F9,0,0,0,62,70,16,72,10,74,0
DATA 26,2,4E,AE,FE,F2,22,4E,2C,78,0,4,4E,AE,FE,62,4C,DF,7F,FF
DATA 4E,75,69,6E,74,75,69,74,69,6F,6E,2E,6C,69,62,72,61,72,79
DATA 0,0,0,0,0,3,0,3,0,7,A0,7,A0,1F,F0,1F,F0,3F,F0,3F,F0,30
DATA F8,3F,F8,3D,FC,3F,FC,7B,FC,7F,FC,30,FE,3F,FE,3F,86,3F,FE
DATA 1F,EF,1F,FF,3F,DE,3F,FE,1F,86,1F,FE,F,FC,F,FC,3,F8,3,F8
DATA 0,E0,0,E0,3,80,3,80,7,E0,7,E0,3,40,3,40,0,0,0,0,0,60,0
DATA 60,0,70,0,70,0,20,0,20,0,0,0,0,0,0,0,0,3,EC,0,0,0,2,0,0
DATA 0,0,0,0,0,A,0,0,0,30,0,0,0,0,0,0,3,F2,0,0,3,F2
DATA BECKER
```

This file is loaded with the LoadSegment routine. Here is a BASIC program that loads and demonstrates the routine:

```
'Load first routine:¶
DEFLNG a-z¶
DECLARE FUNCTION loadseg LIBRARY¶
LIBRARY"T&T2:bmaps/dos.library"¶
a=loadseg(SADD("T&T2:ZZZ"+CHR$(0)))¶
prg=a*4+4¶
'Demo: Mouse sleeping¶
¶
 prg WINDOW(7),0  :'Mouse sleeping¶
¶
FOR i%=0 TO 5000¶
NEXT¶
¶
prg WINDOW(7),1 :'mouse normal¶
¶
'Release memory¶
unloadseg a¶
LIBRARY CLOSE¶
```

4.
Hardware
hacking

4.   Hardware hacking

Why do you spend so much time with the Amiga? It has the software and hardware that make it a quality computer. This chapter deals with the subject of hardware, and some of the neat things you can do using Amiga hardware. You'll even learn some techniques you can use to upgrade your Amiga's hardware.

Before we continue, we need to touch on a few points of information about your hardware:

1.   This is not a course in electronic circuitry, and it was never intended to be. We assume you have some knowledge of electronics, components and circuitry. We also assume that you have some experience operating a soldering iron, and that you know how to use a screwdriver. If you don't possess this knowledge and experience, get it <u>before</u> you start tearing your Amiga apart. **If you still aren't sure of what you're doing to the circuitry, DON'T DO IT! Get someone knowledgeable in electronics to do this tinkering instead.** One wrong solder joint could ruin your Amiga.

2.   If you open your case, you void the warranty (if the warranty is still in effect). Any user-implemented hardware changes to a device violates the warranty. This means that the dealer/manufacturer are under no obligation to repair the machine at their own expense. In short, if you break it, you will probably end up paying to have it fixed, even if the warranty is in effect.

3.   All changes described here were tested by us as explained at the beginning of this book. It isn't always possible for an author to test every version of a computer on the market, so we may have come up wrong on one or two of these things. **If problems crop up, even though the project should theoretically work, <u>change</u> it <u>back</u> <u>to</u> <u>the</u> <u>way</u> it <u>was</u>!**

4.   **Use caution whenever working with electronic components.** Always have the power turned off when doing any electrical work (unplug the equipment just to be extra-safe), for your sake as well as the machine's sake. Remove the components carefully, solder or connect carefully, reconnect components carefully.

5.   **Most importantly, you don't have to do any of this.** We, as developers, had to at least try these things. You, as a user, don't <u>need</u> to try any of these hardware modifications. If

125

you've read the last four warnings, and still feel willing to experiment on your own hardware, fine.

Now that we're done with the warnings, let's take a look at your computer's innards. We'll look at the memory expansion first. With a few small changes, you can configure the memory to not interrupt any programs. The next section goes into detail about disk drives. There will be occasions when you want the disk drive turned off immediately, and this hardware enhancement will show you how. The next item is a real treat—you'll learn how to outfit your Amiga with a 68010 processor. We'll also talk about other processors.

4.1   Disabling memory expansion

Memory expansion offers many advantages. We often get angry at our Amigas because this additional memory is incompatible with many programs. In actuality the problem lies with the programs, not with the expansion. The programs can't tell which memory to use, so they don't work. For example, the sound chip and the graphics chip must access chip RAM, if a program uses them to access fast RAM the program crashes as a result. Many early Amiga programs had this problem.

The next two hardware tricks are based on this problem. There is an alternate software solution (see the *Amiga System Programmer's Guide* from Abacus for a program which disables fast RAM through software). It's easier to turn the Amiga on, flip the switch and run a non-fast-RAM Amiga.

4.1.1   The 2000A board

If you have an Amiga 2000, you should first establish whether you have the A board (this subsection applies only to this board.) If you do not have the A board, skip this section. Look on the circuit board for a PAL chip with the label U3 (you'll also find U1 and U6 labels, but for now these aren't of any interest to us). This PAL chip handles free memory organization. All we have to do is tell this chip not to make the expanded memory available. The memory release control travels over the pins named -OVR (position 19) and -SELECT (position 17).

To disable expanded memory, you must ensure that these two pins are disconnected. If no current flows between these two pins, memory expansion remains disabled. There are two ways to do this:

The first and simplest consists of just breaking the connection between the PAL chip pins and the system. Turn off your Amiga. Carefully disconnect the conducting paths from these pins. Rig a double-pole switch between chip legs 19 and 17 and their connections (you may want to use solderless connectors for the pin legs and connections). Use enough wire to run the switch outside the case with a little slack. Drill a hole in the side of your Amiga case and install the switch in the case. When you turn the switch "on," the system recognizes the expanded RAM. However, when you turn the computer off for five to ten seconds, turn this switch "off" during that time and turn the computer back on, the Amiga won't recognize the memory expansion. All the programs that wouldn't run under expanded memory now run without problem.

The second method is somewhat neater, but also more expensive and more difficult to implement. You'll need the following materials and tools:

Materials: 1 DPST (double-pole, single-throw) switch
approx. 12-16 inches double-strand wire
1 base (20 pole, to fit the PAL chip)
solder

Tools: soldering iron
sharp knife or screwdriver
tweezers

Carefully remove the chip. Take the 20-pin base and cut or snap off the two corresponding pins (position 19 and position 17). Insert your modified base in the old mounting. Now reconnect the removed pins to the mounting using a two-pole switch and some wire. Drill a hole in the side of your Amiga case which allows the switch head to fit through. Make sure the switch is firmly connected. Make sure all solder connections are tight and "clean." Now insert the PAL chip in its new mounting.

Make sure all connections are right (if they aren't, correct the problem), then do a test run of the switch <u>before</u> reassembling the Amiga case.

4.1.2   The Amiga 500: printed circuit board

The Amiga 500 board has a completely different design. Our goal here is to disable the 512K card available from Commodore-Amiga. This expansion card has a battery operated clock and fast RAM. This clock remains undisturbed by the following operations.

Materials: 1 SPST (single-pole, single throw) switch
approx. 12-16" double-strand wire
solder

Tools: soldering iron
sharp knife or screwdriver

Turn off your Amiga and open the expansion "drawer." Remove the expansion card <u>carefully</u> (remember—use caution when removing, modifying and installing any parts). After you remove the card lay it out of the table in front of you, trace side (the side with all the etched connections and solder joints) facing you. You should be able to see the solder joints and traces, and half of the edge card which plugs into the Amiga's expansion port.

Look at pin 32 of the edge card (make absolutely sure that this is pin 32). Follow its route up the printed circuit board. See how the trace (the etching) moves away from the solder point? That's our goal. You must somehow break the conducting path of this trace. Take a sharp screwdriver or sharp knife (an XActo® knife or sharp kitchen knife will work). Carve into the trace to create a space—make sure there's a definite break between the cut (you should be able to see the printed circuit board material through the cut, with no tracing material connecting). You may want to make the space of the cut fairly wide (e.g., 1/8"). Take a piece of two-lead wire and solder each lead at one end to the cut sections of the now-broken trace. Solder the other two ends to the SPST switch. That's all there is to it.

Re-install the expansion card carefully. Make sure all solder connections are tight and "clean." Connect everything up and boot the Workbench. When you have the switch in the "off" position, the Amiga 500 should ignore the memory expansion. When you turn the Amiga off again for five or ten seconds, flip the RAM switch to the "on" position and turn the power switch "on," this enables the memory expansion. If the computer doesn't do what it should when it should, you must have done something wrong. Check your solder joints (cold solder joints frequently occur if you aren't careful, thus not making a tight connection). If you have cold solder joints, re-solder the connections. There really aren't any other errors that could occur.

4.2   Disk drive switching

Additional external disk drives can cause as many problems as memory expansion. External drives are usually automatically configured by the operating system, which uses your working RAM. These autoconfig systems may cause problems, because AmigaDOS can only manage data from the disk drive using chip RAM.

Each drive requires a 30K buffer for file management. Many programs need this memory, but once it's allocated for disk buffers, programs can't access that extra memory. The result: The program either crashes in mid-run or can't be started at all.

On/off switch for disk drives

One solution is to install a switch to disable the drive as needed. You'll need the following equipment:

Materials:

1 SPST (single-pole, single-throw) switch
approx. 4-8" single-strand wire
solder

Tools:

soldering iron
sharp knife
screwdriver

You can easily install a switch if the external drive doesn't have one of its own. The switch interrupts the data direction of the computer by resetting the line which informs the Amiga that another drive is connected. Pin 21 (SEL1) of the drive plug handles the selection of the first external drive.

Turn off the Amiga and unplug it for safety's sake. Determine the correct lead for pin 21 and cut the wire. Solder the cut ends to one end of each strand of wire leading to the switch. Solder the ends of the switch wires to the SPST switch. You can either do this by connecting it at the plug itself, or within the disk drive. If you selected the latter, drill a hole in the disk drive case to match the switch. Mount the switch, reassemble everything carefully and test out the computer.

4.3   Installing a MC 68010

Would you like to make your Amiga faster without spending a lot of cash? Here's your chance. All you have to do is remove the old 68000 and replace it with 68010. This new Motorola chip is 99.99% compatible with the old chip. It has only one disadvantage which you can learn to live with.

But first, on to the advantages! You can install the new processor easily. No soldering (in most cases), no additional expensive components. The 68010 shows speed increases in certain processor commands of up to 80% in tests. If you look at this from a general standpoint, the program uses faster commands as well as those that already exist. All in all, the speed only increases by about 16% over the 68000, but a faster machine is a faster machine.

In addition, you have the option of making the new chip 100% compatible using an additional program (which you will find at the end of this section).

Now let's see to the installation of your new processor. First you must buy a 68010 processor. That shouldn't present a problem: You can find ads for this chip in classified sections of computer magazines, and in any computer journal that deals almost exclusively with sales of components (e.g., *Computer Shopper*). Or perhaps you have an electronics shop in your neighborhood that has the chip available, or can order it for your. Once you have the new processor, you can continue with the installation.

Getting started

First you must open your Amiga case. This takes various amounts of time, depending on the type of Amiga you own. Just take your time dismantling the case, and pay attention to the order in which you take things apart. You'll need to know the order so that it'll be easier putting it back together. You should mark each piece, possibly with masking tape, as you go along.

The 68000 main processor should be easy to find. It's the largest chip on the main printed circuit board, and has a label on it that says "68000" or something similar. You must remove this chip.

Before removing the main processor, we should discuss something important. First off, many of the 68000 chips were merely inserted in a chip socket. However, there may still be a few Amiga motherboards out there that have 68000s with soldered connections. If you are presently looking at a soldered processor, there are only two answers: Either you desolder the chip from the circuit board, or you get someone who has soldering experience to do it for you. If you don't have the soldering experience, you could mess it up badly. The best solution is to use a solder plate (which makes all of the pins hot at the same time) so that the chip can be pulled out as one unit during the desoldering. Solder in an equivalent chip socket to ease chip replacement.

Let's assume for now that you have a socketed 68000. The first step is to remove this from the socket. You can do this using one or two tools: Special tweezers designed for the purpose of removing a chip level (all pins at once); or a screwdriver. The tweezers are expensive, and are only worth the purchase if you want to save the chip for later use (or if you are afraid of injuring the chip).

A flat screwdriver is a little riskier, but achieves the same end result. Insert the blade of the screwdriver flat between the socket and the end of the chip. Rotate the blade gently about 10 degrees or so to pull the processor up from the socket. Repeat the same procedure on the other side. Keep moving from end to end, prying the chip up bit by bit. Before removing the processor completely, note the direction at which the notch of the old processor points. Remove the chip by hand (remember the direction the notch pointed—it's important). This method will work for removing almost any chip, particularly those chips with large numbers of legs.

Before you go on to the next step, we have a warning for you: Electronic components are extremely delicate. The slightest difference in voltage, say from a static charge, can "fry" a chip (render it useless). That's why you should always ground yourself before you handle the chassis or chips.

Next you should insert the new processor. Remove the 68010 from its packaging and place it on the socket from which you removed the 68000. Press down on the chip gently and evenly. Continue this gentle, even pressure until the bottom of the chip is flush with the top of the socket.

Now reassemble the Amiga. Make sure that all parts are accounted for (screws, washers, etc.)—you should have all the parts you removed. Take care that all fasteners are connected properly. Congratulations! You've just replaced the main processor. Now comes the power-on test. Plug in the Amiga and check all power connections. Turn it on. Everything should carry on as normal, except you should notice an increase in speed.

If something's wrong, this may be for one of two reasons:

1.   There may be an improperly connected cable or chip pin. Check this first, before anything else.

2.   Your clothing may have contained a static charge and touched the
      chip. As we mentioned above, chips aren't built to tolerate static
      electricity. If you touched a pin of the chip with your finger and
      your body contained a static charge, you may have destroyed
      your new processor. If nothing helps, you'll have to buy a new
      68010 to test it. Try replacing the old 68000 to see if the entire
      Amiga is defective.

The 68010 has additional debugging instructions, which must be
enabled by software on the Amiga. Programs that start with exception
4 will crash on the 68010, unless these are changes are done. Fred Fish
disk number 18 contains the program DeciGEL which does all of the
setup work for you. The SetAlert command performs the same task
from the startup sequence (you'll find SetAlert on the new
Workbench 1.3 disk). *AssemPro* from Abacus also has a program to do
this, along with the source code.

4.4   The roar of the fans

Do you have an Amiga 2000? In the beginning, we thought the noise
the fan made was a show of quality. After a while the fan noise got
pretty annoying.

We offer you two options. The first suggestion came from a TV
repairman, who advised that we decrease the amount of power running
the fan. We didn't feel that was such good advice, so we chose a more
elegant solution.

The built-in Amiga 2000 fan is a Papst Multi-Fan 8312M. The M at
the end of the number states the amount of noise it makes. After
searching through merchant information, we found a similar model that
performs the same task with half the noise level—the Papst Multi-Fan
8312L.

The hardest part of installing this model is finding it. Once you do, all
the screws and connections are the same as the original equipment. One
disadvantage of the entire process is the price of the new fan—about
$50. Once you've recovered from the shock, remember that the fan will
have a long, quiet life.

For those who think that a new fan is too expensive, we recommend
the method described by the TV repairman mentioned above. He suggested we cut the positive power connection to the fan and insert a
50Ω, 5W potentiometer (the adjustable range should be between 0Ω
and 100Ω). By turning the potentiometer down the noise gets lower and
softer. Make your judgements by the amount of heat accumulation your
Amiga has, rather than fan speed (remember that the degree of heat
increases with expansion cards).

To conclude this section, we leave you with a warning. The Amiga fan
makes so much noise because of the potential amount of hardware it
must ventilate. The developers of the Amiga assumed that every free
expansion slot had a card plugged into it. If this is the case, then the
fan should continue to run at full speed. Otherwise, feel free to
experiment with running the fan at lower and quieter speeds.

4.5   New processor information

Half of the information about new processors usually ends up in technical journals. What can these new processors do for us, exactly? To answer this question, we should take a closer look at these processors.

4.5.1   The 68010: high power, low price

The 68010 is fully compatible with the 68000 command set. All 68000 commands are integrated into the 68010. These commands execute more quickly than in the 68000. In addition, the 68010 features four new commands consisting of a loop mode and three other registers. The amazing part of this chips is its easy replacement over the 68000: Low price, identical size and pinout to the 68000 (see Section 4.3 for installation information).

We should discuss the 68010's architecture. Every assembler supports 68010 programming. Three new registers exist in this chip that the 68000 didn't have: the SourceFunctionCodeRegister (SFC), the DestinationFunctionCodeRegister (DFC) and the VectorBaseRegister (VBR). The last register allows the examination of the beginning of the system vector table (between $0 and $3FF on the 68000). This value changes to $0 after every reset. In addition, it can be very useful to change all vectors simply by switching over.

The Code register consists of only three bits and offers access to Read(SFC) and Write(DFC) just like User and Supervisor modes. Some news for the hardware hobbyist: When you connect pins FC0-FC2 to the address bus, four memory banks accommodate 16 megabytes. The operating system rewrite forces separations in user data/user program and supervisor data/supervisor environments.

Another difference from the 68000 lies in the 68010's loop mode. Prefetch technology makes this possible by reading a command while the processor retains the previous command. The 68000 reads the following loop from the address bus 75000 times and accesses the address bus 75000 times. The 68010 performs this loop only three times, instead of 75000 times:

```
MOVE.W #2499,D0
Loop: MOVE.L (A0)+,(A1)+
DBRA D0,Loop
```

The increase in speed should be evident to you. Unfortunately, only the following machine language instructions function in loop mode:

```
ABCD, ADD, ADDA, ADDX, AND, ASL, ASR, CLR, CMP, CMPA,
EOR, LSL, LSR, MOVE, NBCD, NEG, NEGX, NOT, OR, ROL, ROR,
ROXL, ROXR, SBCD, SUB, SUBA, SUBX, TST
```

The exceptions look somewhat different on the 68010 because more data is needed on the supervisor stack. The last data corresponds to that of the 68000 on the supervisor stack, so the major difference lies in the 68010's larger stack requirements. Bit 15 of the status word is interesting in this context, it tells if the processor executes the exception (0) or ignores it and executes the next command (1). This means that bus and address errors can be trapped using software, solving many Guru problems..

The new commands are called MOVEC, MOVE CCR, MOVES and RTD. The command MOVE SR,Destination only operates in supervisor mode, causing a Guru Meditation. You can program an equivalent exception routine which bypasses this problem. Few programmers are unaware of this problem. Here are the syntaxes of the four instructions (alternate syntaxes are given as needed):

```
MOVEC Register,Destination
```

```
MOVEC Source,Register
```

One of the three new registers or the USP can be substituted here for the Source and Destination arguments. Data size: Word.

```
MOVES Register,Destination
```

```
MOVES Source,Register
```

MOVES transfers data between four data banks according to the methods described above. It serves no purpose in major hardware manipulation on the Amiga.

```
MOVE CCR,Destination
```

MOVE CCR reads the status register.

```
RTD Value
```

RTD is the equivalent of RTS. This instruction adds the value (16 bits) to the stack pointer. This is practical when using the stack as a parameter statement.

4.5.2   The 68012: low cost, high memory

The mere size of the 68012 is the first thing the user notices about the chip. It has a square instead of a rectangular shape, so you can't just plug it into the 68000 socket. The user can take one of two routes to install this chip:

• Install a second socket.

• Buy an adapter board for the 68012.

This 100% 68010 compatible chip allows up to 2 gigabytes of working RAM. The first gigabyte lies in memory locations \$0 to \$3FFFFFFF and the second gigabyte lies in memory locations \$80000000-\$BFFFFFFF. The following diagram shows the pin arrangement as seen from below:

D12	D10	D8	D7	D5	D4	D2	D1	As	|A1
D15	D14	D11	D9	D6	D3	D0	UDS	LDS	DTACK
A22	A23	D13	--	--	--	--	R/W	BG	BGACK
A21	GND	GND					--	VCC	BR
A20	VCC	A2D		MOTOTOLA		GND	GND	CLK	
A19	A18	A25		68012			--	RST	HALT
A17	A15	--		(BOTTOM)		A27	VPA	VMA	
A16	A12	A13	--	A28	A29	--	IPL1	IPL2	E
A14	A11	A10	A8	A5	A2	A31	FC1	IPL0	BERR
-	A9	A7	A6	A4	A3	A1	FC0	FC2	A26

The dashed pins are unused; the A1 pin marks the upper right of the chip.

4.5.3   Monster processors: 68020, 68030, 6888x

68020

Information about the 68020 alone can fill volumes. Here are a few key points about this chip:

• 32-bit address bus: This bus enables direct addressing of 4,294,697,296 bytes (about 4 gigabytes). Pin A0 allows access to odd addresses (the 68000 could only do this by means of elaborate calculations)

• Dynamic bus structure: Allows switching between 8-, 16-, 24-, and 32-bit data buses

- True 64-bit arithmetic

- 62 addressing types (50 of them different)

- Access to individual bits or bit fields

- 28 additional instructions

- Data types: bits, bytes, words, longs, packed BCD numbers, unpacked BCD numbers and bit fields

- Acceptance of internal instructions: three-word prefetch

- Processor internal instruction memory: 256-byte cache

- Coprocessor interface and coprocessor instructions

- Frequency measurement: standard = 16 MHz, others = 24 MHz

- Three stack pointers: `MasterSP`, `InterruptSP`, `USerSP`

- two-cache register and extended `SR`

68030/68851   The 68030 processor surpasses all of this data three to four times over, and still remains compatible. It has 31 registers available for reading and writing. The 68851 coprocessor closely integrates with the 68030, and already runs in hardware-multitasking mode.

68881   Real power comes into play when a floating point arithmetic coprocessor supplies math calculations directly to the 32/64-bit processors. The 68881 processor operates using eight floating point registers, and can process the following operand sizes:

> Byte (8-bit)
> Word (16-bit)
> Long (32-bit)
> Float (32-bit)
> DoubleFloat (64-bit)
> ExtendedFloat (96-bit)
> BinaryCodedDecimal (96-bit)

The math commands encompass any calculations you can think of, including three different logarithms and everything that ever existed in all the Amiga math libraries put together. It is convenient to use general IEEE floating point format, so that a conversion occurs.

68882   The 68882 is an extension of the 68881 processor.

5.
Workbench 1.3

5.   Workbench 1.3

At the time the previous book (*Amiga Tricks and Tips*) hit the market, only two forms of Workbench existed: Version 1.1 and Version 1.2. Commodore-Amiga's development teams have spent a great deal of time refining the Workbench user interface system and AmigaDOS. This chapter discusses a few of the special items offered by the Workbench 1.3 disk, including new devices and FFS (FastFileSystem) access. You'll also read about some of the new AmigaDOS commands and how they can help your productivity in AmigaDOS.

5.1   Using Mount

Users seldom used the Mount command in earlier Workbench implementations. To discover more about the command, we must first understand its main purpose. The Mount command mounts a new device in the Amiga's operating system. First we should look at the existing devices. This can be done easily with the Assign command. If you enter Assign without any arguments, your screen may display the following output:

```
Volumes:

Tips and Tricks [Mounted]
RAM DISK [Mounted]
BeckerText
Workbench 1.3 Wgb [Mounted]

Directories:

FONTS         Volume: BeckerText
ENV   RAM:Env
T     RAM:T
S     Workbench 1.3 Wgb:S
L     Workbench 1.3 Wgb:L
C     Workbench 1.3 Wgb:C
DEVS  Workbench 1.3 Wgb:devs
LIBS  Workbench 1.3 Wgb:libs
SYS   Workbench 1.3 Wgb:

Devices:

NEWCON DF1 DF0 PRT
PAR SER RAW CON RAM
```

Notice the last group (Devices:). This tells us the devices available on the Workbench disk.

DF0: and DF1: should be familiar to you by now. PRT: represents the direct printer interface, and PAR: or SER: represent the parallel and serial interfaces. Output can be sent over RAW: and CON: without access to Intuition. The RAM: may be familiar to you as the RAM disk.

The devices listed above are placed in the operating system for access at any time. Whenever you want to address a new device, Mount must inform the system of the device's existence. This method makes allowances for any further improvements made to the CLI, Shell and editor. See Section 6.2 (Using Workbench 1.3) for more information concerning new operating systems.

We need an entry in the Mount list first, generally found in the DEVS: directory. The following example creates access to an external drive addressed as DF1: (see your Mount list for this example or something similar):

```
DF1:  Device = trackdisk.device
      Unit = 1
      Flags = 1
      Surfaces = 2
      BlocksPerTrack = 11
      Reserved = 2
      PreAlloc = 11
      Interleave = 0
      LowCyl = 0 ; HighCyl = 79
      Buffers = 20
      BufMemType = 3
#
```

Definitions always begin with the new device's name (DF1:) and end with the end mark (#). Everything between them depends on the respective device. Certain arguments are used frequently:

Device　　　This argument tells Mount the name of the device. The DEVS: directory acts as the default directory for devices.

Unit　　　This argument assigns the number of the corresponding device. The first physical disk drive has the number 0, the second (either internal or external) has number 1, and so on. Any 5-1/4" disk drive has a unit assignment of 2. This argument works for disk drives only.

Flags　　　This argument contains a value which changes according to the device.

Surfaces　　　This argument specifies the number of usable surfaces handled by the device. A floppy disk normally has two usable surfaces. A hard disk has four usable surfaces.

Reserved　　　This argument specifies the number of data blocks in the boot block.

BufMemType   This argument specifies the memory type for the data buffer:

0,1 = equal; 2,3 = CHIP-RAM; 4,5 = FAST-RAM

BootPri   Sets the priority of the drive for booting. The higher the number, the sooner this device boots. This option is especially important in Version 1.3 of the operating system, since it allows the user to boot from the RAM disk, hard disk, or almost any device capable of booting. We won't go into detail about each one because the data depends greatly on the device connected.

5.1.1   Renaming commands

If you have a PC or PC compatible, you may be having some problems getting accustomed to the Amiga system's DOS commands. For example, instead of entering A: (MS-DOS) to change access to the first internal drive, you have to enter cd DF0: (AmigaDOS). This becomes especially annoying if you frequently switch between systems, or if you're one of the proud few who own a PC card. In this case it would be the best to rename drive names DF0:, DF1:, etc. to IBM-compatible names.

The AmigaDOS Assign command assigns a new name to each disk. Here's an example:

Assign B: DF1:

Now instead of always having to type DF1:, you can just enter B:. Now remove the disk from the external drive and insert another disk. The Amiga demands the other disk. Assign applies to only the existing directory here, and not the disk drive.

We have a cure for that. Copy the definition for DF1: into the Mount list because it contains all of the necessary data for a disk drive. Then we change the definition name DF1: to B:. After saving, enter:

Mount B:

You can now address drive DF1: as B:.

You can perform the same change on drive DF0:. You must create a copy of the old entry in the Mount list. Change the unit from 1 to 0 so the 0 drive is really addressed. Change the definition name to A:. Finally enter the following:

Mount A:

The table of the devices is supplied with both new devices, which can be checked with `Assign`:

```
Devices:

A B NEWCON DF1 DF0
PRT PAR SER RAW CON
RAM
```

5.1.2   Less is more

`Mount` can do a great deal more than reassign devices. There are very serious applications with which you can save money and amaze your friends. Now we look deep into the arguments which accompany `Mount`.

Here's a scenario: You buy a 10-pack of unbranded disks which were on sale for $10. Unfortunately, they are of inferior quality. The first time you format any of these disks you find that almost all of them have hardware errors on side 1. The formatting stops.

Here's the trick: Enter the `Mount` list and duplicate the definition for `DF1:`. Change this copy definition's name to `WGB:`. Go into the `WGB:` list and change the `Surfaces` argument from 2 to 1. The `WGB:` device formats disk on only one side instead of two sides.

Enter the following in the `CLI`:

```
Format Drive WGB: Name "1 Surface Test"
```

The formatting seems to go faster because only half the disk is being formatted. We recommend strongly that you read and write this disk using this device only; you will have problems reading single-side-format disks using the standard devices (DF0:, etc.). You can also access the data only through your own applications designed to read drive WGB: (i.e., you cannot access data from these disks using normal applications). The main advantage here is that the disks cannot be copied by normal means. One concluding tip: Buy the highest quality disks you can afford, and you won't need to do any of this single-sided disk formatting.

The `Mount` command has two other unusual qualities. The first comes into play when you have a disk with more than one side damaged or defective. `Mount` also regulates the beginning disk track and ending disk track in a formatting process. For example, if you find you have read errors on tracks 0-4, enter the `Mount` list and change the `LowCyl` argument to 5: Formatting begins at track five. Tracks 0-4 remain unformatted, and the rest of the disk formats as normal. The second trick controls the end of the disk: Maybe tracks 71-79 are unreadable. Simply change the HighCyl argument to 70 and format as described above.

Experimental formatting may cause incompatibilities between the Workbench and the disk drive. The first problem is the Workbench. When you connect a new external drive and format a disk on it, you'll get a DF1:NODOS icon. That's okay, but it still creates the second problem. The DF1: drive is no longer addressable whether you insert a disk in the normal Amiga format or not. It responds with "No disk in unit 1" which means that only the new format is accepted. You can address the new format from the Workbench also.

These are some of the interesting applications. When you use a data disk with this format, it is no problem reading it with your own program, but all other programs that shouldn't read the data will not have access, without the correct Mount list.

5.2   Improvements to DOS 1.3

The software development people at Commodore-Amiga added many improvements and upgrades to Workbench 1.3. With a few exceptions, Version 1.3 is fully compatible with Version 1.2. Many of the exceptions appear in default settings. For example, Workbench 1.2 always defaulted to the Topaz font—this doesn't have to be so in Version 1.3. This means that the programmer must furnish all data structures with the desired values, instead of, setting the font address to 0 to assign the Topaz font. There are rules to programming the Amiga and each error in programming produces an undesirable effect in Version 1.3, as was the case in Version 1.2.

Incompatibility occurs only in rare cases. Even then it can be resolved through simple changes in settings. The new devices, libraries, and handler will be of great interest to all. Improvements to existing features and the many new possibilities will also fascinate Amiga users. With these enhancements and improvements, you don't need a Cray to do major computations and applications anymore. Let's start by looking in the DEVS: directory to see what improvements are there.

5.2.1   The PIPE device

The PIPE device is a new member of the DEVS: directory group. To show you what the handler can do, we'll start by viewing a better-known handler—the clipboard device. This device performs temporary data exchange. If you need to exchange data between tasks while in the CLI or Shell, you'd use the clipboard to transfer this data. Once the Mount command places the clipboard in the Mount list, you can direct data to and from this device by output or input.

Unfortunately the Workbench is plagued with frequent read/write errors and delays which extend to this device and its data. Look again in the DEVS: directory, and you'll find an almost empty directory. The clipboard device writes the given data to this directory and removes it as needed.

Disk access takes quite a bit of time. By adding memory expansion (the Amiga can access 4,294,967,296 bytes [over four gigabytes] of main memory through the 68020 processor), the majority of data messages once exchanged on the disk through the clipboard can also be managed in RAM.

Here's where the PIPE device comes into play. You can think of the operation as if a pipeline were placed in RAM which could be filled from one side with your data. The data could them be poured out of the pipeline to the other application when needed. To use the PIPE device the system must first be informed that the PIPE handler should be activated. Enter:

```
MOUNT PIPE:
```

In the DEVS/Mountlist file you can enter the desired size of the pipeline with the editor ED. To fill the pipeline, you only need to make sure that the NewCon device receives the pipeline data instead of the Console device. This can be done with the CLI's output redirection command (>):

```
DIR >PIPE: SYS:
```

This directs the root directory of the boot disk into the pipeline. Nothing else happens after you enter this command, aside from a brief disk access. Enter the following command sequence to empty the PIPE and display its contents on the screen:

```
TYPE PIPE:
```

This command won't work if too much data enters the pipeline, as you may have seen from the above example. Should the pipeline be too full, the error message renders the pipeline data unusable.

5.2.2   The Speak device

The Say command already existed in Version 1.2 but the Speak device in Version 1.3 takes on an entirely different quality.

This device has some similarities to the PIPE device. It connects into the system like PIPE and redirects data. Unlike PIPE the Speak device doesn't allow temporary storage: Whatever goes in, comes out of monitor speakers as speech. Let's test the water a little bit. Enter the following command sequence:

```
MOUNT SPEAK:
DIR >SPEAK: SYS:
```

Perhaps you're tired of reading stories to your children every night, and you'd like a night off from that task. Have the Amiga do it. The following command starts a task and speaks the contents of the file named BedTimeStories:

```
RUN TYPE >SPEAK: "BedTimeStories"
```

Speech synthesis enthusiasts should try the following with the Extras disk in df1:

```
RUN TYPE >SPEAK: df1:AmigaBASIC OPT H
```

It makes more sense to make a prompt audible with Ask:

```
ASK >SPEAK: "Do you like the Amiga?"
```

5.2.3   The NewCon device

The NewCon device is probably the best new command accessible from the Shell. This device is in the startup sequence (Mount NewCon:). NewCon is similar to the Console device that opens CLI windows. Enter a command and press the <Return> key. Now press the <Cursor left> key and observe what happens on the monitor.

You can now edit the command line at any time, similar to what occurs in the List window of AmigaBASIC. When you mistype something in a longer command line, you can now correct this error without having to retype the entire text. Now enter the following commands:

```
DIR df0: DIRS
LIST ram: OPT A
TYPE s/startup-sequence
```

Pretend that you would like to look at the directory of drive DF0:. With the CLI you would have to re-enter the Dir command. Press the cursor up key to scroll up to the previously entered commands. Because only the commands are saved, the memory requirement to do this is small. The cursor keys can be used to edit the commands.

5.2.4   The FastFileSystem

AmigaDOS takes up too much disk space. Version 1.3 uses the external disk media extensively. A new disk format takes advantage of these improvements.

To make you familiar with the file/system relationship, we'll show you a big difference between the versions of AmigaDOS. One data block of an AmigaDOS disk containing program data consists of 512 bytes. Of these 512 bytes DOS only allocates 488 bytes for data—the rest go to data management. When you load a program, the management data executes an elaborate memory transfer. This is where the FastFileSystem comes into play. It ensures that management data is no longer necessary in a data block and that all 512 bytes are ready for use as program data.

When you read sequential multiple data blocks of a program, a single read access can perform this task. Because the data management structure has been removed, this block can be read directly into the desired memory address. The increase in speed is enormous. All disk operations can be increased in speed by a factor of five. The disk space saved by releasing the management data of a disk is also quite large. We calculated that a 20 megabyte hard disk on which you placed the FastFileSystem could save 1.5 megabytes of memory.

The use of FFS boils down to this: You get more disk for the same money. Workbench 1.3 gives you better disk access in any case.

Version 1.3 defaults to an inactive FastFileSystem. You must first inform the system that you need the handler of the same name and from which medium this should come. We recommend that the desired device be entered into the Mount list using ED DEVS/Mountlist. This can later be added to the startup sequence using the Mount command. We've prepared a version of the modified Mount lists to let you quickly adapt to the FFS.

5.2.5   FFS and hard disks

The most cost-effective storage comes from hard disks, because they can hold large amounts of memory. Here is a possible Mount list entry that could be placed in the FastFileSystem of your hard disk. When you integrate it into your Mount list, do the following:

Copy all of the files from your hard disk to normal disks. Enter the following to mount it:

```
Mount FHD:
```

Format your FastHardDisk with the following command sequence:

```
FORMAT DRIVE FHD: NAME "FastHardDisk"
```

Copy your files onto the FHD: device. You'll be surprised how many more files you can put on the hard disk.

```
FHD:        Device = hddisk.device      /* access to  HD */
        FileSystem = L:FastFileSystem /* all clear      */
              Unit = 1                 /* Device 0 waiting
                                          on AmigaDOS    */
             Flags = 0                 /* for OpenDevice */
```

```
        Surfaces = 4           /* Disk surfaces  */
  BlocksPerTrack = 15          /* Number of blocks
                                  per track      */
        Reserved = 2           /* Bootblocks     */
      Interleave = 0           /* Block setup    */
          LowCyl = 10          /* From
                                  cylinder 10    */
         HighCyl = 800         /* to cyl. 800    */
         Buffers = 11          /* Read buffers   */
      BufMemType = 1           /* same
                                  (5=FastRAM)     */
         GlobVec = -1          /* No GlobVec      */
           Mount = 1           /* Load handler
                                  immediately after
                                  entering MOUNT */
         DosType = 0x444F5301  /* Identifier code
                                  for FFS         */
#                              /* End of entry    */
```

You must add the following line to the startup sequence to implement
the FastHardDisk:

```
MOUNT FHD:
```

5.2.8   The new math libraries

Who hasn't dreamt of a 68030 processor and a 68882 floating point
math coprocessor? The prices of these components are a little out of
most people's leagues.

New math libraries in 1.3 provide faster math calculations. The speed
when processing IEEE floats, like those used with the x#- variables in
BASIC, executes much faster. After an exact analysis we determined
that we have found the fastest known floating point routine currently
on the planet. So as not to lead you astray, here is an example of the
way this routine can be used in BASIC:

```
DECLARE FUNCTION IEEEDPSin# LIBRARY
LIBRARY "mathieeedoubtrans.library" 'BASIC does not
                                    'accept pathnames
'use CHDIR [Path for the BMAP-Files]!
PI#=4*ATN(1)        'PI is calculated (fullcircle=2*PI)
CIRC#=2*PI#
FOR I%=1 TO 359                     'circle in degrees
  ANGLE#=CIRC#/I%                   'angle from 2*PI
  HighLong&=PEEKL(VARPTR(ANGLE#))   'first Long of DFloat
  LowLong& =PEEKL(VARPTR(ANGLE#)+4) 'second Long of Float
  SINUS#=IEEEDPSin#(HighLong&,LowLong&) 'Call function
  PSET(I%,90-INT(SINUS#*50)),1      'Draw pixel
NEXT
```

```
FOR I%=1 TO 359              'Just for Demo
 ANGLE#=CIRC#/I%             'Look how fast
 SINUS#=SIN(ANGLE#)          'BASIC is...
 PSET(I%,90-INT(SINUS#*50)),2 'other color
NEXT
LIBRARY CLOSE
```

The first FOR/NEXT loop is slower than the second loop. The VARPTR function must be called 720 times, the slow PEEKL must be called 720 times, the addition of the value four 360 times, and the routines call 360 times with assignment from two long values, which doesn't go quickly. More lines and variable assignments distort the first loop. All of these limitations are amazing. And the end result: The first loop is just as fast as the second loop.

The MathIEEEdoubtrans library includes all the possible transcendental math functions executable on double-precision floating point numbers. The MathIEEEdoubbas library, which contains the simple calculation functions, is fast. Transcendental math functions even come in handy for BASIC users, because they allow you to find the arcsine without using calculation programs at the same speed as the sine function. Here is an overview of the functions:

```
MathIeeeDoubBas-Library
x,y,Double                              Double-precision
                                        floating point
                                        number (BASIC: 2
                                        longs instead of
                                        x and y)
Long                                    Positive/negative
                                        long integer
                                        number
Long        IEEEDPFix    (x)            Double float/long
(D0)        -30          (D0/D1)        integer
                                        conversion
Double      IEEEDPFlt    (Long)         Long integer/
(D0/D1)     -36          (D0)           double float
                                        conversion
Long        IEEEDPCmp    (x,y)          Compare x and y
(D0)        -42          (D0/D1,D2/D3)  (cc set for bcc)
                                        Applies to the
                                        following:
                                        x > y -->1
                                        x=y -->0
                                        x<y -->-1
Long        IEEEDPTst    (x)            Compare x and 0
(D0)        -48          (D0/D1)        (cc set; result
                                        handled as in
                                        IEEEDPCmp when
                                        y=0)
Double      IEEEDPAbs    (x)            Returns absolute
(D0/D1)     -54          (D0/D1)        value of x
Double      IEEEDPNeg    (x)            Function:
(D0/D1)     -60          (D0/D1)        Double=-x
```

MathIeeeDoubTrans-Library

Double	IEEEDPAdd	(x,y)	Function:
(D0/D1)	-66	(D0/D1,D2/D3)	Double=x+y
Double	IEEEDPSub	(x,y)	Function:
(D0/D1)	-72	(D0/D1,D2/D3)	Double=x-y
Double	IEEEDPMul	(x,y)	Function:
(D0/D1)	-78	(D0/D1,D2/D3)	Double=x*y
Double	IEEEDPDiv	(x,y)	Function:
(D0/D1)	-84	(D0/D1,D2/D3)	Double=x/y
Double	IEEEDPFloor	(x)	Returns greatest
(D0/D1)	-90	(D0/D1)	integer less than
			or equal to x
Double	IEEEDPCeil	(x)	Returns smallest
(D0/D1)	-96	(D0/D1)	integer greater
			than or equal
			to x
Double	IEEEDPAtan	(x)	Returns arc-
(D0/D1)	-30	(D0/D1)	tangent of x
Double	IEEEDPSin	(x)	Returns sine of x
(D0/D1)	-36	(D0/D1)	
Double	IEEEDPCos	(x)	Returns cosine
(D0/D1)	-42	(D0/D1)	of x
Double	IEEEDPTan	(x)	Returns tangent
(D0/D1)	-48	(D0/D1)	of x
Double	IEEEDPSincos	(x,VARPTR)	Double calc:
(D0/D1)	-54	(D0/D1,A0)	Compute sine of
			x, put
			cosine of x in
			VARPTR
Double	IEEEDPSinh	(x)	Returns
(D0/D1)	-60	(D0/D1)	hyperbolic sine
			of x
Double	IEEEDPCosh	(x)	Returns
(D0/D1)	-66	(D0/D1)	hyperbolic cosine
			of x
Double	IEEEDPTanh	(x)	Returns
(D0/D1)	-72	(D0/D1)	hyperbolic
			tangent of x
Double	IEEEDPExp	(x)	Exponent of e
(D0/D1)	-78	(D0/D1)	Function:
			Double=e^x
Double	IEEEDPLog	(x)	Returns natural
(D0/D1)	-84	(D0/D1)	logarithm of x
Double	IEEEDPPow	(x,y)	Function:
(D0/D1)	-90	(D0/D1,D2/D3)	Double=x^y
Double	IEEEDPSqrt	(x)	Returns square
(D0/D1)	-96	(D0/D1)	root of x
Float	IEEEDPTieee	(x)	Calc x in IEEE
(D0)	-102	(D0/D1)	floating point
			single precision
Double	IEEEDPFieee	(Float)	Compute single
(D0/D1)	-108	(D0)	precision float
			in double
			precision
Double	IEEEDPAsin	(x)	Returns arcsine
(D0/D1)	-114	(D0/D1)	of x

```
MathIeeeDoubTrans-Library
Double     IEEEDPAcos     (x)              Returns arccosine
(D0/D1)    -120           (D0/D1)          of x
Double     IEEEDPLog10    (x)              Returns base 10
(D0/D1)    -126           (D0/D1)          logarithm of x
```

The BASIC programmer should remember that you can't have a double float in the system routine. You must give this 64-bit variable in the form of two long values which get their values through PEEKL (VARPTR()). The sine demo in this section is an example of this technique. Another feature of BASIC is the short IEEE library name of the command of the same name.

You can give most libraries longer pathnames. With this library the actual pathname may already be so long that no more path data can be given. When you do this, a File not found error ensues. If you want to access the math libraries, you must place the system start disk with the corresponding BMAP files in the current directory or in the LIBS: directory. Or you can add a CHDIR statement before the Library command.

6.
The printer device

6.   The printer device

The printer device gives the BASIC programmer the opportunity to use the printer he has connected to his Amiga. If you have the proper printer driver for your printer and the printer device available, the interfacing usually runs flawlessly, and with a minimum amount of hassle for the user.

This chapter shows you how to set up your printer to perform tasks that are a bit unusual. You'll find a program available to let you control your printer outside of Preferences. In addition, this chapter contains a program which enables easy printed hardcopy from an open window.

6.1   Controlling printer parameters

Open a computer magazine and look through the advertisements. You'll see literally hundreds of printers on the market, all shouting at the user, "Buy me." These printers all carry different price tags, different methods of producing printed matter (dot matrix, daisywheel, inkjet, laser, thermal), and different qualities of printing.

Each printer type has its own special strengths and weaknesses. Here are some general descriptions of these pros and cons:

- Thermal printers are very inexpensive and very quiet, but require special paper and may not be graphic compatible.

- Daisywheel printers produce excellent print for letters, theses, etc., but cannot print any graphics except the most rudimentary graphic output using available characters.

- Dot matrix printers can produce graphics (even in color), but often the NLQ (near letter quality) mode is inadequate for professional text printing.

- Laser printers have speed, high resolution and graphic capability, but the price is prohibitive for the average user.

- Inkjet printers are quiet, efficient and fairly clear printers, but their graphic reproduction varies greatly.

You can easily see that each printer type described above can address at least one of your personal printing needs. The Amiga can help. Once you select the printer you're using in the Change Printer screen of Preferences (on the Workbench disk), the Amiga automatically converts general printer commands and printer-specific command codes to your printer. These codes make your programs either completely compatible with your printer type, or as compatible as possible.

Preferences usually governs this print quality, but you can override the control using the following program. This program should give you some ideas of how the printer device communicates with the printer, and how you can adapt the printer device to your own needs.

The ¶ characters in the following program are not to be entered, they only show where a BASIC line actually ends. When formatting the listing to fit in the book, some lines may be split that should not be. The ¶ character shows where a line actually ends.

```
'****************************************¶
'* Programm: Read Printer Data¶
'* Date: May 28' 88¶
'* Author: tob¶
'* Version: 1.3¶
'****************************************¶
CLS¶
PRINT "Searching for the .bmap files!¶
'EXEC-LIBRARY¶
DECLARE FUNCTION AllocMem& LIBRARY¶
DECLARE FUNCTION DoIO& LIBRARY¶
DECLARE FUNCTION OpenDevice% LIBRARY¶
DECLARE FUNCTION AllocSignal% LIBRARY¶
DECLARE FUNCTION FindTask& LIBRARY¶
LIBRARY "t&t2:bmaps/exec.library"¶
init:        '¶
             GetPrinterData¶
             ¶
             PRINT "Printer-Name        : "; prt.name$¶
             PRINT "Printer-Type        : "; prt.typ$¶
             PRINT "Color capability    : "; prt.color$¶
             PRINT "Characters per line : "; prt.columns%¶
             PRINT "Number of fonts     : "; prt.charsets%¶
             PRINT "Number of raster lines: ";prt.rows&¶
             PRINT "Max. num. Dots horiz  : ";prt.xdots&¶
             PRINT "Max. num. Dots vert.  : ";prt.ydots&¶
             PRINT "Density: Dots/Inch h. : ";prt.xdotspi&¶
             PRINT "Density: Dots/Inch v. : ";prt.ydotspi&¶
             ¶
             END¶
             ¶
SUB GetPrinterData STATIC¶
  SHARED prt.DRPReq&¶
  SHARED prt.typ$, prt.colour$, prt.name$¶
  SHARED prt.columns%, prt.charsets%¶
  SHARED prt.rows&, prt.xdots&, prt.ydots&¶
```

```
                SHARED prt.xdotspi&, prt.ydotspi&¶
                ¶
                DIM prt.color$    (9)¶
                DIM prt.printer$  (3)¶
                ¶
                prt.color$  (1) = "Black-White"¶
                prt.color$  (2) = "Yellow-Magenta-Cyan"¶
                prt.color$  (3) = "Yellow-Magenta-Cyan or Black-White"¶
                prt.color$  (4) = "Yellow-Magenta-Cyan-Black"¶
                prt.color$  (5) = "Blue-Green-Red-White"¶
                prt.color$  (6) = "Black-White Invers"¶
                prt.color$  (7) = "Blue-Green-Red"¶
                prt.color$  (8) = "Blue-Green-Red or Black-White"¶
                prt.color$  (9) = "Blue-Green-Red-White"¶
                ¶
                prt.printer$(0) = "b/w Text Printer"¶
                prt.printer$(1) = "b/w Graphics"¶
                prt.printer$(2) = "Color Text Printer"¶
                prt.printer$(3) = "Color Graphics"¶
                    ¶
                    ¶
                OpenPrinter¶
                ¶
                prt.printerdata&  = PEEKL (prt.DRPReq& + 20)¶
                prt.extendeddata& = (PEEKL (prt.printerdata& + 92) + 12)¶
                prt.name$         = ""¶
                prt.name&         = PEEKL (prt.extendeddata&)¶
                prt.printer%      = PEEK  (prt.extendeddata& + 20)¶
                prt.color%        = PEEK  (prt.extendeddata& + 21)¶
                prt.columns%      = PEEK  (prt.extendeddata& + 22)¶
                prt.charsets%     = PEEK  (prt.extendeddata& + 23)¶
                prt.rows&         = PEEKW (prt.extendeddata& + 24)¶
                prt.xdots&        = PEEKL (prt.extendeddata& + 26)¶
                prt.ydots&        = PEEKL (prt.extendeddata& + 30)¶
                prt.xdotspi&      = PEEKW (prt.extendeddata& + 34)¶
                prt.ydotspi&      = PEEKW (prt.extendeddata& + 36)¶
                ¶
                prt.typ$          = prt.printer$ (prt.printer%)¶
                prt.colour$       = prt.color$   (prt.color%)¶
                ¶
                count = NULL ¶
                char  = PEEK (prt.name& + count)¶
                ¶
                WHILE char <> NULL¶
                   prt.name$ = prt.name$ + CHR$ (char)¶
                   count     = count + 1¶
                   char      = PEEK (prt.name& + count)¶
                WEND¶
                ¶ ,
                ClosePrinter¶
            END SUB¶
            ¶
            SUB OpenPrinter STATIC¶
              SHARED mem.chunk&¶
              SHARED prt.DRPReq&¶
              ¶
```

```
        mem.clear&  = 2^16          'clear memory before task¶
        mem.DRPReq% = 62            '62 Bytes for DRPStruktur¶
        mem.port%   = 37            '37 Bytes for Port-Struct.¶
        mem.label%  = 4             '4  Bytes for Organization¶
        mem.size%   = mem.DRPReq% + mem.port% + mem.label%¶
        ¶
        mem.chunk&  = AllocMem& (mem.size%, mem.clear&)¶
        IF mem.chunk& = NULL THEN ¶
          ERROR 7                   'OUT OF MEMORY ERROR¶
        END IF¶
        ¶
        prt.label&  = mem.chunk&¶
        prt.DRPReq& = mem.chunk& + mem.label%¶
        prt.port&   = mem.chunk& + mem.label% + mem.DRPReq%¶
        prt.name$   = "printer.device" + CHR$(0)¶
        ¶
        POKEL prt.label&, mem.size% 'allocate memory size¶
        ¶
        status%= OpenDevice% (SADD(prt.name$), 0, prt.DRPReq&, 0)¶
        IF status% <> NULL THEN¶
          PRINT "Printer is not available."¶
          CALL FreeMem (mem.chunk&, mem.size%)¶
          EXIT SUB¶
        END IF¶
        END SUB¶
            ¶
        SUB ClosePrinter STATIC¶
            SHARED mem.chunk&¶
            ¶
            mem.size%  = PEEKL (mem.chunk&)¶
            prt.DRPReq& = mem.chunk& + 4¶
            CALL CloseDevice (prt.DRPReq&)¶
            CALL FreeMem (mem.chunk&, mem.size%)¶
        END SUB
```

Variables

prt.DRPReq&	I/O DumpRastPort structure (starting address here)
prt.typ$	Printer category
prt.colour$	Color capability
prt.name$	Printer name
prt.columns%	Characters per line
prt.charsets%	Number of available fonts
prt.rows&	Number of pins available on printhead
prt.xdots&	Max. number of pixels in the X-direction
prt.ydots&	Max. number of pixels in the Y-direction
prt.xdotspi&	Horizontal resolution (pixels per inch)
prt.ydotspi&	Vertical resolution (pixels per inch)

GetPrinterData():

prt.color$()	Array—color types
prt.printer$()	Array—printer types
prt.printerdata&	Starting address, PrinterData structure
prt.extendeddata&	Starting address, ExtendedData structure
prt.name&	Starting address, name string
prt.printer%	Printer type code number
prt.color%	Color type code number
count	Counter
char	Read character

OpenPrinter:

mem.chunk&	Starting address, reserved memory
mem.clear&	= 2^16; set available memory to 0
mem.DRPReq%	= 62; reserve 62 bytes for structure
mem.port%	= 38; reserve 38 bytes for structure
mem.label%	= 4; reserve 4 bytes for organization
mem.size%	Memory requirement in bytes
prt.label&	Starting address, label memory
prt.DRPReq&	Starting address, DumpRastport structure
prt.port&	Starting address, Port structure
prt.name$	Device name
status%	0 = everything's okay

Program description

When you look at it, you discover that the previous program consists of three subprograms:

```
GetPrinterData
OpenPrinter
ClosePrinter
```

The user will find the GetPrinterData subprogram most interesting. This subprogram internally calls the other two subprograms. The structure named PrinterExtendedData contains the information needed by the other subprograms. To arrive at this, it is necessary to first open the printer through printer.device. This is done using the OpenPrinter subprogram.

Next the Exec function AllocMem() allocates memory for two structures: a Port structure and a DumpRastPort structure. In addition, AllocMem() reserves four bytes. These bytes are eventually used as storage for the absolute memory size listed for FreeMem().

When this method is used the Exec function OpenDevice() opens the printer. This call returns a Status report to the system. As long as the Status value doesn't equal zero, the printer cannot be opened.

Possible causes: Another task may be currently accessing the printer, or the printer wasn't properly closed before this access.

When the printer opens, the `DumpRastPort` structure contains a pointer to a structure named `PrinterData`. When the pointer is reset, it points to the `PrinterExtended` data structure, in which the necessary data is saved.

The data is read and stored in the correct variables. Then the printer is closed once again. This is accomplished using a call of the `ClosePrinter` routine. This must be done! When the printer is opened but not closed by the same program it cannot be accessed until the computer is reset.

Here is an example of the program output:

```
Printer-Name          : EpsonQ
Printer-Type          : Color Graphics
Color capability      : Yellow-Magenta-Cyan-Black
Characters per line   :  80
Number of fonts       :  10
Number of raster lines:  24
Max. num. Dots horiz  :  720
Max. num. Dots vert.  :  0
Density: Dots/Inch h. :  90
Density: Dots/Inch v. :  180
```

6.2 Graphic dumps using the printer device

The following program is an example of printer control programming. It shows you the essentials of printing the current contents of your BASIC window to the printer as a graphic hardcopy or screen dump.

This program supports all the special flags included in operating system 1.3. These flags let you reduce the size of a window's contents, enlarge the window, distort its structure, center it and more.

The ¶ characters in the following program are not to be entered, they only show where a BASIC line actually ends. When formatting the listing to fit in the book, some lines may be split that should be on one line in Amiga BASIC. The ¶ character shows where a line actually ends.

```
'***************************************¶
'* Program: Graphic-Dump¶
'* Date: May 28 1988¶
'* Author: tob¶
'* Version: 1.3¶
'***************************************¶
PRINT "Searching for .bmap files!"¶
'EXEC-LIBRARY¶
DECLARE FUNCTION AllocMem& LIBRARY¶
DECLARE FUNCTION DoIO& LIBRARY¶
DECLARE FUNCTION OpenDevice% LIBRARY¶
DECLARE FUNCTION AllocSignal% LIBRARY¶
DECLARE FUNCTION FindTask& LIBRARY¶
LIBRARY "T&T2:bmaps/exec.library"¶
init:  '    ¶
    CIRCLE (100,100),100¶
    PRINT STRING$ (100,"_")¶
    ¶
    special.nothing   = 0 'no Special effects¶
    special.milcols   = 1 'X-Dimension in 1/100      '0
Inch¶
    special.milrows   = 2 'Y-Dimension in 1/100      '0
Inch¶
    special.fullcols  = 4 'Maximale X-measurement    'g¶
    special.fullrows  = 8 'Maximale Y-measurement    'g¶
    special.fraccols  =   16 'fraction of max. X-
measurement¶
    special.fracrows  =   32 'ditto, for Y-measurement¶
    special.center    =   64 'Graphic centered on output¶
    special.aspect    =  128 'correction X-Y-aspect¶
    special.density1  =  256 'Position 1 (lower)¶
    special.density2  =  512 'Position 2 ¶
```

```
            special.density3  =   768 'Position 3¶
            special.density4  = 1024 'Position 4¶
            special.density5  = 1280 'Position 5¶
            special.density6  = 1536 'Position 6¶
            special.density7  = 1792 'Position 7 (high)¶
            special.noformfeed= 2048 'no formfeed¶
            special.trustme   = 4096 'no Reset output ¶
            special.noprint   = 8096 'calculation only, no print¶
            ¶
            Hardcopy (special.center + special.density4), 100&,
       100&¶
            ¶
            'for Black/white printer, black and white screen¶
                                      ¶
            PALETTE 0,1,1,1¶
            PALETTE 1,0,0,0¶
            ¶
            Hardcopy (special.aspect + special.fullcols +
       special.fullrows), 0&, 0&¶
            ¶
            ¶
            END¶
            ¶
       SUB Hardcopy (flags, x&, y&) STATIC¶
            SHARED prt.DRPReq&¶
            ¶
            OpenPrinter¶
            ¶
            POKEL prt.DRPReq& + 52, x&¶
            POKEL prt.DRPReq& + 56, y&¶
            POKEW prt.DRPReq& + 60, flags¶
            InitDRPReq¶
            ¶
            PrtErr% = DoIO& (prt.DRPReq&)¶
            ¶
            PrtErr$  (0)   = "NO ERROR."¶
            PrtErr$  (1)   = "PRINTING STOPPED BY USER."¶
            PrtErr$  (2)   = "PRINTER CANNOT PRINT GRAPHICS."¶
            PrtErr$  (3)   = "./."¶
            PrtErr$  (4)   = "PRINT SIZE IMPOSSIBLE"¶
            PrtErr$  (5)   = "./."¶
            PrtErr$  (6)   = "NO MEMORY FOR INTERNAL VARIABLES."¶
            PrtErr$  (7)   = "NO MEMORY FOR PRINTER BUFFER."¶
            ¶
            result$   = PrtErr$ (PrtErr%)¶
            ¶
            PRINT result$¶
            ¶
            ClosePrinter¶
       END SUB¶
       SUB OpenPrinter STATIC¶
            SHARED mem.chunk&¶
            SHARED prt.DRPReq&¶
            SHARED prt.port&¶
            ¶
            mem.clear&  = 2^16 'Clear memory for task¶
```

```
        mem.DRPReq%  = 62     '62 Bytes, DumpRastport Structure¶
        mem.port%    = 38     '38 Bytes for Port-Structure¶
        mem.label%   = 4      '4  Bytes for Organization¶
        mem.size%    = mem.DRPReq% + mem.port% + mem.label%¶
        ¶
        mem.chunk&   = AllocMem& (mem.size%, mem.clear&)¶
        IF mem.chunk& = NULL THEN ¶
      ERROR 7        'OUT OF MEMORY ERROR¶
        END IF¶
        ¶
        prt.label&   = mem.chunk&¶
        prt.DRPReq&  = mem.chunk& + mem.label%¶
        prt.port&    = mem.chunk& + mem.label% + mem.DRPReq%¶
        prt.name$    = "printer.device" + CHR$(0)¶
        ¶
        POKEL prt.label&, mem.size% 'allocate  memory size¶
        ¶
        status% = OpenDevice% (SADD(prt.name$), 0,
    prt.DRPReq&, 0)¶
        IF status% <> NULL THEN¶
      PRINT "Printer is not free."¶
      CALL FreeMem (mem.chunk&, mem.size%)¶
      EXIT SUB¶
        END IF¶
    END SUB¶
    SUB InitDRPReq STATIC¶
        SHARED prt.DRPReq&¶
        SHARED prt.port&¶
        SHARED p.sigBit%¶
        ¶
        w.window&       = WINDOW(7)¶
        w.rastport&     = PEEKL (w.window& + 50)¶
        w.width%        = PEEKW (w.window& + 112)¶
        w.height%       = PEEKW (w.window& + 114)¶
        w.screen&       = PEEKL (w.window& + 46)¶
        w.viewport&     = w.screen& + 44¶
        w.colormap&     = PEEKL (w.viewport& + 4)¶
        w.vp.modi%      = PEEKW (w.viewport& + 32)¶
        ¶
        p.sigBit% = AllocSignal%(-1)¶
        IF p.sigBit% = -1 THEN¶
      PRINT "No Signalbit free!"¶
      CALL FreeMem(p.io&,100)¶
      EXIT SUB¶
        END IF¶
        p.sigTask& = FindTask&(0)¶
        ¶
        POKE  prt.port&+8,4¶
        POKEL prt.port&+10,prt.port&+34¶
        POKE  prt.port&+15,p.sigBit%¶
        POKEL prt.port&+16,p.sigTask&¶
        POKEL prt.port&+20,prt.port&+24¶
        POKEL prt.port&+28,prt.port&+20¶
        POKE  prt.port&+34,ASC("P")¶
        POKE  prt.port&+35,ASC("R")¶
        POKE  prt.port&+36,ASC("T")¶
```

```
     ¶
     CALL AddPort (prt.port&) ¶
     ¶
     POKE  prt.DRPReq& +  8, 5¶
     POKEL prt.DRPReq& + 14, prt.port&  ¶
     POKEW prt.DRPReq& + 28, 11¶
     POKEL prt.DRPReq& + 32, w.rastport&¶
     POKEL prt.DRPReq& + 36, w.colormap&¶
     POKEL prt.DRPReq& + 40, w.vp.modi%¶
     POKEW prt.DRPReq& + 48, w.width%¶
     POKEW prt.DRPReq& + 50, w.height%¶
     ¶
     IF PEEKL (prt.DRPReq& + 52) = 0 THEN¶
     POKEL prt.DRPReq& + 52, x&¶
     END IF¶
     ¶
     IF PEEKL (prt.DRPReq& + 56) = 0 THEN¶
     POKEL prt.DRPReq& + 56, y&¶
     END IF ¶
  END SUB¶
     ¶
  SUB ClosePrinter STATIC¶
     SHARED mem.chunk&¶
     SHARED prt.port&¶
     SHARED p.sigBit%¶
     ¶
     mem.size%   = PEEKL (mem.chunk&)  ¶
     prt.DRPReq& = mem.chunk& + 4¶
     CALL CloseDevice (prt.DRPReq&) ¶
     CALL RemPort   (prt.port&) ¶
     CALL FreeSignal  (p.sigBit%) ¶
     CALL FreeMem  (mem.chunk&, mem.size%) ¶
  END SUB¶
```

Variables

PrtErr%	Error number of I/O procedure
PrtErr$()	Error message text
result$	Current error message

Program description

As you may have already noticed, this program contains the subprograms OpenPrinter and ClosePrinter were described in the program in Section 6.1. The subs Hardcopy and InitDRPReq are new material. The Hardcopy subprogram should be highly valuable to the user. It ensures that the contents of the current BASIC window transfers to the printer as graphics, then it calls the other subprograms.

The printer must be open before it can print a graphic screen. The OpenPrinter subprogram opens the printer, similar to its task in the program in Section 6.1. The program POKEs the width and the height of the picture to be printed into the DumpRastPort request structure. The same thing happens with the special bits.

The program then calls `InitDRPReq`. This routine fills the rest of the structure with the standard values, and then turns to the BASIC window.

When the time is right, the `Exec` function `DoIO&` sends the `IORequest` structure to the printer. If the printing stops, or if the command cannot be executed for any reason, this function returns an error code to the `Status%` variable. The program converts this error code into readable text and displays this text on the screen. The `ClosePrinter` routine closes off access to the printer, and the program ends.

6.2.1   Hardcopy as an application

The `Hardcopy` function is unusually versatile. It makes use of all the capabilities that the printer device has to offer. The call of the subprograms can look something like the sequence which follows below:

```
Hardcopy flags, width&, height&
        flags: special flags
        height: height of the print out
        width: width of the print out
```

Flags

`special.nothing`
> The printout occurs without any special printing effects

`special.milcols`
> The routine supplies the printed width in 1/1000 inch increments instead of in points (1 inch equals approximately 2.5 cm)

`Hardcopy special.milcols, 9000, 400`
> This call prints a graphic set at the size specified in the arguments. For example, the above sample command defaults to a width of nine inches (22.5 cm) and a height of 400 printed points

`special.milrows`
> Similar to `special.milcols`, but this command controls printable height

`special.fullcols`
> The printable width comes out as wide as the hardware can manage, regardless of the value given as an argument

`special.fullrows`
> Similar to `special.fullcols`, but this command controls printable height

`special.fraccols`
> The given width is interpreted as x/65535ths of the maximum width

`special.fracrows`
> Similar to `special.fraccols`. The given width is interpreted as x/65535ths of the maximum width

`special.center`
> The program prints the graphic centered on the page. The `special.center` flag ignores any previously specified parameters setting printable dimensions

`special.aspect`
> This flag maintains the ratio between height and width, regardless of the changes in height or width assigned by the user

`special.density1-7` (V1.3)
> Print density: 1 = low (default)
>   7= high

`special.noformfeed` (V1.3)
> Disables paper formfeed, useful when printing to laser printers. This allows the user to integrate text and graphics

`special.trustme`
> No reset is sent to the printer

`special.noprint` (V1.3)
> Processes all descriptions and computes all printing dimensions without executing a printout. This command allows the user to double-check printing parameters before doing an actual hardcopy

7.
Workbench
and extras

7. Workbench and extras

The Workbench disk stores all the data you need for doing general "chores" on the Amiga. You'll find files for fonts, printer drivers, CLI commands and libraries. In addition, the Workbench disk features many other support programs and enhancements. The Extras disk also has more than just AmigaBASIC programs.

This chapter introduces you to many enhancements that should make your Workbench sessions easier and more efficient. Here you'll read about many different facets of the Workbench's Preferences program, and how you can adjust some of the parameters set in Preferences through programming. You'll even find a chart of the individual Preferences settings commented in the C language.

Section 7.2 of this chapter looks at a few of the other items on the Extras disk that aren't common knowledge to the average user. These programs also help the user be more productive with Extras data.

7.1 Preferences

The Preferences program is certainly one of the most important programs furnished with the Amiga. This program's importance lies in the amount of control it exercises over the Amiga's working environment. Preferences creates and maintains the environmental settings as specified by the user (e.g., colors, pointer shape, time, etc.). The biggest disadvantage to Preferences comes from the mere size of the program (55K). Many people just don't use Preferences because of the long loading time required to execute the program.

There are many ways to get around this. First you could copy Preferences to the RAM disk for faster access. Later versions of Workbench (1.3 included) have a reset-resistant RAM disk device named RAMB0 which usually retains data in memory after a system reset occurs, so copying Preferences to RAMB0 could be very convenient to the user.

Quite often, you'll find that some programs cannot survive without certain Preferences settings. For example, some word processors won't operate in screen modes, other than in 80-column mode. Or a game may only work with a particular color setting. The following sections will show you how to read and set Preferences data without loading the Preferences program.

7.1.1   Reading and setting Preferences data

First we'll list the Preferences structure to illustrate exactly what goes on in configuring these different parameters. The Preferences structure is presented similar to a C source code. For those of you unfamiliar with this language, we recommend that you learn C as soon as possible. For now we'll discuss the five columns below. First, the hexadecimal number of the C function's location. Then comes the decimal equivalent of the hex number, followed by the function's type and function name. The last column consists of commentary to help you understand the rest of the table, including possible contents:

```
Hex     Dec   Type    Name                   Explanation

struct Preferences
{

0x000   000   BYTE    FontHeight;            Font height: Topaz 8/9
0x001   001   UBYTE   PrinterPort;           $00=parallel, $01=serial
0x002   002   USHORT  BaudRate;              Baudrate: $00=110,
                                             $01=300, $02=1200,
                                             $03=2400, $04=4800,
                                             $05=9600, $06=19200,
                                             $07=MIDI
0x004   004   struct  timeval KeyRptSpeed;   Keyboard repeat rate
0x004   004   ULONG   tv_secs;               in seconds
0x008   008   ULONG   tv_micro;              in microseconds
0x00C   012   struct  timeval KeyRptDelay;   Delay before keyboard
                                             repeat
0x00C   012   ULONG   tv_secs;               in seconds
0x010   016   ULONG   tv_micro;              in micro-seconds
0x014   020   struct  timeval DoubleClick;   Time length of double-
                                             click
0x014   020   ULONG   tv_secs;               in seconds
0x018   024   ULONG   tv_micro;              in micro-seconds
0x01C   028   USHORT  PointerMatrix[36];     Graphic array containing
                                             mouse pointer data
0x064   100   BYTE    XOffset;               X-offset of active
                                             "click"-bit
0x065   101   BYTE    YOffset;               Y-offset of active
                                             "click"-bit
0x066   102   USHORT  color17;               RGB value sprite color 1
0x068   104   USHORT  color18;               RGB value sprite color 2
0x06A   106   USHORT  color19;               RGB value sprite color 3
0x06C   108   USHORT  PointerTicks;          Sensitivity of mouse
                                             pointer to recognizing
                                             click
0x06E   110   USHORT  color0;                RGB value of Workbench
                                             color register 0
0x070   112   USHORT  color1;                RGB value of Workbench
                                             color register 1
0x072   114   USHORT  color2;                RGB value of Workbench
                                             color register 2
0x074   116   USHORT  color3;                RGB value of Workbench
                                             color register 3
```

0x076	118	BYTE	ViewXOffset;	X-offset of top corner of Workbench screen
0x077	119	BYTE	ViewYOffset;	Y-offset of top corner of Workbench screen
0x078	120	WORD	ViewInitX;	Initialization value for ViewXOffset
0x07A	122	WORD	ViewInitY;	Initialization value for ViewYOffset
0x07C	124	BOOL	EnableCLI;	CLI status: $00=on, $01=off
0x07D	126	USHORT	PrinterType;	Printer type
0x080	128	UBYTE	PrinterFilename [FILENAME_SIZE];	Filename of custom printer driver
0x09E	158	USHORT	PrintPitch;	Font pitch: $000=Pica, $400=Elite, $800=Fine
0x0A0	160	USHORT	PrintQuality;	Print quality: $000=Draft, $100=Letter
0x0A2	162	USHORT	PrintSpacing;	Line spacing: $000=6 LPI, $200=8 LPI
0x0A4	164	UWORD	PrintLeftMargin;	Left margin
0x0A6	166	UWORD	PrintRightMargin;	Right margin
0x0A8	168	USHORT	PrintImage;	Printed image: $00=positive, $01=negative
0x0AA	170	USHORT	PrintAspect;	Print direction: $00=horizontal, $01=vertical
0x0AC	172	USHORT	PrintShade;	Graphic shading: $00=b/w, $01=gray scales, $02=color
0x0AE	174	WORD	PrintThreshold;	Degree of contrast
0x0B0	176	USHORT	PaperSize;	Paper size: $00=US Letter, $10=US Legal, $20=Narrow fanfold, $30=Wide fanfold, $40=User-assigned
0x0B2	178	UWORD	PaperLength;	Paper length in lines
0x0B4	180	USHORT	PaperType;	Paper type: $00=Fanfold, $80=Single-sheet

*** Version 1.1 ends here***

0x0B6	182	UBYTE	SerRWBits;	Number of read-write bits
0x0B7	183	UBYTE	SerStopBuf;	Number of stop bits
0x0B8	184	UBYTE	SerParShk;	Parity setting and handshake mode
0x0B9	185	UBYTE	LaceWB;	Workbench interlace status: $00=normal, $01=Interlace
0x0BA	186	UBYTE	WorkName[30];	Printer name buffer
0x0BB	187	BYTE	RowSizeChange;	User-defined line size
0x0BC	188	BYTE	ColumnSizeChange;	User-defined column size

*** Version 1.2 ends here ***

0x0BE	190	UWORD	PrintFlags;	
0x0C0	192	UWORD	PrintMaxWidth;	Maximum printable width in tenths of an inch
0x0C2	194	UWORD	PrintMaxHeight;	Maximum printable height in tenths of an inch
0x0C4	196	UBYTE	PrintDensity;	Print density

```
0x0C5  197  UBYTE  PrintXOffset;     Tabs in tenths of an inch
0x0C6  198  UWORD  wb_Width;         Width of the Workbench
                                     screen
0x0C8  200  UWORD  wb_Height;        Height of the Workbench
                                     screen
0x0CA  202  UBYTE  wb_Depth;         Bitplane depth of the
                                     Workbench screen
0x0CB  203  BYTE   ext_size;         Preferences structure
                                     extension
0x0CD  204
```

```
              /**** Version 1.3 ends here ****/
};
```

Now you know which data the `Preferences` structure accesses, but you still don't have a use for it. It would be nice if you could read the current settings, then alter and save these settings.

Here's where the utility program listed below comes in. This program allows easy BASIC access to the Preferences data using the Intuition functions. Also, this program shows how easily the user can read the structure through two simple examples.

Note: Be careful when using this program if you have Version 1.3 of the Workbench. This Workbench implementation has some expanded data fields. However, the program also runs with Kickstart 1.2.

Two Intuition functions help us perform this task. One function copies the current values into a memory location reserved by the program. You can change the data from this memory location. The second function lets you return these edited settings to Preferences for saving.

The following program changes the colors of the WorkBench screen. The ¶ characters in the following program are not to be entered, they only show where a BASIC line actually ends. When formatting the listing to fit in the book, some lines may be split that should not be. The ¶ character shows where a line actually ends.

```
'*********************************¶
'*                               *¶
'* Add Preferences Data          *¶
'* ----------------------------- *¶
'*                               *¶
'* Author : Wolf-Gideon Bleek    *¶
'* Date   : May 15 '88           *¶
'* Name   : Add-Pref.bas         *¶
'* Version: 1.1                   *¶
'* System : V1.2 & V1.3          *¶
'*                               *¶
'*********************************¶
LIBRARY "T&T2:bmaps/exec.library"¶
DECLARE FUNCTION AllocMem& LIBRARY¶
LIBRARY "T&T2:bmaps/intuition.library"¶
Mainprogram:¶
     Preferences loaded¶
```

```
        GetPreferences Prefs&, 220& ¶
        IF Prefs& = 0 THEN GOTO Ende¶
        ¶
        ' Enter new colors¶
        ¶
        Colour0 = 110¶
        Colour1 = 112¶
        Colour2 = 114¶
        ¶
        POKEW Prefs& + Colour0, 1*15+16*4+256*15¶
        POKEW Prefs& + Colour1, 1*15+16*15+256*0¶
        POKEW Prefs& + Colour2, 1*0+16*15+256*8¶
        ' Save Preferences ¶
        SetPreferences Prefs&¶
      Ende:¶
        FreePreferences Prefs&¶
        LIBRARY CLOSE¶
      END¶
      SUB GetPreferences (Address&, Size&) STATIC¶
        Address& = AllocMem&(Size&+4, 65536&)¶
          IF Address& <> 0 THEN¶
            POKEL Address&, Size&¶
            Address& = Address&+4¶
            CALL GetPrefs(Address&, Size&)¶
          ELSE¶
            Address = 0¶
          END IF¶
      END SUB¶
      SUB SetPreferences (Address&) STATIC¶
          IF Address& <> 0 THEN¶
            Size& = PEEKL(Address&-4)¶
            CALL SetPrefs(Address&, Size&, -1)¶
          END IF¶
      END SUB¶
      SUB FreePreferences (Address&) STATIC¶
          IF Address& <> 0 THEN¶
            Size& = PEEKL (Address&-4)¶
            CALL FreeMem(Address&-4, Size&+4)¶
          END IF¶
      END SUB¶
```

**Program
description**

The program uses three subroutines which calls all of the necessary Intuition functions. The first function (GetPreferences) allocates the necessary memory for the data structure and copies the data proper into this memory. In case the program encounters an error, it returns the value 0. If all went well, then the user can modify every setting in the program. Pay strict attention to the correct starting addresses (e.g., those offsets in the table listed earlier in this section), and to the correct POKE length: POKE for byte values, POKEW for word (i.e., two-byte) values and POKEL for long words (i.e., four-byte values). You get the length from the table, from which you determine the difference between the base address and the next address.

The second function (`SetPreferences`) removes data from the system memory and informs all other programs running of this change, using an identifier of -1. If you prefer not to have the other tasks know about the change, then you must insert the value 0.

The last function (`FreePreferences`) releases the memory occupied by the buffer and `Preferences`. That is important, and signifies good programming style. You should always release memory that you don't need for other programs once you've finished using it.

7.1.2   The new Preferences (Version 1.3)

No discussion of the new operating system would be complete without our mentioning the improvements and changes made to the Preferences program. Possibly the most obvious improvement lies in the upgraded printer control. First, all the printer drivers now execute much faster. A hardcopy which formerly might have taken ten minutes to print, now needs only two minutes for execution time.

Improvements have also been made to the graphic printing configuration. Preferences supported graphic printing to some extent, but not as well as it could have been supported. Now you have much more control over the graphic printout in Version 1.3. We will list the remaining changes before we go into detail in graphic selection.

Workbench screen

At first glance the changes made to the title screen don't look very impressive. For example, the `CLI` gadget gone. You can now work with in the `CLI` without having to go in to click a gadget to activate it first (a change that we believe was long overdue).

One internal improvement that may not be noticeable is in the clock. The setting is passed to the battery-powered realtime clock, so the clock updates whenever you select the Save gadget in this window. That's a great advantage for all 500 and 2000 owners.

A back door to Preferences

Preferences has one extra improvement—the addition of a "back door" to the Preferences program. Just as you have a back door to a house, which allows easier access to the building, Preferences has a rear entrance for users to make a quick change.

Here's an example. You have a new printer and need to test out the printer driver settings until you determine the correct combinations. To do this you would normally select Preferences, change the data in the Change Printer screen and exit Preferences. This operation gets troublesome after a while, since you have to repeatedly select Preferences and Change Printer, change parameters, exit Preferences, test print, select Preferences, and so on.

Workbench 1.3 stores Preferences in a drawer named `Prefs`. If you double-click on this drawer, it opens, revealing the Preferences icon and four additional icons. Three of these icons allow direct access to different sections of Preferences without having to access Preferences itself initially. These icons are as follows:

Pointer   Allows direct access to the Edit Pointer window.
Printer   Allows direct access to the Change Printer window.
Serial   Allows direct access to the Change Serial window.

Select one of these icons. Select the Info item from the Workbench menu to view the Info screen for the icon. Notice that the Default Tool gadget states `Sys:Prefs/Preferences`, and the Tool Types gadget states `Prefs=Icon_name` (`Icon_name` represents either `Printer`, `Serial` or `Pointer`). These specifications tell the Workbench to move to the desired window for changes. This takes much less time than going through Preferences first. If you want to start Preferences from the `CLI`, you can just enter the individual arguments after the word `Preferences`:

Preferences [pointer|printer|serial]

Two other icons can be seen in the Prefs drawer. You'll use the one often, and may never use the other:

Preferences   Accesses the Preferences program.
CopyPrefs   Copies the configuration made by Preferences to
                DF0:DEVS (useful for hard disk systems that
                don't autoboot).

Printing graphics Now, double-click the Printer icon in the Prefs drawer. The Change Printer window appears. You'll note that this window contains two gadgets for selecting graphic modes—Graphic 1 and Graphic 2.

Graphic 1 Clicking the Graphic 1 gadget has the same effect as clicking the Graphic Select gadget in Workbench 1.2's Change Printer window. A window appears, listing the parameters for selecting different print parameters: `Aspect`, `Image`, `Shade` and `Threshold`. Note the gadget in the `Shade` parameter that wasn't in Workbench 1.2:

Gray Scale2   Supplies extended four-shade gray scaling (the
                Commodore-Amiga A2024 monitor supports
                this degree of gray scaling).

Graphic 2   Clicking the Graphic 2 gadget takes us into a new window. This window lists additional gadgets for greatly improved printed graphic control.

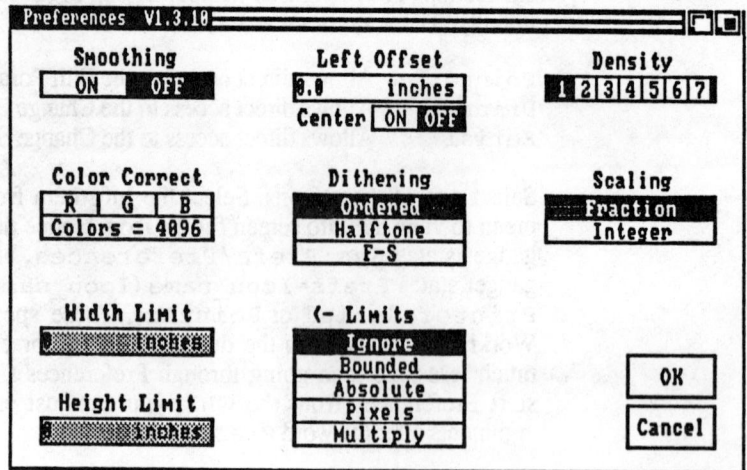

```
╔═════════════════════════════════════════════════════════╗
║ Preferences  V1.3.10                              ▢▣▢    ║
║                                                          ║
║    Smoothing          Left Offset          Density       ║
║   ┌────┬─────┐      ┌──────────────┐    ┌─────────────┐   ║
║   │ ON │ OFF │      │0.0    inches │    │1│2│3│4│5│6│7│   ║
║   └────┴─────┘      └──────────────┘    └─────────────┘   ║
║                     Center ┌──┬───┐                      ║
║                            │ON│OFF│                      ║
║                            └──┴───┘                      ║
║   Color Correct         Dithering          Scaling       ║
║   ┌───┬───┬───┐      ┌───────────┐      ┌───────────┐     ║
║   │ R │ G │ B │      │  Ordered  │      │  Fraction │     ║
║   ├───┴───┴───┤      ├───────────┤      ├───────────┤     ║
║   │Colors=4096│      │  Halftone │      │  Integer  │     ║
║   └───────────┘      ├───────────┤      └───────────┘     ║
║                      │    F-S    │                        ║
║                      └───────────┘                        ║
║   Width Limit          (- Limits                          ║
║   ┌────────────┐     ┌───────────┐                        ║
║   │░░░░inches░░│     │  Ignore   │                        ║
║   └────────────┘     ├───────────┤                        ║
║                      │  Bounded  │      ┌─────────┐       ║
║                      ├───────────┤      │   OK    │       ║
║   Height Limit       │  Absolute │      └─────────┘       ║
║   ┌────────────┐     ├───────────┤                        ║
║   │░░░░inches░░│     │  Pixels   │      ┌─────────┐       ║
║   └────────────┘     ├───────────┤      │ Cancel  │       ║
║                      │  Multiply │      └─────────┘       ║
║                      └───────────┘                        ║
╚═════════════════════════════════════════════════════════╝
```

Preference 1.3 Graphic 2 Screen

Smoothing   This function enables the smoothing of diagonal lines. In many cases, printed diagonal lines may have the "jaggies" (a jagged appearance) in some Amiga graphic applications. Click the ON gadget to enable it and the OFF gadget to disable it. The Smoothing function defaults to OFF.

Note: You cannot have smoothing enabled at the same time you have F-S dithering enabled (see the paragraph entitled Dithering below). If you select F-S then select Smoothing ON, the dithering mode changes to Ordered.

Left Offset   Now look at the next function to the right. The Left Offset parameter controls the left margin of the graphic (if you want one). If you enter 0.0 inches (default setting) no left offset occurs.

Note: Selecting the Center ON parameter (see below) disables Left Offset.

Density   The Density parameter controls the density (darkness) of the printout. A higher density requires more printing time. The lower the density setting, the faster the printing. Density 1 is the default setting.

Color Correct   This parameter attempts to control color compensation in printing. Either the red (R), blue (B) or green (G) shades appear on the printer as on the screen. The normal amount of color available is 4096 colors. However, this amount decreases if you select color correct. Color correct can often produce a better output. Default is no color correction (none of the three gadgets is selected).

Dithering

Dithering can be defined as another form of color control. Dithering prints different color dots close together so that the multiple colors appear to the naked eye as one color. You have three options for dithering:

| Ordered | This enables dithering in an orderly pattern of printed dots. |

| Halftone | This enables dithering in halftone style, similar to the method used in printing newspapers, comic books and other media of this type. |

| F — S | F-S stands for Floyd-Steinberg. F-S refers to the Floyd-Steinberg error distribution method, which takes a set of points to be combined into one color and randomizes the dithering slightly. If you don't have a color printer to see a Floyd-Steinberg configured printout, you should see one sometime—it's really interesting. |

Scaling

Earlier Workbench graphic printouts all came out in the same size and format, regardless of the size of the original graphic. Workbench 1.3 provides two scaling modes:

| Fraction | Executes normal scaling as found on Workbench 1.2. |

| Integer | Enables different sized printouts as specified in the Width Limit and Height Limit gadgets. For example, if you enter ones in both these gadgets, the graphic appears in 1:1 scaling. Entering higher values doubles and triples the scaling. If you enter 0 in each gadget, the printout appears at the size of the sheet as was stated by selecting Fraction. |

< - Limits

This last function specifies the given graphic measurement limits, as stated in the Width Limit and Height Limit gadgets. You can choose from one of five limiting modes:

| Ignore | Ignores given values and prints the graphic in the normal format specified by the application used to create the graphic. |

| Bounded | Sets the maximum measurements as specified by Width Limit and Height Limit. Many graphics may print in smaller sizes than specified due to distortion. |

| Absolute | Sets the measurements as absolute values in increments of one-tenth of an inch. For example, A Height Limit of 40 and Width Limit of 50 prints a graphic four inches high by five inches wide. |

| Pixels | Similar to Absolute, except that values are read in pixels instead of tenths of an inch. |

Multiply | Similar to Absolute. However, Multiply allows a printout in multiples of original graphic size, as specified in the Height Limit and Width Limit gadgets. For example, if you have a Height Limit of 2 and Width Limit of 3, the printout appears twice the normal height and three times the normal width. These settings vary with the original graphic size. If the original was 320x200, the printout here would be 640 pixels wide by 600 pixels high.

These are the additions to The Version 1.3 implementation of Preferences. If you don't quite get the printout you intended, keep experimenting. Practice makes perfect, and this saying is very true in printing graphics. If you haven't yet bought a printer, we recommend that you ensure that the printer you're buying has a matching printer driver included in Workbench 1.3.

Note: If you can't find the driver for your printer, look on the Extras disk: There are a few printer drivers that the Amiga developers couldn't fit on the Workbench disk. You'll find these other drivers on the Extras disk instead.

7.1.3   The 1.3 Utilities drawer

In addition to system data and work environment control, the Workbench disk contains a number of utility programs. Utilities are useful and helpful programs that aid the user in programming or other tasks. You'll find these utilities in the Utilities drawer of the Workbench disk.

Double-click the Utilities drawer to open it. Many of the programs carried over from Version 1.2 underwent some upgrading for Version 1.3. New additions include extra parameters and settings, and little known methods of CLI access.

Clock parameters from CLI You can set the clock parameters easily from menus. However, every time you reboot the Workbench, all the parameters return to their original status. You can control the clock parameters using a new CLI command named Clock.

The argument template for Clock looks like this:

```
CLOCK [ANALOG|DIGITAL1|DIGITAL2] [=<x>,<y>[,<width>,
<height>]] [12HOUR|24HOUR] [SECONDS] [DATE]
```

The arguments represent the following:

ANALOG|DIGITAL1|DIGITAL2
>Specifies one of the three clock types available from the Workbench (default=ANALOG).

<x>,<y>
>Specifies clock placement on the screen. <x> represents the number of horizontal pixels from the left screen border; <y> represents the number of vertical pixels from the top of the screen (default=10,15).

<width>,<height>
>Specifies the height and width of the analog clock only. Digital clocks ignore the <height> and <width> arguments.

12HOUR|24HOUR
>Specifies the AM/PM (12-hour) or military (24-hour) clock type (default=12HOUR).

SECONDS
>Enables or disables seconds display (default=OFF).

DATE
>Enables or disables date display (default=OFF).

The following CLI command displays the time and date during the current Workbench session:

```
Utilities/Clock DIGITAL2 24HOUR DATE
```

ClockPtr
You can execute ClockPtr by executing or running the program from the CLI or by double-clicking its icon. When you access ClockPtr, the pointer changes into a digital clock whenever the pointer rests on the Workbench screen. ClockPtr can display different time parameters. Moving the pointer to the left side of the Workbench screen displays minutes and seconds; moving the pointer to the right side of the screen displays hours and minutes.

To disable ClockPtr, press <Ctrl><C> if you started it using Execute from the CLI, enter Break if you started it using Run from the CLI, or double-click the icon again if you started it from the Workbench.

CMD
This new program sends CMD_WRITE output to a file that would normally be sent to a parallel or serial output device. This command has great potential for user control. A CMD_WRITE transfers data to a printer, whether through the CLI or through program control.

The argument template for CMD looks like the following:

```
CMD <devicename><filename>[OPT s|m|n]
```

181

The arguments are as follows:

`<devicename><filename>`
> Specify the original parallel or serial device (`<devicename>`) and the file to which you want the information sent (`<filename>`). You cannot use PAR: or SER: as device names.

`OPT s`
> Do not execute any short initial write (usually occurs after a reset). The short initial write sets the printer to its power-up status in some printer drivers. You won't need this mode for sending data to a file. So, if your printer driver sends this code, use s.

`OPT m`
> Use with multiple files until `Break` occurs or `<Ctrl><C>` is pressed. `Cmd` normally disables itself after writing a file. This option keeps the command open for writing more than one file or copies of the same file.

`OPT n`
> Enable notify mode. This mode keeps the user informed of progress during the file transfer.

Install Printer

You'll recall reading a bit earlier about the printer drivers placed on the Extras disk, since the Workbench disk didn't have enough room on it. You'll also remember reading earlier about the `IconX` configured script file named `InstallPrinter`. `InstallPrinter` copies a printer driver from the Extras disk to the appropriate directory on the Workbench disk (the DEVS: directory).

You can execute this program from the `CLI` or double-click its icon. The program displays a list of printer drivers available on the Extras disk. Enter the name of the desired driver at the prompt (you may use wildcards if you wish to copy more than one driver) and press the `<Return>` key. This script file copies the driver to the DEVS: directory and adds the driver name to the list found in the `Change Printer` window of Preferences. Press the `<Return>` key without entering any driver names if you wish to exit `InstallPrinter` without copying any drivers.

More

This command lets you display ASCII text files on the screen. You can access `More` from either the `CLI` or from the Workbench. The `CLI` syntax:

`More <filename>`

To access `More` from the Workbench, double-click the `More` icon. If you wish to access an icon equipped text file direct from `More`, click once on the `More` icon, press and hold the `<Shift>` key and double-click the text icon you want to read.

The following keys move you through the text file:

<Space>	next page
<Backspace>	previous page
<Return>	next line
<<>	(less than) first page of file
<>>	(greater than) last page of file
<%n>	display the n% segment of the file
<Ctrl><L>	refresh window
</><string>	execute case sensitive search of characters following the </> character (e.g., /March will not find march)
<.><string>	execute non-case-sensitive search of string following the <.> character (e.g., .March will find both March and march)
<n>	find next occurrence of string stated in either </> or <.>
<h>	help list
<q>	(or <Ctrl><C>) quit
<E>	edit with editor found in the ENV:EDITOR variable

More displays the percentage of the file at the bottom of the screen. When you reach the end of the file, the message changes to −Less−.

When you access More using the CLI or Shell, you can access an editor immediately for editing the file you're viewing, provided that the ENV:EDITOR variable contains a specification. This variable should contain the correct editor path (e.g., C:ED). If ENV:EDITOR is defined, press <Shift><E> to invoke the editor.

PrintFiles This command copies files to your printer. You can print more than one file at a time by accessing the file from the CLI and using the multiple file arguments.

You can access PrintFiles from the Workbench or from the CLI. The argument template for the CLI command looks like this:

```
PrintFiles [-f]<filename>[[-f]<filename>][[-f]<filename>]…
```

The arguments are as follows:

-f   Enables form feed mode. This mode adds a form feed between each file and at the end of the file or set. You can enable this mode from the Workbench by selecting Printfiles's info screen and entering FLAGS=formfeed in the TOOL TYPES gadget.

<filename>
    Specifies the name of the file(s) you want printed.

If you want to access PrintFiles from the Workbench, click on the icon of the file you want printed. Press and hold the <Shift> key and click on any other file icons you want printed. Continue to hold the <Shift> key and double-click on the Printfiles icon.

7.1.3.1   Other Workbench 1.3 utilities

Graphic
Dump

This command does a screen dump of the Intuition screen in the fore-ground to the printer. The 1.3 version of GraphicDump allows you to specify the size of the screen dump.

You can access GraphicDump either by double-clicking its icon or by accessing it from the CLI. The argument template for the CLI implementation of GraphicDump looks like this:

GraphicDump [TINY|SMALL|MEDIUM|LARGE|xdots:ydots]

The arguments are as follows:

TINY   Prints the screen dump about one quarter the size of the printable width (height adjusts proportionately).

SMALL   Prints the screen dump about one half the size of the printable width (height adjusts proportionately).

MEDIUM Prints the screen dump about three quarters the size of the printable width (height adjusts proportionately).

LARGE   Prints the screen dump the full printable width (height adjusts proportionately). This is the default value when you access graphicDump from the Workbench.

7.2 Tools on the Extras disk

We mentioned a few pages back that the Extras disk contains more than just AmigaBASIC. You can find a few extra printer drivers on this disk (accessible from the `InstallPrinter` script file), and a number of additional utility programs. This section discusses a number of them found on Extras 1.3. Look in the `Tools` directory for these:

FED

FED is the abbreviation for Font EDitor. This utility lets you either change existing fonts or create your own.

Note:

Two warnings about FED. First, never experiment with the fonts on your original Workbench disk. Second, FED cannot edit fonts any larger than 32 pixels by 32 pixels.

You can access FED by double-clicking on its icon. A window appears containing gadgets and characters. The following is a list of the menu names, their items and the available gadgets.

Project

This menu provides you with file management. The following items are available:

New	Clears available fonts in memory.
Open	Allows the user to open a font from disk.
Save	Saves the current font to disk.
Save As	Saves the current font to disk under a new name.
About	An info screen—tells you who wrote FED.
Quit	Quits FED and returns you to the Workbench.

Edit

This menu provides editing facilities for the *entire* font (you cannot change just one letter, and some edits may be irreversible).

Make italic	Italicizes font.
Make bold	Bolds font.
Make underlined	Underlines font.
Copy to	Copies character from one box to another box. Select the character you want copied. Select Copy to and select the box to which you want the character copied. Copy mode is enabled until you select Copy to again.
Erase	Deletes the character from the box selected.
All right	Moves all characters of the font to the right by one pixel.
All left	Moves all characters of the font to the left by one pixel.
All up	Moves all characters of the font up by one pixel.
All down	Moves all characters of the font down by one pixel.

Attributes   This menu provides facilities for setting the font's type and style bits.

> **Font type**   You can select either Proportional spacing or Fixed width spacing.
>
> **Font style**   Choose from Normal, Italic, Bold, Underlined or Extended style. Most fonts work best in Normal style.
>
> **Rendering**   Choose from Forward or Reverse.

KeyToy2000   This utility displays the current global keymap. The first screen display shows unshifted keyboard output. If you want to see keys displayed through the use of <Shift>, <Ctrl>, etc., click on the appropriate gadget in the KeyToy window, or press the appropriate key on the keyboard.

Here are a few "ground rules" in using `KeyToy2000`:

- Blue labeled keys cannot be accessed by `KeyToy` (the <CTRL> <SHIFT> and <ALT> keys can be accessed.)

- Yellow labeled keys cannot be accessed (the <Caps Lock> key and the <Commodore> and right <Amiga> keys).

- $$-labeled keys contain strings with more than one character.

- Characters beginning with ^ or ~ are control characters.

- Blank labeled keys are undefined.

Memory display   You have three options for displaying memory. The first option displays available memory when on the Workbench screen. This has a couple of disadvantages. First, this screen can supersede any other windows or screens. In addition, this memory display appears only when the Workbench screen is active. The Extras disk includes two utility programs written expressly for displaying free memory.

FreeMap   FreeMap creates a new screen and graphically displays the memory allocation. This screen displays both chip RAM and fast RAM. Older versions of `FreeMap` only displayed chip RAM, so the fast RAM display is a new addition. `FreeMap` also shows how the memory is divided into segments when multiple tasks are running in memory. The output is graphic.

The `Info` menu displays a description of how `FreeMap` displays memory. Select the `Please` item from the `Quit` menu to exit `FreeMap`.

PerfMon   PerfMon is a performance monitor program that indicates both free
chip RAM and free fast RAM. A peculiarity is that both displays show
the amount of processor time currently in use. It's interesting to see in
what way the 68000 is used or unused. A black line indicates the max-
imum ideal configuration. Some disadvantages to PerfMon: It uses its
own window and chip RAM, as well as its own text window on the
screen.

Palette   This tool allows the user to change screen colors. Unlike Preferences,
which limits itself to the Workbench colors, Palette offers you
access to any color in the Amiga's available spectrum. You can open
Palette by double-clicking its icon or by accessing it from the CLI.

The argument template for accessing Palette from the CLI looks
like this:

Palette [<bitplanes>][<screentype>]

The arguments represent the following:

bitplanes
    Specifies the bitplane depth involved in the new color palette
    setting. 1 gives you two colors; 2 gives you four colors; 3 gives
    you eight colors; 4 gives you 16 colors; and 5 gives you 32
    colors.

screentype
    Specifies the resolution of the screen currently being tested. 0
    gives a resolution of 320x200 pixels; 1 gives an interlaced reso-
    lution of 320x400 pixels; 2 gives a resolution of 640x200
    pixels; and 3 gives an interlaced resolution of 640x400 pixels.

The window displayed by Palette has a number of gadgets and
sliders allowing user color control.

Note: Palette color changes are temporary—you cannot currently save this
information to disk.

MEMACS   This is another item in the Tools: directory of the Extras disk, it is a
text editor. Many versions of MEMACS (short for MicroEmacs) exist for
many different brands of computers. MEMACS is a screen oriented text
editor which is much more powerful than ED. It allows you to edit
more than one file at a time, providing that enough RAM exists for
you to have all those multiple programs in memory.

You can execute MEMACS by double-clicking the Workbench icon, or
by access from the CLI. The argument template for MEMACS looks
like this:

Memacs [<filename>][goto <n>][OPT W]

The arguments represent the following:

[<filename>]
    Specifies the file you want loaded into MEMACS.

[goto <n>]
    Moves the cursor to line n of filename.

[OPT W]
    Places MEMACS in a Workbench window.

MEMACS allows the use of both key combinations and mouse access. The menus are self-explanatory, but be sure to look at the keyboard shortcuts listed on the menus. The beauty of MEMACS is that the keyboard shortcuts are the same on any machine it is running on. This means that if you learn to use the keyboard shortcuts on the Amiga version, you will know how to operate an IBM or UNIX version of MEMACS.

8.
Personalizing the Workbench

8. Personalizing the Workbench

You may have wondered about the possibility of changing the Workbench messages to give your Workbench the "personal" touch. Or perhaps you wanted to change the Workbench texts to another language other than English. It's not as easy as changing a BASIC program, but it can be done.

This chapter shows Amiga 1000 owners how you can change the Workbench texts. All you need are a backup copy of the Kickstart disk and a disk monitor. Use <u>backups</u> of Kickstart and Workbench! Do NOT use your originals when editing important files.

If you've never used a disk monitor, these programs allow you to read, edit and write blocks of disk memory. If you don't have a disk monitor, look for one in the public domain. Many such programs are available, under titles like `Diskmon` or `TSEditor`. Or if you prefer, get the disk monitor listed in Abacus' *Amiga Disk Drives Inside and Out*. Learn the essentials of using a disk monitor <u>before</u> starting this project, since one error in typing could destroy data.

Note: **The instructions in this chapter are intended for the Amiga 1000 Kickstart disk only.** Those of you who own Amiga 500 and 2000 models have Kickstart in ROM, so you can't easily change that. If you really want to edit your Kickstart ROM, you'll have to somehow extract the ROM code using a machine language monitor, change that code and burn it into a new EPROM. You'll probably have to find someone who has expertise in EPROM burning and machine language to do this for you, if you don't have the experience yourself. Amiga 500 and 2000 users may prefer to skip this chapter. However, you can still learn a great deal about the workings of Kickstart by reading this chapter.

8.1   Making preparations

First let's go through the parts list one more time. You need the following equipment to make these changes to the Kickstart disk:

Kickstart backup

We repeat, **do not use your original Kickstart disk for this project.** Take your Kickstart disk, enable the write protect and make a backup or two of the disk. Use the `Duplicate` item from the Workbench menu, or use the `Diskcopy` command from the `CLI`. Once you've made backups put your original Kickstart disk away. Use the backup for making changes, and keep the second backup handy in case you accidentally destroy the backup currently in use. In fact, making more than two backups is always a good idea for any disk.

Disk monitor

As described above, disk monitors read data from a disk (usually in increments of a sector). You can examine this data, edit it and write it back to the disk.

You can find disk monitor programs from a number of sources. Many public domain disks have disk monitors, and a number of books contain listings for powerful monitors in C, AmigaBASIC and machine language.

One necessary feature the disk monitor must have: It must be capable of displaying the data in ASCII characters, and allow text entry into the disk block. The disk monitor program in the Abacus book *Amiga Disk Drives Inside and Out* has this ability and is the one we used when preparing this book to modify our KickStart disks.

You do not need the Workbench disk for the modifications. Your inclination might be to look on the Workbench disk for the texts. If you haven't looked there yet, we'll tell you right now that you won't find the texts needed on the Workbench disk. The Kickstart disk (or ROM) contains any messages that go into the operating system. These messages load during the booting process. Therefore, you only need the Workbench disk when you test out your new system.

Here are a few ground rules which you should know while editing your backup Kickstart disk:

1)   <u>Always</u> use backups whenever using a disk monitor to write disk blocks. If you use original disks, you risk destroying important data. Certain areas of disks shouldn't be tampered with, one error could render an entire disk useless for anything other than reformatting.

2)   When writing to disk, test boot the disk often at first (after every change works well). This way if something goes wrong, you can at least figure out when the problem arose. As you gain confidence in editing disks, you can test reboot less often.

3)   Use compatible versions of Workbench and Kickstart (i.e., 1.2 Kickstart with 1.2 Workbench, 1.3 Kickstart with 1.3 Workbench). Intermixing versions of Kickstart and Workbench may cause problems.

4)   When rebooting with a modified Kickstart, the Amiga does an internal checksum to see if Kickstart is compatible with itself. A "normal" Kickstart disk invokes the Workbench hand icon when you reset the computer. However, a modified Kickstart disk will cause the system to ask for the Kickstart disk. This is perfectly normal—just keep both Kickstart and Workbench handy when booting up and rebooting.

5)   Take your time when using a disk monitor. One misplaced space or character can crash the system. Just take the time to observe the structure of a text, and keep that structure the same length. If you rush the editing process, the odds of making a major error increase. Take it slowly and carefully.

So much for the warnings. Let's do some disk editing.

8.2 Getting started with text editing

We've got the groundwork done. Now let's get started with the editorial process. We can now begin with looking for the texts we want changed. Section 8.3 give a complete listing of the texts.

8.2.1 Starting messages and the `AmigaDOS` window

Boot up your monitor and do whatever you have to do to read your Kickstart backup. Read block 454 decimal ($01c5 hexadecimal) for Kickstart 1.2 and block 453 decimal ($01c4 hex) for Kickstart 1.3. Look for some system names like LIBS, DEVS or FONTS (you may have to scroll up and down through the blocks until you find the text mentioned here, depending on the type of Kickstart you have). Now search for the following text in this block or the block immediately following this block:

```
CON:0/0/640/200/AmigaDOS
```

This line opens a console window named AmigaDOS. That's the first thing you see as the Workbench does its task. This creates the window during booting, before the screen appears in AmigaDOS. This command configuration sets the window height at 200 pixels, the standard value for American (NTSC video) Amigas. If you have a PAL video Amiga (the European standard), you can change the Y value from 200 to 256. Or if you prefer, you can make your AmigaDOS window smaller. For instance, we changed the 200 to 150. The altered line should now look like this:

```
CON:0/0/640/150/AmigaDOS
```

Make your changes and write the block back to the disk. Exit the disk monitor. Turn the computer off for ten seconds. Turn it on again and try booting with the modified Kickstart disk. The Amiga eventually asks for the Workbench disk. Insert the Workbench disk as usual. The AmigaDOS window should appear on the screen, about 3/4 the height of the original window. This may not seem like much of an accomplishment, but better things are coming.

Turn the computer off for ten seconds and remove the experimental disks. Turn it back on and reboot with the Kickstart and Workbench disks you normally use. Execute the disk monitor again.

Let's do our first real text modification—change the name of the AmigaDOS window to something else. Read the block you modified earlier (454 decimal [$01c5 hex] for most versions of 1.2, and 453 decimal [$01c4 hex] for versions of 1.3). Look again for the following text (you modified this line earlier to reduce the size of the AmigaDOS window):

```
CON:0/0/640/150/AmigaDOS
```

The Abacus product development department has a favorite user named Elmer who's been a noted media personality since the 1930s. His accent is—well, unusual. We'll change the AmigaDOS window title to match Elmer's personal DOS. The new name can be whatever we want, just as long as the new name is the same length as or shorter than the number of characters present in the existing name. **Do not make your replacement texts any longer than the originals. If the text is shorter, pad it to the proper length using spaces.** Here are some examples of correct text replacements and incorrect text replacements:

Original	`CON:0/0/640/150/AmigaDOS`
Correct	`CON:0/0/640/150/FredDOS`
Correct	`CON:0/0/640/150/Doug_DOS`
Incorrect!!	`CON:0/0/640/150/Richard_DOS`

AmigaDOS occupies eight characters. Change the window title to read as follows:

```
CON:0/0/640/150/ElmerDOS
```

Make your changes and write the block back to the disk.

Exit the disk monitor. Turn the computer off for ten seconds. Turn it on again and try booting with the modified Kickstart disk. The Kickstart eventually asks for the Workbench disk. Insert the Workbench disk as usual. The new DOS window should appear on the screen with the title ElmerDOS instead of AmigaDOS. If the system crashes, turn the computer off and reboot with the regulation Kickstart and Workbench.

Turn the computer off for ten seconds and remove the experimental disks. Turn it back on and reboot with the Kickstart and Workbench disks you normally use. Execute the disk monitor again.

Read the block you read when you changed the ElmerDOS title (454 decimal or so). Let's change the copyright message. Look for one of the following texts:

```
Copyright . 1985, 1986 Commodore-Amiga
Copyright . 1988 Commodore-Amiga
```

Change this text to read as follows (don't touch the period between the word Copyright and the copyright year—it's machine code, and not just a period):

```
Copywight . 1988, 1989 Commodore-Amiga
Copywight . 1989 Commodore-Amiga
```

Write that block to disk as usual. Now look for one of the following texts (you may have to scroll around to the next block to find it):

```
All rights reserved..Release 1.2
All rights reserved..Release 1.3
```

Change this to:

```
All wights weserved..Wewease 1.2
All wights weserved..Wewease 1.3
```

Write this block to disk. Now turn off the computer for ten seconds and do an experimental bootup. Watch the screen carefully, and look at your efforts. Congratulations; you now have an alpha version of ElmerDOS!

As we said above, you can change the messages to whatever you want (limited only by line length) later, but do it our way for the moment. It may seem silly now, but once you get accustomed to this process, you can handle it easily.

8.2.2   Changing the title bar and menus

Most of the Workbench's functions are accessible through menus. You can also change these menu titles and items to your own needs, or to make them understandable to people who speak in other languages.

Let's continue with our ElmerDOS concept. If you boot the disk monitor, you'll find the menu texts beginning at block 384 decimal in Kickstart 1.2. and at block 383 decimal in Kickstart 1.3. There you'll see the Workbench's menu title and its menu items. The other menu titles and items are in this block and the next block. Before thinking about overwriting these, remember that the new name must be no longer than the original, and that a shorter name may be padded with ending spaces.

One item of interest before we continue: Look for the last item of the Special menu (Version). If you look a few characters past that item, you'll see a number of blank spaces. This is actually another menu. This other menu comes into play when an error occurs. The Amiga jumps to a debugger in the Kickstart ROM which allows the user to examine the error in detail, providing that a terminal is connected to the Amiga's RS-232 interface.

You can enable this menu and call the data from here. This only makes sense if you're a developer—the average Amiga user doesn't need this menu.

To use this hidden menu, you must add the word Debug to the loadWB command in the startup sequence. You'll also have to insert the word Debug in the blank spaces. For now we'll skip this item and continue with the menus that apply to the everyday user. If you want more information about the Debug menu, see the *Amiga ROM Kernel Reference Manual: Exec* from Commodore-Amiga for details on ROM-Wack and this menu.

8.2.3   New menu items and messages

Maybe you have the ambition to translate the menu titles and items into a foreign language. Or perhaps just change the names to something more "fun." This can be interesting—renaming menu items to humorous functions or foreign languages.

Just by scrolling through the disk blocks, you can see that the Amiga has many, many menu items and messages. We are only going to concentrate on the most important ones in this chapter. If you wish to explore on your own, you'll find a collection of these and other messages listed at the end of this section.

Any time you work with the Amiga, the Workbench screen is active. You can only work with the Workbench if the startup sequence loaded it using LoadWB. In any case, the screen title bar reads Workbench Screen.

Let's continue customizing the Kickstart for ElmerDOS. Select block 247 for Kickstart 1.2 (block 245 for Kickstart 1.3). Look for the following screen:

```
Workbench Screen
```

Change it to the following:

```
Wuhkbench Scween
```

Write the block to disk as usual. You may want to reboot and see how well the new Kickstart is holding up. If nothing crashes, we can continue.

The title bar of the Workbench screen lies in block 359. It reads as follows:

```
Workbench release 1.2.  %ld free memory
```

When you make the change to this text, do so with extreme caution! The period, two spaces, %ld and space are statements specific to C. These statements allocate room for the system to insert the number of bytes free. Leave these characters intact! Now, change this line to match our current ElmerDOS Kickstart:

```
Wuhkbench wewease 1.2.  %ld fwee memowy
```

Write the block to disk.

Let's go in and change some menu items. Remember, the menu texts start at block 384 decimal (Kickstart 1.2.) or at block 383 decimal (Kickstart 1.3.). You'll see the Workbench menu listed as follows:

```
Workbench.Open.Close.Duplicate.Rename..Info..Discard..
```

Convert it to ElmerDOS by changing this text to the following (notice the two spaces used to pad the replacement for Discard:

```
Wuhkbench.Opun.Cwose.Dupwicate.Wename..Huh?..Bwast  ..
```

Write the block back to disk as usual.

Now, look for the Disk menu title. It should read as follows:

```
Disk..Empty Trash.Initialize
```

Change it to read:

```
Disk..Empty Twash.Initiawize
```

Remember, do not touch the periods separating the menu titles and items. Write the block to disk.

Now for the Special menu (which may be spread over the course of two blocks on your Kickstart). The original reads:

```
Special.Clean Up..Last Error..Redraw..Snapshot..Version
```

Change it to the following (remember to leave the periods alone):

```
Special.Cwean Up..Wast Ewwow..Wedraw..Snapshot..Wuhsion
```

Write the block to disk and do a test reboot. Pull down each menu and see the result.

We should also change the requester called by the replacement for Discard (Bwast). Go to block 385 (Kickstart 1.2) or block 383 (Kickstart 1.3). The original text:

```
Warning: you..cannot get back.what you discard.
```

Change it to the following (remember to leave the periods alone):

```
Warning: you..cannot get back.what you bwast! .
```

Write the block to disk.

We need to modify the gadgets for this requester message. Go to block 381 (Kickstart 1.2) or block 379 (Kickstart 1.3). Here you'll find the text for the gadgets used by the discard requester:

```
ok to discard.forget it!
```

Replace this text with the following (notice the padding spaces after bwast):

```
ok to bwast  .fawget it!
```

Write the block to disk. Do a test reboot. Open the Workbench disk icon. Click once on a file icon and select the Bwast item from the Wuhkbench menu. The following requester should appear:

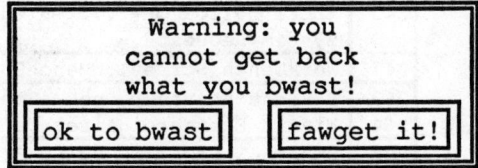

```
┌─────────────────────────────────────┐
│            Warning: you             │
│          cannot get back            │
│          what you bwast!            │
│ ┌─────────────┐   ┌─────────────┐   │
│ │ ok to bwast │   │ fawget it!  │   │
│ └─────────────┘   └─────────────┘   │
└─────────────────────────────────────┘
```

Click on the fawget it! gadget to exit without bwasting (discarding) the file.

This should give you some idea of the basics of changing your Kickstart disk. The ElmerDOS example given here was intended as a generic tutorial on editing the disk. Now you can customize your own Kickstart disk.

8.3 A guide to Kickstart messages

The following is a list of messages available on your Kickstart disk. The entry begins with the block number as found on our Kickstart 1.2 disk (other Kickstart disks may require some scrolling up or down by a block or two). Then follows the text itself. Just remember that your replacement texts can be no longer than the original texts. Shorter replacement texts must be padded using spaces or punctuation marks.

Some of these messages may not be visible by any means other than access through a disk monitor. However, we chose to include a few of them just to show you what's on your disk that you might not ordinarily be aware of.

Blk.	Message
25-	Not enough memory
26	.&.Software failure. .&.Recoverable Alert. Press left mouse button to continue Guru Meditation # ...
26	ROM Wack commands: alter.boot.clear.fill.find.go. iq.limit.list.regs.reset.resume.set.show.user.
56	The Amiga Wizards bring this power to you
245	=LEFT BUTTON OK=.....=RIGHT BUTTON CANCEL= System Request
247	Workbench Screen..WBenchPort
263-	Brought to you by not a mere Wizard, but the
264	Wizard Extraordinaire: Dale Luck!
292	DMC68343 FLOATING POINT FIRMWARE(C) COPYRIGHT 1981 BY MOTOROLA INC.
341	read error %ld, track %d
348	Please insert volume..in any drive Retry.Cancel
349	Error while ...
351	examining directory.accessing %s.opening %s. reading.writing.moving %s.removing %s.examining %s.. writing %s.
353	This drawer is not really a directory
358	Can't rename this disk
359	Workbench release 1.2. %ld free memory
373	SYS:System/DiskCopy
375	Icons cannot be moved into this window
376	This disk cannot be copied
378	'%s' cannot be moved out of its window.. Disks are of incompatible type and cannot be copied
381	OK to discard.forget it! Kickstart version %ld.%ld. Workbench Version %ld.%ld
384	Info not available Workbench Open Close Duplicate Rename Info Discard

Blk.	Message
384– 385	Disk Empty Trash Initialize Special Clean up Last Error Redraw SnapShot Version Debug.flushlibs Warning: you..cannot get back.what you discard
391	Cannot read info file %s
394	Enter the new name. Press return when done... Do not use '%lc' in names Ran out of memory. Please free some and try again
396	DOS
401	The icon(s) have no default tool
407	This drawer cannot be opened
418	kodiak andy carl Initial CLI
422– 423	Disk corrupt - task held Software Error - task held Finish ALL disk activity Select CANCEL to reset/debug
425	Retry.Cancel
426	Fault.Error code %N
428	Volume..in Unit 0x!!.. is not validated is write protected.. Please replace volume... in any drive.... is full..... Not a DOS disk.. No disk present..... has a read/write error.. You MUST replace volume
432	Please insert volume....in any drive
454– 455	SYS.:...LIBS....DEVS....FONTS...C...L...S...DFX.CLI Restart.FileHandler. CON:0/0/640/200/AmigaDOS Copyright . 1985, 1986 Commodore Amiga, Inc.. All rights reserved.. Release 1.2 :S/STARTUP-SEQUENCE
456	CON.RAW.SER.PAR.PRT devs:system-configuration
460	*** BREAK-CLI c:..Unknown command %S Unable to load %S .%S failed return code %N Error in command name
462– 463	Too many > or < command too long Unable to open redirection file. Syntax error CLI error: %S
488	BUSY

Blk.	Message
510	Out of memory Cannot open disc device :L/Disk-Validator...L:Disk-Validator Unable to load disk validator
511- 512	out of range slready set Error validating disk Disk structure corrupt Use DISKDOCTOR to correct it out of range Disk is unreadable checksum error
880	Empty
882	Trashcan
883	Trashcan.info

You've probably noticed the many markers such as %ld,%s, etc. These are C format specifiers, which must stay untouched in the disk. They act as reference points for inserting text and numeric data.

Appendices

Appendices

A. Error messages

This section lists AmigaDOS error messages by number.

103 insufficient free store

AmigaDOS can't load the program due to insufficient memory.
End any other tasks or close any other open CLI windows.

105 task table full

AmigaDOS can only manage 20 CLI tasks at once. As soon as
the internal task table is full, no more CLIs can be opened.

120 argument line invalid or too long

This error message appears if an AmigaDOS command has a
problem with the given parameters.

121 file is not an object module

Only program files can be started by directly entering their
names (e.g., script files must be started with Execute).

122 invalid resident library during load

A problem occurs when opening or loading a library.

202 object in use

This message prevents file writing or directory deletion while
another task accesses the file or directory.

203 object already exists

A given name already exists and cannot be erased.

204 directory not found

AmigaDOS cannot find a given directory.

205 object not found

A file or directory cannot be found from AmigaDOS.

206 invalid window description

The syntax was incorrect when opening a window. Check the
window coordinates and syntax (e.g., con:0/0/635/100/).

209 packet request type unknown

A driver cannot fulfill a desired access. This only occurs because of programming errors.

211 invalid object lock

A programming error created an invalid lock code.

212 object not of required type

Confusion between files and directories causes this error.

213 disk not validated

The disk in the drive is probably damaged.

214 disk write-protected

It is not possible to write to this disk. The write protect clips are probably in the wrong position.

215 rename across devices attempted

Rename cannot rename from one disk to another.

216 directory not empty

Trying to erase a directory that is not empty causes this error.

218 device (or volume) not mounted

AmigaDOS cannot find the requested disk.

219 seek failure

A false argument was given when calling the Seek function.

220 comment too big

File comments added to a file with `FileNote` cannot be longer than 80 characters.

221 disk full

No memory available on the given disk for the desired action.

222 file is protected from deletion

The file is probably protected from deletion with Protect.

223 file is write protected

224 file is read protected

Both of these commands react to the protection flags set using Protect. These two error message are not used because the present version of DOS only supports the D flag.

225 not a valid DOS disk

Either the disk structure of the disk is completely destroyed or it was not formatted under AmigaDOS.

226 no disk in drive

There is no disk in the requested drive at the time.

232 no more entries in directory

This programming error informs you that the access of the ExNext routine in a directory cannot find any more entries.

B.   CLI shortcuts

The CLI and Shell commands include <Ctrl> and <Esc> command sequences that can be entered from the keyboard. The command characters can also be used in script files through the Echo command. The Escape sequence appears in quotation marks, beginning with an asterisk acting as the <Esc> key (e.g., echo "*ec" clears the screen). You can change the type style, enter a color, move the cursor and more by entering these codes in a CLI window.

<Esc> c	Clear screen and disable all special modes
<Esc> [0m	Disable all special modes (normal characters)
<Esc> [1m	Bold type
<Esc> [2m	Black type (color number 2)
<Esc> [3m	Italic type
<Esc> [30m	Blue type (color number 0)
<Esc> [31m	White type (color number 1)
<Esc> [32m	Black type (color number 2)
<Esc> [33m	Orange type (color number 3)
<Esc> [4m	Underlining
<Esc> [40m	Blue background (color number 0)
<Esc> [41m	White background (color number 1)
<Esc> [42m	Black background (color number 2)
<Esc> [43m	Orange background (color number 3)
<Esc> [7m	Inverse presentation (normally blue on white)
<Esc> [8m	Blue type, invisible (or color number 0)
<Esc> [nu	Width of CLI window in characters (n)
<Esc> [nx	Left margin of the CLI window in pixels (n)
<Esc> [ny	Distance of window from top in pixels (n)
<Esc> [nt	Number of lines in CLI window (n)

<Ctrl><H>   Deletes the last character entered or <Backspace>

<Ctrl><I>   Moves the cursor to a tab position to the right or
                 <Tab> (default 5 character)

<Ctrl><J>   Enters line feed without executing the entered
                 command. This allows multiple command entry.
                 Pressing the <Return> key executes all commands in
                 sequence

<Ctrl><K>   Moves the cursor to a position as above. The text that
                 is there cannot be changed

<Ctrl><L>   Clears the screen

<Ctrl><M>   Ends the line and executes the entered or <Return>
                 commands

<Ctrl><N>   Enables the Alt character set. Only special characters are
                 printed

<Ctrl><O>   Disables the Alt character set and returns to the normal
                 character set

<Ctrl><X>   Deletes the current line

<Ctrl><\>   Signals the end of a file in AmigaDOS. Also ends
                 input in Con: windows

C. Printer escape sequences

The following printer Escape sequences are translated using the printer drivers included in Preferences.

Escape sequence	Meaning
<Esc>c	Initialize (reset) printer
<Esc>#1	Disable all other modes
<Esc>D	Line feed
<Esc>E	Line feed + carriage return
<Esc>M	One line up
<Esc>[0m	Normal characters
<Esc>[1m	Bold on
<Esc>[22m	Bold off
<Esc>[3m	Italics on
<Esc>[23m	Italics off
<Esc>[4m	Underlining on
<Esc>[24m	Underlining off
<Esc>[xm	Colors (x=30 to 39 [foreground] or 40 to 49 [background])
<Esc>[0w	Normal text size
<Esc>[2w	Elite on
<Esc>[1w	Elite off
<Esc>[4w	Condensed type on
<Esc>[3w	Condensed type off
<Esc>[6w	Enlarged type on
<Esc>[5w	Enlarged type off
<Esc>[2"z	NLQ on
<Esc>[1"z	NLQ off
<Esc>[4"z	Double strike on
<Esc>[3"z	Double strike off
<Esc>[6"z	Shadow type on
<Esc>[5"z	Shadow type off
<Esc>[2v	Superscript on
<Esc>[1v	Superscript off
<Esc>[4v	Subscript on
<Esc>[3v	Subscript off
<Esc>[0v	Back to normal type

<Esc>[2p	Proportional type on
<Esc>[1p	Proportional type off
<Esc>[0p	Delete proportional spacing
<Esc>[xE	Proportional spacing = x
<Esc>[5F	Left justify
<Esc>[7F	Right justify
<Esc>[6F	Set block
<Esc>[0F	Set block off
<Esc>[3F	Justify letter width
<Esc>[1F	Center justify
<Esc>[0z	Line dimension 1/8 inch
<Esc>[1z	Line dimension 1/6 inch
<Esc>[xt	Page length set at x lines
<Esc>[xq	Perforation jumps to x lines
<Esc>[0q	Perforation jumping off
<Esc>(B	American character set
<Esc>(R	French character set
<Esc>(K	German character set
<Esc>(A	English character set
<Esc>(E	Danish character set (Nr.1)
<Esc>(H	Swedish character set
<Esc>(Y	Italian character set
<Esc>(Z	Spanish character set
<Esc>(J	Japanese character set
<Esc>(6	Norwegian character set
<Esc>(C	Danish character set (Nr.2)
<Esc>#9	Set left margin
<Esc>#0	Set right margin
<Esc>#8	Set header
<Esc>#2	Set footer
<Esc>#3	Delete margins
<Esc>[xyr	Header x lines from top; footer y lines from bottom
<Esc>[xys	Set left margin (x) and right margin (y)
<Esc>H	Set horizontal tab
<Esc>J	Set vertical tab
<Esc>[0g	Delete horizontal tab
<Esc>[3g	Delete all horizontal tabs
<Esc>[1g	Delete vertical tab
<Esc>[4g	Delete all vertical tabs
<Esc>#4	Delete all tabs
<Esc>#5	Set standard tabs

D.   Guru meditation codes

Guru Meditations supply information about system crashes. Guru
Meditations return two eight-digit numbers. The first number gives
detailed error information in the following format:

System ID code	Error class	Error number
xx	xx	xxxx

The second eight-digit number gives the starting address of the task that
started the interrupt.

System ID codes

00	CPU trap
01	Exec library
02	Graphics library
03	Layers library
04	Intuition library
05	Math library
06	CList library
07	DOS library
08	RAM library
09	Icon library
0A	Expansion library
10	Audio device
11	Console device
12	GamePort device
13	Keyboard device
14	Trackdisk device
15	Timer device
20	CIA resource
21	Disk resource
22	Misc resource
30	Bootstrap
31	Workbench
32	Diskcopy

Error classes

01	Insufficient memory
02	MakeLibrary error
03	OpenLibrary error
04	OpenDevice error
05	OpenResource error
06	I/O error
07	No signal

Special guru meditation codes

When a system ID code begins with a number greater than or equal to 8, the error is non-recoverable. Subtract 8 from the first digit to get the true system ID code.

CPU traps

00000002	Bus error
00000003	Address error
00000004	Illegal instruction
00000005	Divide by zero
00000006	CHK instruction
00000007	TRAPV instruction
00000008	Privilege violation
00000009	Trace
0000000A	Opcode 1010
0000000B	Opcode 1111

Exec library

81000001	Error in 68000 exception vector checksum
81000002	Error in ExecBase checksum
81000003	Error in a Library checksum
81000004	Insufficient memory for MakeLibrary
81000005	Memory list scrambled
81000006	No free memory for interrupt server
81000007	Problem with InitAPtr
81000008	Semaphore scrambled
81000009	Double call from free
8100000A	"Bogus Exception"

Graphics library

82010001	Insufficient memory for Copper display list
82010002	Insufficient memory for Copper command list
82010003	Copper list overflow
82010004	"Copper Intermediate" list overflow
82010005	Insufficient memory for header of Copper list
82010006	Memory absence at Long Frame
82010007	Memory absence at Short Frame
82010008	Insufficient memory for Flood Fill
82010009	Insufficient memory for TmpRas
8201000A	Insufficient memory for BltBitMap
8201000B	"Region Memory"

Layers library

83010001	No available memory for layers

Intuition library

84000001	Gadget type unknown
84010002	Insufficient memory to add port
84010003	Insufficient memory for Item Plane Alloc
84010004	Insufficient memory for Sub Alloc
84010005	Insufficient memory for Plane Alloc

84000006	Original coordinate smaller than RelZero
84010007	Insufficient memory to open screen
84000008	Insufficient memory for Raster Alloc
84010009	Unknown type at Open Sys Screen
8101000A	Insufficient memory for gadgets
8101000B	Insufficient memory for window
8100000C	Faulty return code encountered in Intuition
8100000D	IDCMP sent a faulty message
8400000E	Answer was incomprehensible
8400000F	Error when opening Console device

DOS library

07010001	Memory problem at startup
07000002	Problem with EndTask
07000003	Problem with Qpkt
07000004	Receiver packet not expected
07000005	Problem with FreeVec
07000006	Error in DiskBlock sequence
07000007	Faulty bitmap
07000008	Key already erased
07000009	Checksum false
0700000A	Diskette error
0700000B	Incorrect value for key
0700000C	Problem at overlay

RAM library

| 08000001 | Faulty Segment-List |

Expansion library

| 0A000001 | Problem at Expansion Free |

Trackdisk device

| 14000001 | Seek error at calibrate |
| 14000002 | Error at timer delay |

Timer device

| 15000001 | Incorrect request |
| 15000002 | Incorrect transfer |

Disk resource

| 21000001 | Get drive has prepared the diskette |
| 21000002 | Interrupt: no active drive |

Bootstrap

| 30000001 | Boot code error |

Index

68000 commands	135	Command description	78
68010 processor	126	Computer viruses	109
		CON handler	3
Accessing directories	84, 88	Console device	6, 148
AllocMem()	22, 84	Control key.	4
Amiga hardware	125	ConvertFD	20
AmigaBASIC	8	Copy more!	5
AmigaDOS	76	CurrentDir()	88
AmigaDOS commands	141		
Archival listings	92	DATA statements	47
ASCII file	57	DeciGEL	133
ASCII format	9	Default Tool gadget	177
ASCII text	10	DefChip()	22
Assign	72	DeleteFile() function	90
Autoknob	53	Density parameter	178
Automatic backups	3	Device	142
		DEVS	11
BASIC editor	10	Direct file control	90
BCPL language	116	Directory menu	98
Block	73	Directory files	88
Boot block	109	Directory handling	87
BootPri	143	Directory listing	85
Border	31	Directory management	92
Borderless CLI	6	Disk drive switching	130
BufMemType	143	Disk icons	6
Byte Bandit virus	109	Disk monitor	192
		Disk routines	76
C programming language	105	Diskcopy command	192
CHR$(27)	11	DiskDoctor	13
CLI	3	Dithering	179
CLI output	3	Division by zero handler	106
CLI text modes	3	DOS lock access	83
Clipboard device	146	DrawBorder()	47
Clock	180	DumpRastPort structure	162
Clock parameters	180		
ClockPtr	181	Echo	3
CloseAll	23	ElmerDOS	196
ClosePrinter routine	162	Examine()	84
CMD_WRITE	181	Exception routine	106
Code register	135	Exec.library	10
Color correct	178	ExNext() function	85
ColorCycle	120	Extras disk	171

FED   185
FFS (FastFileSystem)   141
File access   76
File control   77
File menu   98
File monitor   58
Filled gadgets   40
Flags   142
Floating point variables   114
Font Attributes   186
FreeMap   186
FreeMem()   161
FreePreferences   176

Gadget   23, 31
GadgetDef   24, 29
GetDir subroutine   100
GetMsg()   25
GetPreferences   175
GetPrinterData subprogram   161
Graphic 1   177
Graphic 2   177
Graphic dumps   163, 184
Graphics.library   40
Guru Meditation   13

Hardcopy   166
Height Limit   179
Hexadecimal   58
Hidden texts   14
HighCyl   145

Info file   53, 90
Info()   88
InitDRPReq   167
Install command   109
InstallPrinter   182
Instruction register   106
IntuiText   29
Intuition   57
Intuition knob graphic   52
Intuition library   9
Intuition window   20
IntuitionMsg   25
IORequest   167

JAM2   30

JSR (Jump to SubRoutine)   117

KeyToy2000   186
Kickstart   14
Kickstart backup   192
Kickstart messages   200
Knob graphic   52

LIBRARY   40
Link module   116
LoadIt routine   100
LoadSeg   116
LoadWB   6
Lock() function   83
LowCyl   144
LPRINT   12

Machine language   105
MEMACS   187
Memory display   186
Memory   9
Memory allocation routine   24
Memory expansion   126
Mlist   22
Modular work   8
More   182
Motorola chip   131
Mount command   141
MOVE CCR   136
MOVE SR,Destination   136
MOVES   136

NewCLI   6
NewCon   5
NewCon device   148
NewShell   5
NewSuffix routine   101
NIL device   150
Numerical array   79

OpenAll   23
OpenDevice()   161
OpenPrinter subprogram   161
OpenWindow()   23

PAL   73
Palette   187

PAR	11	Shell	5
ParentDir() function	87	Sliders	52
Patching	74	Smoothing function	178
PerfMon	187	Sort routine	100
PIPE device	146	SourceFunctionCodeRegister (SFC)	135
PolyDraw()	47	Speak command	147
Power LED	115	Special menu	196
Preferences	11	SpecialInfo	52
Preferences program	171	SPST switch.	130
Prefs	177	Standard icons	8
Printed circuit board	128	Startup sequence	3
Printer device	157	Status display	73
Printer parameters	157	Status register	106
PrinterData	162	String gadgets	52
PrinterExtendedData	161	Superstate word	106
PrintFiles	183	Supervisor stack	106
Process handling	77	Surfaces	142
PropInfo	52	System vectors	110
Proportional gadget	52	System-Configuration	13
PRT:	11		
		TabOut	47
RAM disk RAD	150	Temporary files	3
RAMB0	6	Text editing	194
Random file access	80	TOOL TYPES	183
Read(SFC)	135	Tool	11
RectFill	40	Tool Types gadget	177
Rename() function	91	Topaz font	146
Renaming commands	143	Trap vector	108
Renaming menu items	197		
Reserved	142	UnDef()	22
RTD	136	UNDERLINE	4
RTE (ReTurn from Exception)	106	Undo buffer	73
RTS	136	Undo gadget	73
		Unit	142
SaveData routine	100	UnloadSeg routine	116
Say command	147	Unlock()	83
SCA virus	109	Utilities drawer	180
Dcaling	179	Utility program	174
screen names	9		
Script file	5	Variables	160
Scrolling tables 4	5	VectorBaseRegister (VBR)	135
SER	11		
SetAlert command	106, 133	Width Limit	179
SetDrMd	40	WinDef() 2	2
SetPreferences	176	Window name	9
SetProtection()	91	Workbench	6
Settings menu	99	Workbench disk	171

Workbench screen   176
Write(DFC)   135

xClose() function   79
xOpen() function   78
xRead() function   78
xWrite() function   79

AssemPro

Machine Language Development System for the Amiga

Bridge the gap between slow higher-level languages and ultra-fast machine language programming: AssemPro Amiga unlocks the full power of the AMIGA's 68000 processor. It's a complete developer's kit for rapidly developing machine language/assembler programs on your Amiga. AssemPro has everything you need to write professional-quality programs "down to the metal": editor, debugger, disassembler & reassembler.

Yet AssemPro isn't just for the 68000 experts. AssemPro is easy to use. You select options from the dropdown menus or with shortcut keys, which makes your program development a much simpler process. With the optional Abacus book *Amiga Machine Language* (see page 3), AssemPro is the perfect introduction to Amiga machine language development and programming.

AssemPro also has the professional features that advanced programmers look for. Lots of "extras" eliminate the most tedious, repetitious and time-consuming m/l programming tasks. Like syntax error search/replace functions to speed program alterations and debugging. And you can compile to memory for lighting speed. The comprehensive tutorial and manual have the detailed information you need for fast, effective programming.

AssemPro Amiga offers more professional features, speed, sheer power, and ease of operation than any other assembler package we've seen for the money. Test drive your AssemPro Amiga with the security of the Abacus 30-day guarantee.

Suggested retail price: $99.95

Features

- Integrated Editor, Debugger, Disassembler and Reassembler
- Large operating system library
- Runs under CLI and Workbench
- Produces either PC-relocatable or absolute code
- Create custom macros for nearly any parameter (of different types)
- Error search and replace functions
- Cross-reference list
- Menu-controlled conditional and repeated assembly
- Full 32-bit arithmetic
- Advanced debugger with 68020 single-step emulation
- Written completely in machine language for ultra-fast operation
- Runs on any Amiga with 512K or more and Kickstart version 1.2
- Not copy protected

Machine language programming requires a solid understanding of the AMIGA's hardware and operating system. We do not recommend this package to beginning Amiga programmers

DataRetrieve

A Powerful Database Manager for the Amiga

Imagine a powerful database for your Amiga: one that's fast, has a huge data capacity, yet is easy to work with.

Now think **DataRetrieve** *Amiga*. It works the same way as your Amiga—graphic and intuitive, with no obscure commands. You quickly set up your data files using convenient on-screen templates called masks. Select commands from the pulldown menus or time-saving shortcut keys. Customize the masks with different text fonts, styles, colors, sizes and graphics. If you have any questions, Help screens are available at the touch of a button. And **DataRetrieve's** 128-page manual is clear and comprehensive.

DataRetrieve is easy to use—but it also has professional features for your most demanding database applications. Password security for your data. Sophisticated indexing with variable precision. Full Search and Select functions. File sizes, data sets and data fields limited only by your memory and disk storage space. Customize up to 20 function keys to store macro commands and often-used text. For optimum access speed, **DataRetrieve** takes advantage of the Amiga's multi-tasking.

You can exchange data with **TextPro** *Amiga*, **BeckerText** *Amiga* and other packages to easily produce form letters, mailing labels, index cards, bulletins, etc. **DataRetrieve** prints data reports to most dot-matrix & letter-quality printers.

DataRetrieve is the perfect database for your Amiga. Get this proven system today with the assurance of the **Abacus 30-day MoneyBack Guarantee.**

Suggested retail price: $79.95

Features

- Select commands and options from the pulldown menus **or** shortcut keys
- Enter data into convenient screenmasks
- Enhance screen masks with different text styles, fonts, colors, graphics, etc.
- Work with 8 databases concurrently
- Define different field types: text, date, time, numeric & selection
- Customize 20 function keys to store macro commands and text
- Specify up to 80 index fields for *superfast* access to your data
- Perform simple or complex data searches
- Create subsets of a larger database for even faster operation
- Exchange data with other packages: form letters, mailing lists etc.
- Produce custom printer forms: index cards, labels, Rolodex•cards, etc. Adapts to most dot-matrix & letter-quality printers
- Protect your data with passwords
- Get Help from online screens
- Not copy protected

- Max. file size
- Max. data record size
- Max. data set
- Max. no. of data fields
- Max. field size

Limited only by your memory and disk space

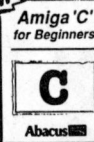

Books for the AMIGA

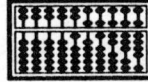

Amiga for Beginners

Amiga For Beginners- the first volume in our Amiga series, introduces you to Intuition (Amiga's graphic interface), the mouse, windows, the CLI, and Amiga BASIC and explains every practical aspect of the Amiga in plain English. The glossary, "first-aid" appendix, icon appendix and technical appendix are invaluable to the beginner.

Topics include:

- Unpacking and connecting the Amiga components
- Starting up your Amiga
- Customizing the Workbench
- Exploring the Extras Disk
- Taking your first steps in the AmigaBASIC programming language
- AmigaDOS functions
- Using the CLI to perform 'housekeeping' chores
- First Aid, Keyword, Technical appendixes
- Complete set-up instructions
- Backing up important diskettes
- Setting Preferences
- Creating your own icons

No Optional Disk Available

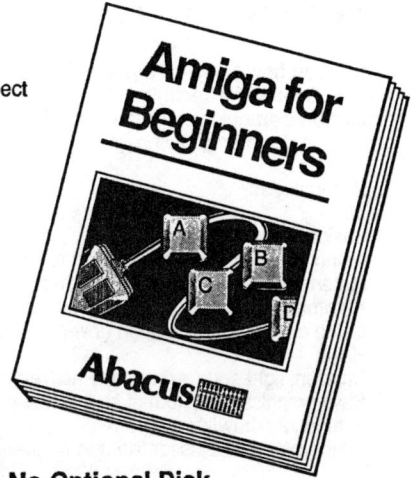

Volume 1   Suggested Retail Price $16.95   ISBN 1-55755-021-2

AmigaBASIC: Inside & Out

AmigaBASIC- Inside and Out- THE definitive step-by-step guide to programming the Amiga in BASIC. Every AmigaBASIC command is fully described and detailed. Topics include charts, windows, pull down menus, files, mouse and speech commands.

Features:

- Loaded with real working programs
- Video titling for high quality object animation
- Windows
- Pull-down menus
- Moused commands
- Statistics
- Sequential and random files
- Exciting graphics demonstrations
- Powerful database
- Charting application for creating detailed pie charts and bar graphs
- Speech utility for remarkable human voice syntheses demonstrations
- Synthesizer program to create custom sound effects and music.

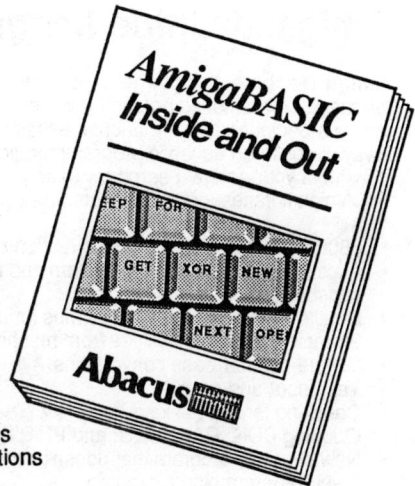

Volume 2   Suggested retail price $24.95   ISBN 0-916439-87-9

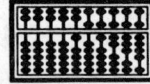

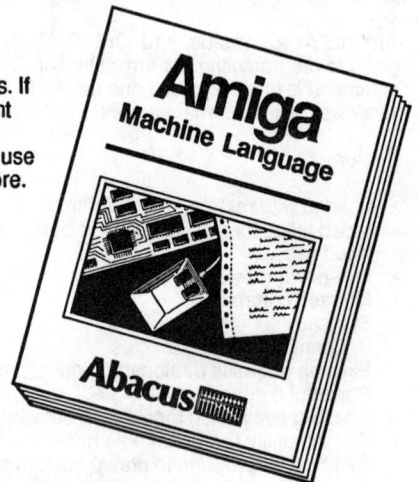

Books for the AMIGA

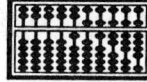

Amiga Tricks & Tips

Amiga Tricks & Tips follows our tradition of other Tricks and Tips books for CBM users. Presents dozens of tips on accessing libraries from BASIC, custom character sets, AmigaDOS, sound, important 68000 memory locations, and much more!

Topics include:

- Diverse and useful programming techniques
- Displaying 64 colors on screen simultaneously
- Accessing libraries from BASIC
- Creating custom character sets
- Using Amiga DOS and graphics
- Dozens of tips on windows
- Programming aids
- Covers important 68000 memory locations

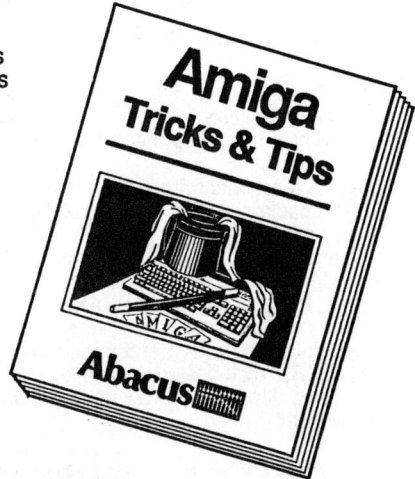

Volume 5   Suggested retail price $19.95   ISBN 0-916439-88-7

Amiga System Programmer's Guide

Amiga System Programmer's Guide is a comprehensive guide to what goes on inside the Amiga in a single volume. Explains in detail the Amiga chips (68000, CIA, Agnus, Denise, Paula) and how to access them. All the Amiga's powerful interfaces and features are explained and documented in a clear precise manner.

Topics include:

- EXEC Structure
- Multitasking functions
- I/O management through devices and I/O request
- Interrupts and resource management
- RESET and its operation
- DOS libraries
- Disk Management
- Detailed information about the CLI and its commands

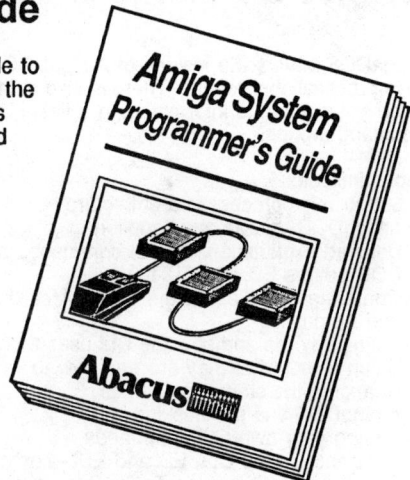

Volume 6   Suggested retail price $34.95   ISBN 1-55755-034-4

Books for the AMIGA

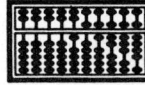

Amiga C for Beginners

An introduction to learning the popular C language. Explains the language elements using examples specifically geared to the Amiga. Describes C library routines, how the compiler works and more.

Topics include:

- Particulars of C
- How a compiler works
- Writing your first program
- The scope of the language (loops, conditions, functions, structures)
- Special features of C
- Important routines in the C libraries
- Input/Output
- Tricks and Tips for finding errors
- Introduction to direct programming of the operating system (windows, screens, direct text output, DOS functions)
- Using the LATTICE and AZTEC C compilers

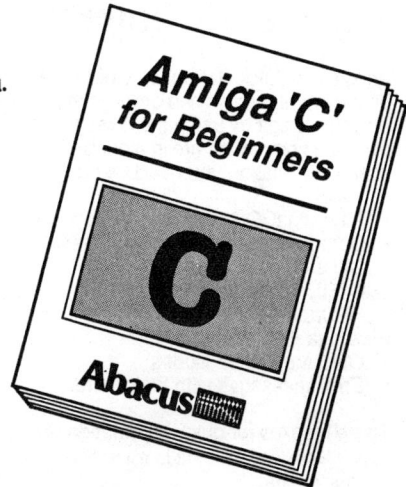

Volume 10   Suggested retail price $19.95   ISBN 1-55755-045-X

Amiga C for Advanced Programmers

Amiga C for Advanced Programmers- contains a wealth of information from the pros: how compilers, assemblers and linkers work, designing and programming user friendly interfaces using Intuition, managing large programming projects, using jump tables and dynamic arrays, coming assembly language and C codes, and more. Includes complete source code for text editor.

Topics include:

- Using INCLUDE, DEFINE and CASTS
- Debugging and optimizing assembler sources
- All about Intuition programming (windows, screens, pulldown menus, requesters, gadgets)
- Programming the console devices
- A professional editor's view of problems with developing larger programs
- Using MAKE correctly
- Debugging C programs with different utilities
- Folding (formatting text lines and functions for readability)

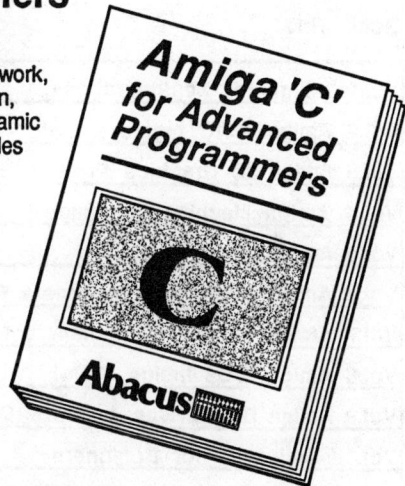

Volume 11   Suggested retail price $24.95   ISBN 1-55755-046-8

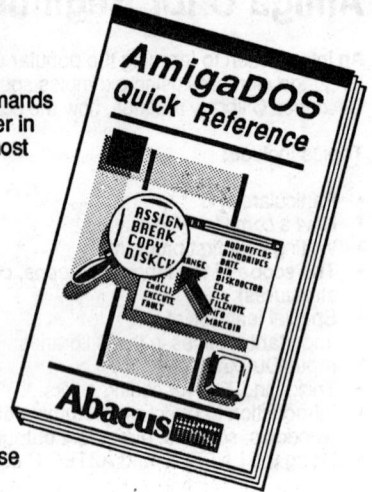